The Beaches of Maui County

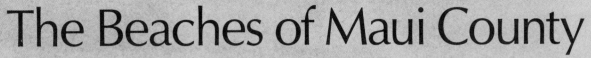

The Beaches of Maui County

Second Edition

John R. K. Clark

A KOLOWALU BOOK
University of Hawaii Press
Honolulu

Photo Credits
On the cover: Polihua Beach, Lāna'i,
photos by Grant Tanoura
Title page spread: Polihua Beach, Lāna'i,
photo by Alexis Higdon
Maui: photos by Grant Tanoura
Moloka'i: photos by Grant Tanoura
Lāna'i: photos by Alexis Higdon
Kaho'olawe: photos by Jeanette Foster,
except Hakioawa Bay by Rick
McCloskey

Library of Congress Cataloging-in-Publication Data

Clark, John R. K. 1946–
    The beaches of Maui County / John R. K. Clark. — 2nd ed.
        p.   cm. — (A Kolowalu book)
    Bibliography: p.
    Includes index.
    ISBN 0-8248-1246-8
    1. Maui County (Hawaii)—Description and Travel—Guide-books.
2. Beaches—Hawaii—Maui County—Guide-books. I. Title.
DU628.M3C55   1989   89–4794
919.69'21044—dc19   CIP

∞ *The paper used in this publication meets the minimum require-*
ments of American National Standard for Information Sciences—Per-
manence of Paper for Printed Library Materials
                                                    ANSI Z39.48-1984

To my son
Jason Keliiaumoana Clark

Contents

Maps

Preface

The first edition of *The Beaches of Maui County* was published in 1980. During the interim between the first edition and its revision, Maui County developed a number of new beach parks and public rights-of-way. This edition includes all of the new developments and the improvements that were made to the existing parks. In short, the second edition brings *The Beaches of Maui County* completely up-to-date.

This book is a guide to all the beaches, sandy and rocky, on all four of the large islands that comprise Maui County—Maui, Moloka'i, Lāna'i, and Kaho'olawe—and the small island of Molokini as well. Like its predecessor, *The Beaches of O'ahu,* it provides information on beach activities and water safety, and is also a study in Hawaiiana, giving historical sketches of each beach. Much of this material has been gleaned from personal interviews and has never before appeared in print. My intention in making this information available is not only to provide interesting reading but to record it before it is lost for good. I also hope it will stimulate further research by others. With this end in mind, I would like to invite serious students of Hawaiiana who wish to pursue any of the leads in this book to contact me personally. There is still a tremendous amount of historical material about each island's shoreline that has yet to be recorded.

The first section of the book provides specific information about each individual beach or section of shoreline. Each island is circled in a clockwise direction from these starting points: Waihe'e Beach Park on Maui, Kaunakakai Wharf on Moloka'i, Mānele Bay on Lā-na'i, and Hanakanae'a on Kaho'olawe. Preceding the text for each island is a chart providing a consolidated description of the island's beaches and what they have to offer in the way of shoreline activities and park facilities. The stories for each individual beach follow, accompanied by strip maps pinpointing the exact locations of the beaches.

The second section provides general information on water safety and is intended primarily for people unfamiliar with the ocean and its dangers. Visitors to Hawai'i are strongly urged to read this section before hitting the beach.

Water conditions at any beach are subject to change with variations in tides, winds, and surf. Many beaches also exhibit dramatic variations in appearance through seasonal erosion and accretion of beach sand. *The Beaches of Maui County* points out these changes and many potential dangers, but anyone unfamiliar with a beach should also exercise some common sense. If a beach looks dangerous to you, don't go in the water. One of the best indicators of the safety of a beach is the presence of local residents and their families in the water. If they are in the area, but not in the water, ask them why before you jump in.

All beaches in the State of Hawai'i are public property, but only below the upper reaches of the waves as evidenced by the vegetation line. Access to a beach is designated unlimited in the book if the beach is on county or state land that is always open to the general public—primarily public parks. Anything less than unlimited access means that the coastline of the beach or a portion of it is private property. Coastline areas that are private property, but whose owners allow the public to cross their land, are noted, as are public rights-of-way and access routes other than those that trespass.

The island of Lānaʻi presents a unique access situation. Except for the state harbor area at Mānele Bay, the coastline above the vegetation line around the entire island is private property. Castle and Cooke, Inc., is the major landowner. The public is allowed access to the island only as guests of the owner or of a Lānaʻi resident. Tourists and hunters are considered guests of the owner. For further information check with the Kōʻele Company, Castle and Cooke's representative in Lānaʻi City.

The island of Kahoʻolawe also presents a unique access situation. There is none. Kahoʻolawe was taken over by the U.S. Navy in 1941, and the Navy, together with the other military services, has used the island for training ever since. Recreational use of the waters within the surface danger zone, a specific area of ocean surrounding the island, has been permitted since 1968, when the Navy commenced a program to open these waters when the target complex is not in use. The waters generally are open to the public on weekends and holidays. Weekly news releases are issued to the local news media and to the state Division of Fish and Game, to advise the public if the waters will be open or closed. The Coast Guard issues notices to mariners which contain the same information. Recreational use of the island itself has not been deemed safe by the Navy because of the accumulation of unexploded ordnance since 1941.

Some of the terms used for specific areas of the beaches described in this book are defined as follows:

Foreshore. The area actively shaped by the waves that slopes into the water.

Backshore. The area between the foreshore and the vegetation line.

Coastline. The area from the vegetation line inland.

The beaches themselves are made up of several different kinds of substance, defined as follows:

White sand. Composed primarily of calcarious material.

Detrital sand. Composed primarily of a mixture of calcarious sand and material eroded from the land. These beaches are brown, grey, or black, depending on the type of material and the proportions of the mixture.

Shingle. Composed primarily of pebble to fist-sized rocks that are usually flat with well-rounded corners; the Hawaiian word for these stones is ʻiliʻili.

Cobblestone. Composed primarily of fist- to head-sized rocks.

Cinder. Composed primarily of volcanic cinder eroded from shoreline cinder cones. Kaihalulu in Hāna is the only cinder beach in Maui County, although a number of tiny cinder pocket beaches can be found around Kaʻuiki Head and Ka Iwi O Pele.

Acknowledgments

During the course of my research for *The Beaches of Maui County,* I interviewed many individuals, either personally, by mail, or by telephone. It would be impossible for me to acknowledge all of them by name, but to all I extend my warmest *mahalo*. For each island, however, there are a number of people whose help was of major importance and whose contributions are directly responsible for the success of this book. I would like to recognize them individually:

Maui. Charlie Aikala, Alex Akina, Charlie Akina, Irmgard Aluli, Henrietta Apo, Bob Carroll, Eddie Chang, Kenneth Chong Kee, Allen Corell, James Dunn, Joe English, Lucy Farden, David Fleming, James Fleming, Sid Getzner, Sonny Hoopii, Garner Ivey, Alice Johnson, John Kaaiea, Dallas Kalepa, Mary Kalua, Martha Kekona, Helen Kenolio, Leslie Kuloloio, Marion Lee Loy, Alice Lum, Henry Maio, Moses Maliikapu, J. R. Mac McConkey, Calvin McGregor, Russell Morris, Ellen Oliveira, Marie and Willy Olsen, Kiyoshi Oshiro, Helen Peters, Stanley Raymond, Joe Rosa, Lori Sablas, Allen Silva, George Smith, Joe Swezey, Rene Sylva, Donald Uchimura, Teruo Uchimura, Katheryn Watson, Ann Wilmington, Cable Wirtz, Betty Young.

Moloka'i. Charles Busby, John Cambra, Reginald Colotario, Pat and Peppy Cooke, Mary Duarte, Aka Hodgins, Larry Joao, Lucy and John Kaona, Lani Kapuni, Rose Lelepali, Elroy Malo, Lucy Mikasobe, Rachael Nakoa, John Naughton, Noah Pekelo, Sanford Smith, Catherine Summers, Mary Summers, Audrey Sutherland.

Lāna'i. A. Duane Black, Edean and Swede Desha, Alexis Higdon, Lydia and Sol Kaopuiki, Gwen Leong, Hector Munro.

Kaho'olawe. Michael Clemens, Jamie Davidson, Jeanette Foster, Louis Hubbard, Rick McCloskey, Nathan Napoka, David K. Pedro, Leo T. Profilet, Richard Sawyer, Farley Watanabe.

In addition, there is a small group of people whose assistance and support spanned more than one island and whose contributions were vital to the successful completion of the entire book. They are: Inez Ashdown, Jim Bier, Janyce Blair, Betty Bushnell, Alice and George Clark, Camille Clark, Judy Clark, Rick Gaffney, Harald Hauff, Stuart Kiang, Kathy and Richard Longstaff, Ross Mace, J. Cline Mann, Ralph Moberly, Bridget and Karl Mowat, Harry J. Mowat, Sarah Requilman, Rosalynn Rodrigues, Violet and Herbert Santos, Grant Tanoura.

I would finally like to acknowledge the work of Elspeth P. Sterling, who covered the same ground, and much more, long before I did. Her unpublished fourteen-volume set, "The Sites of Maui County," proved invaluable to me in my research and is probably the best single source of historical and archaeological information that has ever been compiled on Maui County.

Island of Maui

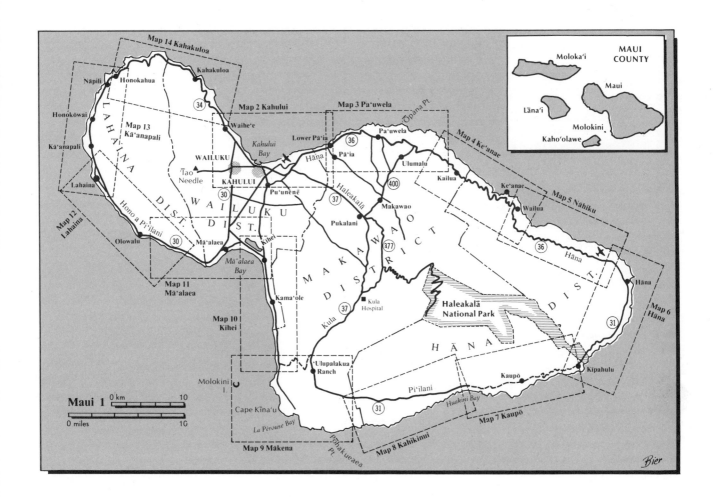

MAUI COUNTY

Moloka'i

Maui

Lāna'i

Molokini

Kaho'olawe

Map 14 Kahakuloa

Kahakuloa

Nāpili
Honokahua

Honokōwai

Kā'anapali

LAHAINA

Map 13
Kā'anapali

34

Waihe'e

Map 2 Kahului

Map 3 Pa'uwela

'Ōpana Pt.

Pa'uwela

Map 4 Ke'anae

Lower Pā'ia

36

Hāna

Pā'ia

Ulumalu

Kahului Bay

WAILUKU

'Īao Needle

KAHULUI

Pu'unēnē

Haleakalā

Kailua

Ke'anae

Map 5 Nahiku

Wailua

30

Lahaina

WAILUKU DIST.

37

Makawao

Hāna

36

Map 12 Lahaina

Hono a Pi'ilani

Pukalani

DIST.

Olowalu

30

Mā'alaea

MAKAWAO

377

Hāna

Kīhei

Mā'alaea Bay

Map 11 Mā'alaea

DISTRICT

Haleakalā National Park

Hāna

Map 6 Hāna

Kama'ole

37

Kula Hospital

31

Map 10 Kīhei

Kula

HĀNA

Molokini I.

'Ulupalakua Ranch

DIST.

Kīpahulu

Kaupō

Cape Kīna'u

Pi'ilani

31

Huakini Bay

Map 7 Kaupō

La Pèrouse Bay

Pōhakueaea Pt.

Map 8 Kahikinui

Map 9 Mākena

Maui 1

0 km   10

0 miles   10

Bier

BEACHES OF MAUI

BEACH & LOCATION	BEACH ACTIVITIES				PUBLIC FACILITIES			BEACH COMPOSITION			ACCESS	
	SWIMMING	SNORKELING	SURFING	BODY-SURFING	COMFORT STATION	PICNIC EQUIPMENT	PAVED PARKING	SAND	DETRITAL SAND	ROCK	PUBLIC	PRIVATE
1) WAIHE'E BEACH PARK, WAIHE'E	✔	✔	✔		✔	✔	✔	✔			✔	
2) WAIEHU BEACH PARK, WAIEHU		✔	✔		✔	✔		✔			✔	
3) PAUKŪKALO BEACH, PAUKŪKALO			✔							✔	✔	
4) KAHULUI HARBOR, KAHULUI	✔		✔	✔		✔		✔			✔	
5) KANAHĀ BEACH PARK, KAHULUI	✔				✔	✔	✔	✔			✔	
6) SPRECKELSVILLE BEACH, SPRECKELSVILLE	✔	✔	✔					✔			✔	
7) H. A. BALDWIN PARK, SPRECKELSVILLE	✔		✔	✔	✔	✔	✔	✔			✔	
8) LOWER PĀ'IA PARK, LOWER PĀ'IA	✔		✔	✔	✔	✔		✔			✔	
9) MANTOKUJI BAY, LOWER PĀ'IA								✔				✔
10) KŪ'AU BAY, KŪ'AU	✔		✔	✔				✔			✔	
11) FATHER JULES PAPA, KŪ'AU								✔			✔	
12) H-POKO PAPA, HĀMĀKUA POKO			✔					✔			✔	
13) HO'OKIPA BEACH PARK, HĀMĀKUA POKO	✔		✔	✔	✔	✔	✔	✔			✔	
14) MĀLIKO BAY, MĀLIKO	✔	✔	✔							✔	✔	
15) KUIAHA BAY, PA'UWELA	✔	✔								✔		✔
16) HONOMANŪ BAY, HONOMANŪ	✔	✔	✔							✔	✔	
17) KE'ANAE, KE'ANAE										✔	✔	
18) WAILUA, KO'OLAU			✔							✔	✔	
19) LOWER NĀHIKU, LOWER NĀHIKU										✔	✔	
20) WAI'ĀNAPANAPA STATE PARK, HĀNA	✔				✔	✔	✔			✔	✔	
21) WAIKOLOA BEACH, HĀNA	✔		✔							✔	✔	
22) HĀNA BEACH PARK, HĀNA	✔	✔			✔	✔	✔		✔		✔	
23) KAIHALULU BEACH, HĀNA	✔	✔							✔			✔
24) LEHO'ULA BEACH, HĀNA								✔				✔
25) KŌKĪ BEACH PARK, HĀNA	✔		✔	✔		✔		✔			✔	
26) HĀMOA BEACH, HĀNA	✔		✔	✔				✔				✔
27) MAKA'ALAE BEACH, MAKA'ALAE	✔								✔			✔
28) WAILUA, KĪPAHULU									✔			✔
29) PEPEIAOLEPO BEACH, KĪPAHULU									✔			✔
30) SEVEN POOLS PARK, KĪPAHULU	✔						✔			✔	✔	
31) MOKULAU BEACH, KAUPŌ									✔		✔	
32) NU'U BAY, KAUPŌ	✔	✔							✔		✔	
33) HUAKINI BAY, KAUPŌ									✔		✔	
34) KANAIO BEACH, HONUA'ULA										✔	✔	
35) LA PÉROUSE BAY, HONUA'ULA	✔	✔	✔							✔	✔	
36) 'ĀHIHI-KĪNA'U NATURAL AREA RESERVE, KANAHENA		✔								✔	✔	
37) ONELOA BEACH, PU'U ŌLA'I	✔	✔	✔	✔				✔				✔
38) PU'U ŌLA'I BEACH, PU'U ŌLA'I	✔	✔	✔	✔				✔				✔
39) ONEULI BEACH, PU'U ŌLA'I	✔	✔							✔		✔	
40) MALUAKA BEACH PARK, MĀKENA	✔	✔		✔				✔			✔	
41) MĀKENA LANDING BEACH PARK	✔	✔			✔		✔	✔			✔	
42) PO'OLENALENA BEACH PARK, PO'OLENALENA	✔	✔		✔				✔			✔	

BEACH & LOCATION	BEACH ACTIVITIES				PUBLIC FACILITIES			BEACH COMPOSITION			ACCESS	
	SWIMMING	SNORKELING	SURFING	BODY-SURFING	COMFORT STATION	PICNIC EQUIPMENT	PAVED PARKING	SAND	DETRITAL SAND	ROCK	PUBLIC	PRIVATE
43) PALAUEA BEACH, PALAUEA	✓	✓		✓				✓				✓
44) POLO BEACH, WAILEA	✓	✓		✓			✓	✓			✓	
45) WAILEA BEACH, WAILEA	✓	✓		✓			✓	✓			✓	
46) ULUA BEACH, WAILEA	✓	✓		✓			✓	✓			✓	
47) MŌKAPU BEACH, WAILEA	✓	✓	✓	✓			✓	✓			✓	
48) KEAWAKAPU BEACH, KEAWAKAPU	✓	✓		✓			✓	✓			✓	
49) KAMA'OLE III BEACH PARK, KAMA'OLE	✓	✓		✓	✓	✓	✓	✓			✓	
50) KAMA'OLE II BEACH PARK, KAMA'OLE	✓	✓		✓	✓	✓	✓	✓			✓	
51) KAMA'OLE I BEACH PARK, KAMA'OLE	✓	✓		✓	✓	✓	✓	✓			✓	
52) KALAMA BEACH PARK, KAMA'OLE	✓	✓	✓		✓	✓	✓	✓			✓	
53) KALEPOLEPO BEACH PARK, KALEPOLEPO	✓	✓			✓	✓	✓	✓			✓	
54) MAI POINA 'OE IA'U BEACH PARK, KĪHEI	✓	✓	✓		✓	✓	✓	✓			✓	
55) MĀ'ALAEA BEACH, MĀ'ALAEA	✓	✓	✓	✓				✓			✓	
56) KAPOLI BEACH PARK, MĀ'ALAEA		✓	✓							✓	✓	
57) McGREGOR POINT, McGREGOR POINT	✓	✓						✓			✓	
58) PĀPALAUA STATE WAYSIDE PARK, PĀPALAUA	✓	✓				✓			✓		✓	
59) UKUMEHAME BEACH PARK, UKUMEHAME	✓	✓	✓				✓		✓		✓	
60) OLOWALU BEACH, OLOWALU	✓	✓	✓						✓		✓	
61) AWALUA BEACH, AWALUA	✓		✓	✓					✓		✓	
62) LAUNIUPOKO STATE WAYSIDE PARK, LAUNIUPOKO	✓		✓		✓	✓	✓	✓			✓	
63) PUAMANA BEACH PARK, LAHAINA	✓		✓			✓	✓	✓			✓	
64) LAHAINA, LAHAINA	✓	✓	✓				✓	✓			✓	
65) PU'UNOA BEACH, LAHAINA		✓	✓				✓		✓		✓	
66) WAHIKULI STATE WAYSIDE PARK, WAHIKULI	✓	✓			✓	✓	✓			✓	✓	
67) HANAKA'Ō'Ō BEACH PARK, KĀ'ANAPALI	✓	✓	✓	✓	✓	✓	✓	✓			✓	
68) KĀ'ANAPALI BEACH, KĀ'ANAPALI	✓	✓		✓				✓			✓	
69) HONOKŌWAI BEACH PARK, HONOKŌWAI	✓	✓			✓	✓	✓	✓			✓	
70) KAHANA BEACH, KAHANA	✓	✓						✓			✓	
71) KEONENUI BEACH, 'ALAELOA	✓	✓						✓			✓	
72) 'ALAELOA BEACH, 'ALAELOA	✓	✓	✓					✓				✓
73) HONOKEANA, HONOKEANA	✓	✓								✓		✓
74) NĀPILI BAY, NĀPILI	✓	✓	✓	✓				✓			✓	
75) KAPALUA BEACH, KAPALUA	✓	✓		✓	✓		✓	✓			✓	
76) ONELOA BEACH, KAPALUA	✓	✓		✓				✓			✓	
77) D. T. FLEMING BEACH PARK, HONOKAHUA	✓	✓	✓	✓	✓	✓	✓	✓			✓	
78) MOKULĒ'IA BEACH, HONOLUA	✓	✓		✓				✓			✓	
79) HONOLUA BAY, HONOLUA	✓	✓	✓	✓						✓	✓	
80) PUNALAU BEACH, PUNALAU		✓	✓					✓			✓	
81) HONOKŌHAU BAY, HONOKŌHAU			✓							✓	✓	

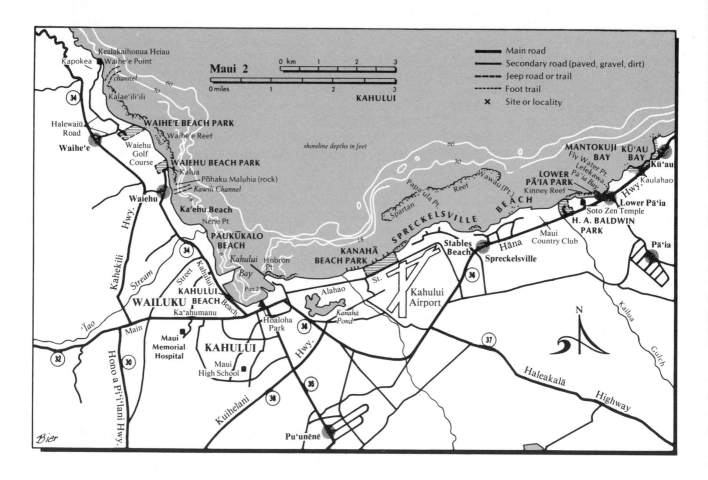

(1)
Waihe'e Beach Park

Four of the most famous streams on the island of Maui are located on the eastern side of the West Maui Mountains. Waikapū, Wailuku, Waiehu, and Waihe'e, collectively known as Nā Wai 'Ehā, "the four waters," are noted throughout the Hawaiian Islands for their beauty. In 1948 composer Charles E. King published his second book of Hawaiian songs and included " 'Inikimālie" (Gentle Pinches). This song, written by James Kahale, honors the four Maui streams whose names begin with *wai* and their companion winds.

VERSES:

Waikapū, makani kokololio	Waikapū, gusty wind
Wailuku, makani lawe mālie	Wailuku, easygoing wind
Waiehu, makani hō'eha 'ili	Waiehu, skin-hurting wind
Waihe'e, makani kili 'o'opu	Waihe'e, graceful wind

CHORUS:

Makani houhou 'ili	Skin-stinging wind
'Ini'iniki mālie	Gently pinching

(Reprinted by permission of the Charles E. King Music Co.)

Waihe'e translates as "slipping water" and its accompanying wind, the makani kili 'o'opu, appears in the song as the "graceful wind.' An alternate translation is the "wind (carrying the) faint odors (of the) gobie fish." A legend says that the 'o'opu nopili was the *kapu* fish of a Waihe'e chief. Someone attempted to eat one secretly, however, and was detected and caught by the drifting aroma of the cooking fish.

Waihe'e Beach Park is located on the *makai* side of the Waiehu Municipal Golf Course driving range. This seeming contradiction in place names is a result of the golf course having the bulk of its land in the Waiehu district. When the course opened in 1928, the main en-

4

WAIHEʻE BEACH PARK. This narrow sand beach strewn with coral rubble and seaweed fronts the beach park and also forms the *makai* boundary of Waiehu Municipal Golf Course. When the ocean is calm, the shallow reef inshore pro-vides some safe swimming areas and excellent diving grounds. In the distance the lower slopes of Haleakala are visible under the low ceiling of clouds.

trance and the clubhouse were constructed in Waiehu. The course has retained its original name even though the main entrance is now in Waiheʻe and the clubhouse has been relocated to the Waiheʻe side of the greens. Waiheʻe Beach Park is fronted by a brown detrital sand beach that begins at Papamoku below the 6th hole. The beach passes through Wahieliʻiliʻi, the name of a *papa* between the 7th and 8th holes, and Kaukalā, a *papa* fronting the 8th hole. Offshore from the park is one of the widest sections of Waiheʻe reef, itself one of the longest and widest reefs on Maui. Beginning at Waiheʻe Point the reef reaches a width of over one thousand feet off Waiheʻe and narrows to about half this width at Paukūkalo, where it terminates. The inshore areas fronting Waiheʻe Beach Park are moderately shallow with sandy channels providing good areas for swim-ming, snorkeling, diving, and shoreline fishing. The narrow beach is also a popular area for beachcombing and *limu* gathering. Strong alongshore currents are infrequent, usually accompanying winter surf or storm surf conditions. Ironwood trees and *naupaka* bushes line the backshore and are scattered throughout the small park. Park facilities include restrooms and show-ers, picnic tables, and a paved parking lot. To reach the area, follow Halewaiū Road in Waiheʻe to the Waiehu Municipal Golf Course parking lot and then turn *makai* on the park access road along the driving range.

To the left of Waiheʻe Beach Park the sandy beach

curves around to the rocky point fronting Waiheʻe Dairy. The access road to this area is appropriately named Halewaiū Road, *halewaiū* meaning "house (of) milk" or dairy. Midway down the beach is a small point called Kalaeʻiliʻili, or Kaʻiliʻili. It is the site of a crudely constructed fishing shack and is a popular gathering place for fishermen. The more common name for this area is "the Round Table," referring to the large spool table fronting the shack.

The west end of the sand beach also marks the end of the reef. A large channel angles offshore and usually has a very powerful rip current running through it, making swimming or diving very dangerous. The water is also usually murky, this end of the beach having suffered considerable erosion. Many ironwood trees and *naupaka* bushes have fallen across the sand as the ocean has stolen the ground from under them. On the driftwood-strewn point beyond the sand beach are the ruins of a *heiau*. It was called Kealakaihonua and is situated in an area called Kapokea. The *heiau* walls are visible from Waiheʻe Beach.

(2)
Waiehu Beach Park

Waiehu means "water spray" and is one of the four famous streams on Maui known as Nā Wai ʻEhā, "the four waters." The name Waiehu probably refers to the mists that form around the *mauka* waterfalls on windy days. The ocean counterpart of these mists is the *ʻehukai* or sea spray.

Waiehu Beach Park is adjacent to the east end of Waiehu Municipal Golf Course. The narrow, coarse white sand beach fronting the park begins at a boulder retaining wall that was constructed to retard erosion of the golf course. This area was called Kauapo, "the wharf," for an old landing that once stood there. All traces of it were destroyed by the tsunami of 1946. *Uapo* or *uwapo* is the Hawaiianization of the English word "wharf." The shoreline fronting the improved portion of the park was formerly called Kalua. The ocean bottom at Kalua is very shallow and rocky, making a poor swimming area. This beach is frequented primarily by fishermen, *limu* gatherers, and beachcombers. The park facilities include a pavilion with restrooms, showers, picnic tables, barbecue grills, and an unpaved parking lot. The park offers a beautiful view of Haleakalā on cloudless days and also an excellent view of the mountain's infrequent snow caps during the winter months. Waiehu Beach Park is located at the end of Lower Waiehu Beach Road. The beach at Waiehu continues for about a mile toward Paukūkalo beyond the park.

Just offshore from the first beach homes is a channel called Kawili, "the swirl." It was named for the movements of a strong rip current that often runs seaward through the channel. Beyond Kawili is a rock in the ocean named Pōhaku Maluhia, "peaceful rock," that can only be seen at low tide on a calm day. The reef surrounding Pōhaku Maluhia is broken, allowing strong currents to come ashore unchecked during times of heavy surf. The offshore bottom is rocky with scattered patches of sand. The area is frequented primarily by fishermen. During the late 1920s the residential shoreline development at Waiehu took its name from Pōhaku Maluhia and was called the Maluhia Beach Lots. Maluhia Church in the center of these homes also took its name from the same source.

The beach that begins at Kalua, the site of Waiehu Beach Park, ends at a small bay called Kaʻehu, "the sea spray." Kaʻehu Beach is a narrow, curving dark detrital sand beach that fronts a swampy marshland sometimes called Paukūkalo Marsh. The coastline is a low sandy plain covered with strand vegetation. Like the rest of the beach preceding it, Kaʻehu offers poor swimming but fair diving conditions on calm days. During heavy surf, strong rip currents run seaward through several sand channels in the reef. The beach ends at a rocky point that marks the mouth of ʻĪao Stream. Kaʻehu can be reached by following the shoreline from Waiehu Beach Park or from Paukūkalo.

(3)
Paukūkalo Beach

Paukūkalo means "taro piece," and is the name of a Hawaiian homestead area and a shoreline residential-industrial neighborhood to the rear of a rocky beach. The beach at Paukūkalo is composed entirely of boulders, many of which are covered with *kaunaʻoa*. The *kaunaʻoa* is a mollusk which solidly affixes itself to rocks in its adult stage and often has very strong, razor-sharp edges. The Hawaiians considered cuts from the *kauna'oa* to be deadly poisonous. The offshore bottom is a continuation of the beach and is very rocky. The entire Paukūkalo shoreline is unprotected from the open ocean and is subject to very strong alongshore and rip currents, especially during heavy surf. Occasionally the waves offshore are good enough for surfing, usually when a north swell and *kona* wind occur at the same time. The boulder beach is frequented primarily by fishermen and beachcombers. It can be reached from the ends of a number of public streets in Paukūkalo that run *makai* from Waiehu Beach Road.

(4)

Kahului Harbor

In 1790 King Kamehameha I brought his war canoes from the island of Hawai'i and landed them on the beach at Kahului. He routed the forces of the Maui chief Kalanikūpule in a famous battle that was later called Kepaniwai o 'Īao. Kahului means "the winning," but the name probably has older origins than this invasion by Kamehameha.

The first Western building erected in Kahului was a warehouse near the beach, built by Thomas Hogan in 1863. It was followed ten years later by Kimble's Store, also constructed near the shoreline. The development at Kahului Bay continued as sugar cane made its commercial debut on Maui and proved to be an economically viable crop. In 1879 a small landing was constructed to serve the sugar planters, and in 1881 the Kahului Railroad Company was incorporated, making its headquarters on the shores of the bay. Kahului Railroad Company was the first railroad in the Hawaiian Islands and initially connected Kahului and Wailuku. Hobron Point, the right point of Kahului Harbor, was named for Captain Thomas Hobron, the founder of the railroad company. Hobron was a sea captain turned merchant, and together with William O. Smith and William H. Bailey, his two sons-in-law, he formed the partnership that began the company.

In 1900 the town of Kahului, infected with bubonic plague, was deliberately burned to the ground to destroy the infected rats spreading the disease. With the rebuilding of Kahului also came the first of the alterations that changed Kahului Bay into a full-scale commercial harbor. By 1910 the Kahului Railroad Company, acquired in 1884 by Samuel G. Wilder, had built at its own expense an 1,800-foot-long rubblemound breakwater, had dredged a basin, and had constructed a 200-foot wharf to accommodate vessels with a 25-foot draft. A newspaper writer of the day observed that the shoreline of Kahului Bay would be a natural place for a hotel: "Here would be found bathing of the best and a splendid beach as well as many other things which would appeal to visitors and which, if properly advertised, would bring many additional tourists to the Valley Island."

On December 7, 1941, the United States entered World War II when a devastating air attack was launched on Pearl Harbor and other target areas on O'ahu by aircraft of the Japanese Imperial Navy. Contrary to popular belief, however, this was not the only attack on American soil during World War II. During the early hours of January 1, 1942, Japanese submarines shelled Kahului Harbor and fire was returned by 75 mm shoreline artillery. Hilo and Nāwiliwili harbors also were shelled at the same time. In November 1945 a Captain Omae, liaison officer from the Japanese Imperial Navy records section, was reassembling destroyed information for General Douglas MacArthur. Omae said that the 1942 assaults were carried out purely for harassment. Their purpose was to keep Americans worried about coastal attacks so that aircraft that might have been used overseas would be kept home. Submarines also shelled Fort Stevens, Oregon, near the mouth of the Columbia River, and the Goleta oil fields near Santa Barbara, California. On February 7, 1942, an airplane was launched from a submarine and sent over the southern Oregon coast to attack military installations, but the lone pilot could not find any.

After World War II Kahului began another era of expansion. Harry and Frank Baldwin wanted to create a "Dream City" on Maui, with reasonably priced homes, primarily for sugar and pine workers, and with parks, industrial and commercial centers, and a memorial hospital. In 1949 the first homes in the Hale Koa subdivision were started and development has continued ever since. Today Kahului houses the largest population on Maui.

Kahului is also the site of the first publicly funded permanent artistic earthwork built in a public place in the United States. Located on the grounds of Maui High School on Lono Avenue, the work resembles a set of three ocean waves on the earth's surface. The work was commissioned by the State Foundation on Culture and the Arts, and executed by Thomas Woodruff. Woodruff's sculpture, created by simply rearranging the former surface with a bulldozer, offers a pleasing contrast to the otherwise flat surroundings.

Kahului Harbor is the only deep-draft harbor on Maui. Except for two sections of beach, the shoreline within the harbor is made up of artificial structures. The existing harbor consists of a 2,315-foot west breakwater, a 2,760-foot east breakwater, and a 600-foot-wide entrance channel between the two breakwaters. In 1963 a 14-foot-wide concrete boat ramp was constructed in the harbor's west breakwater. It includes a protective groin, a rigging catwalk, and unlimited unpaved parking. Boaters unfamiliar with the Kahului area would be well advised to check with local boaters before launching from the ramp. The offshore bottom is shallow and rocky at low tide and the access channel is poorly defined. During the prevailing trade winds, surf often breaks on the reef just outside the ramp, creating a great deal of inshore turbulence. The area is popular with surfers. A small narrow shingle beach lies inshore of the ramp, but it is not a particularly good swimming area. The offshore bottom is shallow and rocky and the water is usually murky. This area of Kahului Harbor is sometimes called Kahului Breakwater Park and is frequented primarily by fishermen, surfers, boaters, and *limu* gatherers.

Kahului Beach begins at a revetment lining the *makai* edge of Kahului Beach Road and ends at Pier 2. The brown detrital sand beach fronts four hotels, Hoaloha Park, and a restaurant. Four narrow boulder-settings front the hotels to retard erosion of the shoreline. The offshore bottom, a mixture of sand and rocks, is shallow and safe for swimming, but usually does not attract swimmers. The inner harbor waters are almost invariably murky. Occasionally small waves break offshore from Hoaloha Park that are good enough for surfing or bodysurfing.

Hoaloha Park is located on Kaʻahumanu Avenue directly across from the Kahului Shopping Center. The park area was formerly occupied by an unsightly con-glomeration of rubbish, discarded junk, and several abandoned, decaying buildings. In 1970 Helen Toms, the charter president of the newly formed Soroptimist Club, suggested to the club that they clean up the area as a service project. The club members agreed and enlisted the help of numerous other community organizations and private companies. The project began in February 1971 and was completed by Kamehameha Day, June 11, of the same year, when the park was blessed and officially opened. The park has since been the focal point of Kamehameha Day festivities every year. All of the time and effort that went into the park's creation was ultimately made possible through the courtesy of Alexander and Baldwin, Inc., which owns the land but has made it available for public use. Alexander and Baldwin, Inc., maintains the park and Mrs. Toms is in charge of its use. The name Hoaloha means "beloved companions" and was chosen to express the positive community spirit and the united effort that were demonstrated in the park's creation.

(5)
Kanahā Beach Park

Kanahā means "the shattered (thing)" and is the name of a pond, a wildlife sanctuary, and a beach park. Kanahā Pond and its twin, Mauoni, are said to have been constructed during the reign of the famous Maui chief Kihaapiʻilani. His name is also associated with Nā Hono a Piʻilani, "the valleys (acquired) by Piʻilani," six valleys in the West Maui Mountains that were part of his domain.

In 1871 the Hawaiian newspaper *Ke Au ʻOkoʻa* told a legend involving a man named Kapoi who lived with his wife at Kaimuheʻe, just above the two waters Kanahā and Mauoni. One day Kapoi's wife went out to gather *ʻūhini* (grasshoppers) and found an owl's nest with seven eggs. Thinking they were duck's eggs, she took them and gave them to Kapoi. He realized what they were, but refused to give them back to the owl who appeared and requested their return. Kapoi then smashed the eggs against the stone wall surrounding the house. Infuriated over the senseless loss, ʻAʻapueo, the mother owl, and her mate, Pueokaia, gathered owls from all the islands. All of the men and chiefs of the area, including Kapoi and his wife, were destroyed. The place *mauka* of the ponds where the cruel breaking of 'A'apueo's eggs was avenged was called Wailuku, "water (of) destruction."

During World War II the military took over large portions of Maui for training and defense sites. One of them was the present airport area, where Naval Air Station Kahului was established in March 1943 as a maintenance station for fleet units. It was a training and staging area, and served also as the central fuel storage and supply depot for all naval activities on Maui. Naval Air Station Kahului was often abbreviated as N.A.S.Ka. and this soon resulted in a new name for the area, Naska. Naska today is the site of Kahului Airport and a small industrial-commercial complex. Some of the old World War II structures can still be found in the area, including the now empty Naska Swimming Pool.

Naska also included the present Kanahā Beach Park, a long park that includes about one mile of shoreline. The entire park is fronted by a wide white sand beach that is broken into numerous pockets by a series of boulder groins. These rock piles were placed in the ocean for the purpose of sand and land retention, as the entire shoreline from Kū'au to Waihe'e has had serious erosion problems for many years. The inshore bottom is shallow and is composed of a mixture of sand and rocks, making a swimming area that is attractive primarily to children. The water is almost invariably murky. The beach begins *makai* of Kahului Airport and ends at Hobron Point, the east point of Kahului Harbor. It is frequented by fishermen, *limu* pickers, picnickers, and windsurfers. The waters offshore the park are highly regarded as one of the best board sailing sites on Maui for both beginning and advanced windsurfers.

Facilities in the park include restrooms, showers, picnic tables, barbecue grills, and several paved parking lots. The primary shade tree is *kiawe,* so all park goers are advised not to come barefoot. Kanahā Beach Park is a very pleasant, peaceful park situated just beyond the hustle and activity of Kahului's town and airport. It offers a beautiful view of the West Maui Mountains, including the town of Wailuku and 'Īao Valley.

The major portion of the beach park is undeveloped and consists of *kiawe* forests crisscrossed by a number of well-used dirt roads. Directly *makai* of the end of Keolani Road, the access road to the park, one of the many dirt roads leads to a sandy knoll, the highest point in the park. This knoll is the site of an old park pavilion that was constructed before the military took control of the area. Its twelve lava rock pillars and high peaked shake-roof are still standing firmly.

Kanahā Beach Park takes its name from Kanahā Pond, a large brackish waterpond located inland of the west end of the park. Kanahā Pond is an important bird sanctuary that supports major populations of stilts, coots, gallinules, and heron, and also serves as wintering grounds for a number of ducks and shoreline birds. In ancient times the pond was used by the Hawaiians as a fishpond. In more recent times the area was controlled for many years by a sugar plantation and then, during World War II, by the U.S. Navy. Kanahā Pond was designated a wildlife refuge in 1952 and declared a Registered National Natural History Landmark in 1971. The pond and its wildlife can best be viewed at the junction of Highway 36 and Highway 396, where a parking lot and an observation shack have been constructed for the public.

(6)
Spreckelsville Beach

Claus Spreckels was a sugar refiner from San Francisco. An efficient but ruthless businessman, he set up his own sugar growing operation in 1878 when he founded the Spreckelsville Plantation on Maui. Samuel Alexander and Henry P. Baldwin had started their sugar plantations in the 1870s, and by 1876 they knew that they had to have water to irrigate their fields. They obtained a government lease authorizing them to build a ditch to carry water from Nāhiku to their Pā'ia plantation. Alexander and Baldwin were allowed two years to complete the project, at which time the lease would expire if the ditch were not completed. Spreckels arrived in Hawai'i while the Hāmākua Ditch was under construction. He quickly ingratiated himself to King Kalākaua and secured a lease for a second ditch on Maui, as well as the rights to Alexander and Baldwin's ditch if they failed to complete it. Much to Spreckel's disappointment, and to the kingdom's surprise, the Hāmākua Ditch was finished before the deadline of September 30, 1878. Undaunted, Spreckels constructed his own ditch and irrigation system and ran a successful plantation.

The type of political maneuvering that Spreckels used against Alexander and Baldwin was typical of his transactions and dealings with the Hawaiian business community and with the monarchy as well. Spreckels became an extremely powerful political figure during the 1880s and had great influence over King Kalākaua and Walter Murray Gibson, the premier and minister of foreign affairs. Both Gibson and Kalākaua had gotten themselves heavily in debt to Spreckels, primarily through gambling at cards. By 1886 Spreckels wanted Kalākaua's crown and this proved to be the turning point in their relationship. Kalākaua was able to secure a loan from a financial syndicate in London, and the debt to Spreckels was paid off. Spreckels' hold on the king and Hawai'i was broken, and he left the islands.

In subsequent years, Henry P. Baldwin himself acquired the Spreckelsville Plantation and changed its name to the Hawaiian Commercial and Sugar Company. This was the beginning of a series of mergers that has resulted in today's H. C. & S. Co., the largest sugar plantation in the state, with mills at Pā'ia and Pu'unēnē. In September 1900 Lowrie Ditch, named for William J. Lowrie, the manager of H. C. & S. Co.'s plantation and mills at Spreckelsville, was completed. Water was brought a distance of twenty-two miles from Kailua to the arid uplands *mauka* of Spreckelsville. As the plantation prospered and grew, so did Spreckelsville. At the peak of its expansion, the area included many plantation camps, two schools, and several large, exclusive shoreline residential areas. Today very little remains to distinguish Spreckelsville as a former center of population. Most of the land occupied by the camps has been reclaimed for sugar cane.

Spreckelsville Beach stretches for over two miles, beginning at a cluster of residential homes at the end of Spreckelsville Beach Road and ending at the Maui Country Club. This long reach of shoreline is broken into a series of short beaches by points of lava, boulders, beach rock, and groins constructed to retain sand. Over the years Spreckelsville Beach has had serious erosion problems, as evidenced in several places by beach rock in the ocean, marking the limits of former shorelines, and also by banks of earth at the present shoreline. Large sand dunes lie behind much of the beach, although many of them have been excavated for beach-home construction. The largest existing dunes front the

golf course and were used as burial grounds by the Hawaiians.

The offshore bottom along most of Spreckelsville Beach is rocky with scattered patches of sand. The water is often murky, but many good swimming areas can be found. The prevailing current runs toward Kahului Harbor and usually is not strong enough inshore to pose any problems. The beach is frequented primarily by fishermen and beachcombers. Public access is available in several places. The most popular area is called Stables, for the H. C. & S. stables at the intersection of Hāna Highway and Spreckelsville Beach Road. In the early years the plantation kept saddle horses for the supervisors, dray horses to pull the plows and wagons, and mules to carry seed and fertilizer. Pack animals are still kept there and used today to haul "seeds," short pieces of cane which will sprout, into the fields to replant dead areas, that is, isolated plots that have failed to grow after the initial cane planting. These horses are also used to carry barrels of weed poison, which is sprayed by hand. Adjoining the H. C. & S. stables is an open expanse of low sand dunes covered with strand vegetation. Located near the end of one of the airport's runways, this vacant area was formerly the site of a plantation camp. It was razed and the residents relocated because of the danger of the camp's proximity to the runway. This open shoreline between the stables and a residential community is the only public section of Spreckelsville Beach. Other areas of the beach can be easily reached by following the shoreline from Kanahā Beach Park or Baldwin Park. To provide further access, Alexander and Baldwin, Inc., has agreed to lease to the County of Maui a beach parcel of almost 47,000 square feet at Spreckelsville. This area is located at the end of Kealakai Place.

(7)

H. A. Baldwin Park

Harry A. Baldwin, a son of Henry P. Baldwin, was born on January 12, 1871, while his father and his uncle, Samuel Alexander, were developing their first sugar plantation on Maui. Harry Baldwin became a builder in his own right, a delegate to Congress, and a member of the state senate. He was also the manager of Maui Agriculture and a partner with Angus MacPhee in the Kaho'olawe Ranch Company. Harry Baldwin died in

1946. The park is a memorial to him, his achievements, and his contributions to the island of Maui.

The park was originally developed as a company recreational facility by Hawaiian Commercial and Sugar Co., now a division of Alexander and Baldwin, Inc. From 1949 to 1963 it was leased to the East Maui Community Association. In 1963 the park was leased to the County of Maui and converted into a public beach park.

To the right of the park are two well-known shoreline landmarks, the Rinzai Zen temple and the Lime Kiln. The Rinzai Zen temple was founded by the Reverend Nashin Okamoto in 1932. Today the Reverend Kiyoshi Oshiro, the Reverend Okamoto's pupil, services and maintains the temple. The Reverend Oshiro designed the present temple and built it after the original temple was demolished by the 1946 tsunami. Beyond the Rinzai Zen temple is the Lime Kiln, which belongs to Hawaiian Commercial and Sugar Co. The kiln dates back to the 1920s. The lime-producing process involves converting beach sand into a lime powder. The bulk of the powder is bagged and sent to the sugar mills, where it is vital to the processing of sugar cane. After the cane is crushed, lime is added to the juice to prevent deterioration and also to aid in clarification, or the removing of impurities. All of the lime is used locally on Maui.

H. A. Baldwin Park is the most popular beach park on the windward side of Maui. The beach and the adjoining picnic areas are always crowded. The major attraction is the surf that breaks along the entire length of the park's long, wide white sand beach. This shorebreak draws bodysurfers from all the nearby centers of population, such as Wailuku, Kahului, and Pā'ia, making Baldwin Park a natural gathering place for the island's youth. Tourists and older residents also utilize the area, because of the convenient facilities as well as the beach. The large playing field to the rear of the beach is used by many sports organizations. Occasionally the waves offshore from the pavilion are good enough for board surfing and it is not uncommon to find surfers in the park.

The long white sand beach fronting the park begins *makai* of the Maui Country Club golf course at Red Hill and ends at the Lime Kiln. Usually the shorebreak is small, but good enough to sustain bodysurfing on almost any day. Occasionally it gets big enough to be dangerous for anyone unfamiliar with the impact of shorebreak surf. The bottom slopes quickly to overhead depths. The constantly incoming surf frequently creates small rip currents, but they are usually of little consequence to anyone experienced with the ocean. Alongshore currents generally run toward the left end of the beach. The safest swimming area for little children and those seeking calmer conditions is in the lee of a narrow length of beach rock that angles seaward from the shoreline near the pavilion. Another safe area for children can be found at the far west end of the long beach. There, too, a section of beach rock exposed by erosion forms a protected swimming area. The natural pond is shallow and sandy.

Facilities in the park include one pavilion with picnic tables, kitchen facilities, and appliances; barbecue grills; picnic tables on the park grounds; restrooms; showers; one baseball field; one soccer field; a swing set; and paved and unpaved parking. The park is located on the Hāna Highway between Spreckelsville and Lower Pā'ia. The access road from the highway to the beach is bordered by a narrow, unfenced drainage ditch that is usually filled with stagnant water. Little children should not be allowed to wander in the area.

The first bodysurfing contest on Maui was held at Baldwin Park on February 5, 1977. The event was initially a St. Antony's School project coordinated with the county's Youth Services Office. It was intended only for students, but was opened to the general public on the day of the contest. Baldwin Park was selected as the contest site not because it has the best bodysurfing waves, but because it has the most consistent waves.

(8)
Lower Pā'ia Park

Pā'ia means "noisy," but the origin of the name is now unknown. The town of Pā'ia is best known as the site of the first sugar plantation formed by Henry P. Baldwin and his brother-in-law, Samuel Alexander. Pā'ia was also the original destination of the famous Hāmākua Ditch, the first major aquaduct constructed on Maui. After growing sugar cane for several years, Alexander and Baldwin realized that their fields in the central lowlands needed to be irrigated. Baldwin conceived the idea of carrying water from the Nāhiku district near Hāna over the eastern slope of Haleakalā to the old Pā'ia Plantation by irrigation ditches and tunnels. The project was started in November 1876 and completed in September 1878. The Hāmākua Ditch was one of the major engineering feats of its day and an important example for the rest of the sugar industry.

The inland town of Pā'ia grew considerably around the sugar mill on Baldwin Avenue, moving both *mauka* and *makai*. As homes and stores began to concentrate around the Hāna Highway, a new village formed that was simply called Lower Pā'ia. Today Lower Pā'ia still retains a picturesque plantation-town profile, but most of the old wooden buildings now house tourist-oriented shops and restaurants. Caravans of rental cars laden with tourists daily assail the rigors of the Hāna Highway, which passes directly through Lower Pā'ia.

There are two sandy beaches in Lower Pā'ia, one is on Pā'ia Bay and the other is on Mantokuji Bay. The wide, sloping white sand beach in Pā'ia Bay begins at the Lime Kiln and ends at a rocky point. The most popular section of the beach fronts Lower Pā'ia Park, a public beach park on the Hāna Highway. The surf in this area often breaks far enough offshore for surfing. The shorebreak also provides good waves for bodysurfing and is sometimes better than Baldwin Park on the same swell. However, Lower Pā'ia Park is not a popular bodysurfing spot. During a big winter swell the shorebreak is often huge and pounding, creating very powerful rip currents. The alongshore currents are also strong and make staying in the lineup a constant effort. The bottom drops to overhead depths very close to the water's edge. The beach is much safer for swimming on calm days when there is no surf, but even then the alongshore currents can be persistent. The ocean is usually murky.

Lower Pā'ia Park is located on Hāna Highway on the Kahului side of the town of Lower Pā'ia. This shoreline area, once an unsightly rubbish dump, was cleared and converted into a park in 1934 as a community service project of the Outdoor Circle. Maui Agriculture Company leased the land to the County of Maui and in 1947, in a land exchange, title was conveyed to the Territory of Hawaii. Maui Agriculture Company subsequently was merged with Alexander and Baldwin, Inc. Facilities in the park include restrooms, picnic tables, a basketball court with lights, a softball field, and a swing set. The park is a popular gathering place for Christians, un-doubtedly because of the Pā'ia Christian Youth Center adjacent to the grounds.

To the west of the beach park and beyond the small rocky point is Kinney Reef. It was named for Claud Kinney, an ex-seafaring man who made his home next to the Lime Kiln and was the foreman of the H. C. & S. warehouse. He was a colorful figure and many interesting stories are still told about him. To the east of the beach park is a rocky point marking the end of the sand beach. The side of the point that faces Pā'ia Bay was called Lelekawa, "to jump from a high place into the water." Children from the neighborhood used to jump into the ocean off these rocks. The outer point beyond Lelekawa is commonly called Fly Water Point. Heavy surf breaking across the point crashes into a large flat-surfaced rock, causing the white water to fly skyward.

(9)
Mantokuji Bay

The narrow white sand beach in Mantokuji Bay is the second of the two beaches in Lower Pā'ia. The bay and the beach take their name from the Mantokuji Mission, located on the shoreline *makai* of the Hāna Highway. The mission was founded in 1907 by the Reverend Sokyo Ueoka, who was ordained in Tokyo as a minister of the Soto Zen sect. The Reverend Sokyo Ueoka was succeeded by his son, Sokan Ueoka, who was in turn succeeded by his son, Shuko Ueoka, the present resident minister. Mantokuji Bay is also known as Otera Bay, *otera* meaning "temple" in Japanese. The small white sand beach to the rear of the temple lies between two rocky points. The offshore bottom is rocky, offering poor swimming conditions. This area has had severe erosion problems, and the water is usually murky. A pillbox on the beach is a remnant of World War II shoreline defenses. Similar structures can be found at Pā'ia Bay and at many other shoreline areas on Maui. The area is frequented primarily by fishermen. There is no public access.

(10)
Kū'au Bay

Kū'au means "handle" and is the name of a point and a small residential community on the Hāna Highway. Kū'au Bay to the west of the point is primarily rocky, with several interspersed pockets of white sand. The most popular area is Kaulahao, "iron chain," which adjoins the left point of the bay. Kaulahao is a small, wide, coral-rubble and white sand beach that is fronted along its entire seaward edge by a shelf of beach rock. Offshore the bottom is rocky and swimming is poor. Inshore of the shelf are small tidal pools which can accommodate children as long as the ocean is calm and surf is not washing over the rocks. Kaulahao, locally often pronounced Kalahao, fronts a field of sugar cane owned by Alexander and Baldwin, Inc. The company allows the public access to the shoreline, but has had problems with people dumping rubbish in the area. Warning signs are posted along the backshore of the beach.

The other popular place in Kū'au Bay is a small cove that was called Lamalani. Lamalani is better known today as Tavares Bay, for Antone F. (A. F.) Tavares, a well-known Maui resident, whose family still lives near the bay. The beach of Tavares Bay is only a tiny pocket of white sand fronted by rocks and backed by a concrete retaining wall. The primary attraction is the surf. Surf-

ers and bodysurfers constitute the majority of those who frequent the area. There is no public access.

(11)
Father Jules Papa

During the early 1900s the rocky point that now houses most of the Kū'au residential community was the home of an elderly man named Ako. He was the oldest person living in the area, so the point was known by his name, Ako Point. A channel through the rocks in the middle of the point was called Ako Channel. These names are still used today by local fishermen. Ako was buried on his property next to two other family graves. All evidence of the graves and the ruins of a small fishing shrine that stood on the property were eradicated when the lot was bulldozed for construction of a private home.

To the east of Ako Point is a beautiful pocket of white sand that is commonly called Kū'au Cove. The entire cove is fronted by a wide shelf of exposed reef, a *papa* in Hawaiian. *Makai* of the *papa* the ocean is deep, and strong alongshore currents usually pull from east to

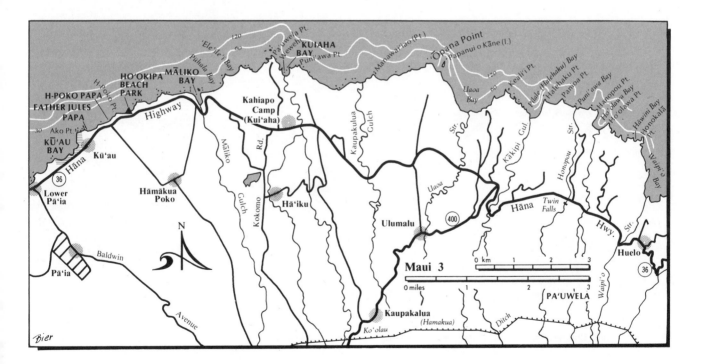

west. At the west end of the cove a rip current runs seaward along Ako Point. The inner edge of the *papa* has several large tidal pools which are ideal places for children to get wet along this otherwise dangerous coastline. The tidal pools are safe except when heavy surf sweeps completely over the *papa*. In former times this was a favorite place for fishermen to leave their families while they went diving in the reefs offshore.

Kū'au Cove is better known among local residents as Father Jules Papa. Father Jules Verhaeghe was born in Belgium, on March 28, 1885. He arrived in Kū'au in 1922 to take over the Holy Rosary Church, which had been built about 1900. The church was located between Kū'au Store and the Catholic cemetery. In 1928 Father Jules built the Holy Rosary Church in Pā'ia and vacated the old building in Kū'au. The beach below the former church and the cemetery, however, still retained the name Father Jules Papa.

The best-known landmark in the area today is Mama's Fish House. Floyd Christenson bought the former nightclub in 1973, remodeled the building, and leased it to Hilda Costa, the original "Mama," who operated the restaurant as a family venture. In 1976 the Costas left the restaurant, so Christenson himself took over the operation. Public access over a privately owned unimproved lot at the right end of the beach is allowed.

(12)
H-Poko Papa

Around the east point from Father Jules Papa is an almost identical beach known as H-Poko Papa. H-Poko is a common abbreviated form of Hāmākua Poko that is almost invariably used by Maui residents. *Papa* is the Hawaiian word for the wide shelf of exposed reef that fronts the short, narrow white sand beach. Hāmākua, which means "long corner," is the name of two districts

H-POKO PAPA. *Papa* is the Hawaiian word for the flat, table-like shelf of reef that sits between the sand and the ocean. H-Poko is an abbreviated form of Hāmākua Poko, the name of the district in which this *papa* is located. H-Poko Papa is popular with both shoreline fishermen and skin divers. During the winter months many surfers gravitate to this area, attracted by the often excellent waves breaking across the reefs offshore.

14

on Maui, Hāmākua Loa, "long Hāmākua," and Hāmākua Poko, "short Hāmākua." H-Poko Papa, located below the intersection of the Hāna Highway and Holomua Road, was named not only because it is in Hāmākua Poko, but because it is directly *makai* of the former H-Poko Mill and H-Poko Camp. The ruins of the mill, constructed in 1880, are located behind the old Maui High School buildings on Holomua Road. The ruins are not apparent at first glance because they are completely covered by vegetation. Maui High School is now located in Kahului.

H-Poko Papa is fronted by deep water, with strong alongshore currents. There are several large tidal pools that can accommodate wading children except during heavy surf when waves sweep across the rocks. The area is frequented primarily by fishermen. To the east of H-Poko Papa is a sea cliff called H-Poko Point. The large dusty vacant lot on top of the point is one of the most popular drive-in spots on Maui to watch surfers in action. During the winter and spring months the huge surf that forms on the offshore reefs attracts surfers from all over the island. H-Poko Point offers an excellent view not only of the riders directly offshore but of those at nearby Ho'okipa Park as well. The land surrounding both H-Poko Papa and H-Poko Point is privately owned but the public is allowed access.

(13)
Ho'okipa Beach Park

Ho'okipa Beach Park, the original home of contemporary surfing on Maui, is one of the island's best-known shoreline landmarks. Maui Agriculture leased the land for the park to the County of Maui in 1933 and in a land exchange conveyed title to the Territory of Hawai'i in 1947. The name Ho'okipa means "hospitality." Probably the foremost promoter of the park's fame not only on Maui but throughout Hawai'i is a beautiful song that is today a Hawaiian standard. It was written by Alice Johnson, who because of her beautiful voice is still called "the Songbird of Maui." In 1936, while Alice was singing with the Royal Hawaiian Band, her family moved from Lower Pā'ia to Kū'au. In 1937, after returning to Maui, she and her sister decided to walk over and have a look at the park in their new neighborhood. A close family friend was the parkkeeper, and when the two young girls arrived, their friend had just finished her *poi* lunch. Then she lay down on the lawn under a *hau* tree and fell asleep for the remainder of her lunch hour. At that time there were many *hau* trees and a wide white sand beach fronting the park's present seawall. The serenity and beauty of the setting inspired Alice to write the song she entitled "Ho'okipa Park Hula."

The surf offshore from Ho'okipa Beach Park provides surfers with waves almost all year round, as the reefs pick up both summer and winter swells. The most spectacular waves, however, occur during the winter and often reach heights of ten to fifteen feet. This tremendous surf is some of the best on Maui.

Contemporary surfing got started on Maui at Ho'okipa in the early 1930s, and in 1935 a small group of surfers formed the Ho'okipa Surf Club. A small building that served as a clubhouse and a set of surfboard racks were donated and constructed in the park by Harold Rice. Foremost among the charter members were two brothers, Donald and Teruo Uchimura, who have both been avid surfers as well as great promoters of the sport of surfing since the founding of the club.

During the later 1930s Ho'okipa Beach Park was also used by the Hui Makani, a youth organization for the children of Lower Pā'ia and Kū'au. It was started by a policeman, Curtis Sylva, who often brought the children to the park to swim and surf. During World War II the park became a favorite party site of the men of the Fourth Marine Division, whose camp was at Kokomo.

The destructive tsunami of April 1, 1946, completely altered the natural features of the park. Many of the *hau* trees and most of the wide sand beach were lost, and the high seawall that now borders the seaward edge of the park was constructed to prevent further damage.

During the early 1960s a second Ho'okipa Surf Club was formed on Maui. Originally called the Maui Surf Club, the members decided on the name Ho'okipa Surf Club because the park was their usual meeting and surfing place. The guiding forces behind the new club were Barbara and William Meheula. Under their leadership the club became an outstanding and influential youth organization. The club participated in many community service projects, initiated the first Lāna'i-Lahaina surfboard race, and coordinated a weekend of festivities that evolved into the annual Lahaina Whaling Spree. The club members were also the first to surf many of

Maui's then virgin surfing grounds. They conceived names still familiar to surfers, such as Hot Sands, Lone Palm, and Pine Tree.

In the early 1970s a new ocean sport called windsurfing was introduced to Hawai'i. Its popularity swept O'ahu first and then moved to Maui. By the 1980s the international windsurfing community had discovered that the wind and waves on Maui, particularly at Ho'okipa Beach Park, offered some of the most exciting board sailing sites in the world. Today the surf at Ho'okipa hosts windsurfers from every corner of the globe and provides the venue for a number of major windsurfing competitions.

The beach fronting the park is little more than a strip of white sand behind a wide, rocky shelf. This *papa* makes entries into the ocean precarious during periods of high surf. The bottom offshore is a mixture of reef and patches of sand. Longshore currents are often strong and run toward the high point at the west end of the beach. The beach park is not particularly suitable for swimming, especially during periods of high surf. However, during periods of calm seas some swimming occurs at both ends of the beach. The primary shoreline activities are fishing, surfing, and windsurfing. Facilities at the park include restrooms, showers, picnic pavilions, and paved parking. A large parking lot on Ho'okipa Point offers an excellent view of the park and the surf offshore. The park borders the Hāna Highway.

(14)
Māliko Bay

Māliko means "budding," as in the appearance and growth of young flowers. Māliko Bay sits at the head of Māliko Gulch, a very long and deep gulch that originates above Makawao. A well-known incident involving Henry P. Baldwin occurred at Māliko during the construction of the Hāmākua Ditch. In November 1876 Baldwin organized the Hāmākua Ditch Company to carry water by tunnel and ditch from the Nāhiku district in East Maui to the dry lowlands of central Maui. The water was needed to irrigate the sugar cane fields of his Pā'ia Plantation. One of the project's major problems was crossing the deep gulches that run down to the ocean on the flanks of Haleakalā. Pipes had to be run down one side and up the other. When the workers reached Māliko, they balked at the extremely high and steep cliffs. Henry Baldwin personally went to the site and lowered himself down the cliff, to show that it could be done safely. The most impressive aspect of this feat was that Baldwin had only one arm, having lost the other in an industrial accident at his Pā'ia Mill.

In 1913 the Kahului Railroad Company constructed across Māliko Gulch a steel railroad tressel that became a famous landmark. It was 684 feet long and 230 feet high, the highest railroad tressel ever constructed in Hawai'i. The Hawaiian Consolidated Railroad on the Big Island had the longest at 1,006 feet, but it was only 193 feet high. The Māliko tressel was located just below Pu'u o Umi and was also used to support the irrigation conduit of the Hāmākua Ditch across the gulch. The huge structure was dismantled and scrapped in the 1960s, but many of the old concrete foundation blocks can still be easily located.

Māliko Bay is a small, narrow bay with steep rocky sides. A small boulder beach lies at the head of the bay. The inshore water is usually murky, a result of the discharge from Māliko Stream. Large rocks sitting on the shallow ocean bottom protrude above the surface of the water. Sometimes small surf forms on these rocks. The bay is not a good swimming area, especially during heavy surf. Large waves create powerful rip currents and a tremendous amount of surge at the mouth of the bay. Very large surf sometimes completely closes the narrow entrance channel. The major attraction at Māliko is its public boat ramp. Constructed in 1976, the concrete ramp is located on the east side of the bay. Its location affords some protection from the prevailing currents and winds, but not from heavy surf. The ramp is popular and well used, however, because of the long distances between launching facilities on Maui. Māliko Bay is considered to be one of the best *akule* and *'ōpelu* grounds on Maui. Both private and commercial fishermen frequent the area to net those schooling fish. Māliko Bay can be reached by following the access road that turns off the Hāna Highway on the Hāna side of the bridge.

To the rear of the boulder beach is a large coconut grove with several corrals and a riding arena. Known as the Double A Arena, it was built and is owned by two brothers, Daniel and Wilfred Awai.

(15)
Kuiaha Bay

The shoreline from Māliko to Honomanū is characterized by high, steep sea cliffs. Within this long reach of cliffs are a number of bays that are usually little more than wide, moderately deep indentations in the shoreline, usually where streams meet the ocean. The beaches in these areas are narrow stretches of large boulders lying directly at the base of the sea cliffs. Many of these boulder beaches are not accessible at all by land, and if they are, it is only by a hazardous climb using a rope or cable to get down the cliffs. During the winter and spring months these bays are assaulted by heavy surf that sweeps completely across the boulders against the sea cliffs. There are no fringing reefs to check the advance of surf or strong currents. Over the years many fishermen have lost their lives along this dangerous coastline. These rough waters have long been excellent grounds for netting *akule* and *'ōpelu* and for hooking *'ū'ū*, *'āweoweo,* and *āhole*. The open bays include Pūhala, 'Ele'īle'ī (also called Watercress), Uaoa (also known as Keone or Black Sand to the old-time *akule* fishermen), Halehaku (also known to fishermen as Kākipi for the gulch inland and frequently labeled Pīlale on maps), Puni'awa (at the end of Honopou Stream), Hāwini, Waipi'o, Hoalua, and Hanawana. There is no public access to any of these shoreline areas except from the ocean. Many of the bays are over one mile away from the Hāna Highway, and all of the land between the highway and the shoreline is private property replete with locked gates and No Trespassing signs.

Within the reach of sea cliffs between Māliko and Honomanū are also several bays which are fairly accessible by land. These bays, which include Kuiaha, Ho'olawa, and Makaiwa, are narrower and more recessive than their neighbors and offer a greater degree of protection from the heavy surf and powerful currents that sweep the coastline. For these reasons they are more attractive to anyone wishing to visit the shoreline. However, there is no public access by land to any of these bays, either.

Kuiaha Bay is probably the best representative of these inaccessible areas, in light of all the attention that has been focused on it. Kuiaha Bay is located in an area known as Pa'uwela. The east point of the bay was formerly known as Puniawa. Puniawa is also an alternate name of the bay as well, but should not be confused with Puniawa Bay at Honopou, a short distance up the coast. Kuiaha is also known as Coconut Grove, for the small stand of twenty-five coconut trees on the coastline of the bay. At the west point of the bay is a cluster of huge rocks in the ocean that was called Wewehi. Wewehi was the sentinel who indicated the conditions of the ocean. The inhabitants of Kuiaha lived upland some distance from the ocean, but by looking at Wewehi they could determine the conditions in the bay from the amount of white water and surge at these rocks. They could also see what the tide was doing. While the people lived inland, their canoes and nets were stored in sheds on the shoreline. Residents of surrounding villages also used the bay, along with the people of Kuiaha. The village at Kuiaha today is called Kahiapo Camp. It was named for the Reverend Moses Kahiapo, who founded the Ho'omana Na'auao Church there, one of the first Hawaiian churches built in the area.

The situation of people living *mauka* and going *makai* to fish or simply to enjoy the ocean was ordained by geographical necessity in all the areas along this stretch of coastline. In recent times, however, many of the old trails and access roads to the shoreline have been fenced off or closed with locked gates, not only to the general public but to local residents as well. In June and November of 1977 Leslie Kuloloio and Charles Maxwell led two marches to Kuiaha to protest the lack of public access. The two leaders were joined by their families, friends, and supporters, including several longtime residents of the Pa'uwela area. There is still no public access to the area.

Pa'uwela Point on the west side of Kuiaha Bay is another area popular among fishermen and other local residents. The point has been the site of the Pa'uwela Lighthouse since 1910. In 1978 the 3.3 acre parcel surrounding the light station was declared surplus by the Coast Guard and turned over to the Department of Health, Education and Welfare (HEW). In 1981 ownership of the land was transferred from federal jurisdiction to Maui County for use as a public park. The park is called Pa'uwela Point Park. Improvements to the site included demolition of the lighthouse keeper's quarters which were badly vandalized, installation of a water line and a fence along the cliff, and landscaping. The park is open only during daylight hours.

Below the sea cliffs on the Kuiaha side of Pa'uwela Point is a wide, rocky terrace with several large tidal pools. It is a popular area for fishing and exploring, but only when the ocean is calm. Otherwise it is an extremely dangerous place where fishermen have been swept off the rocks and drowned in heavy surf. Adjoining the terrace is a deep cove that is popularly known as Shark Hole. Shark Hole received its name because a group of men formerly fished there for sharks. They began their sport-fishing about 1924. On the terrace they built a large boom that extended out over the cove. From the base of the boom a length of fence wire was stretched across the mouth of the cove and secured to a pipe anchored in the opposite point. A baited hook was hung from the wire. The carcasses of unlicensed dogs shot by the camp police at Hāmākua Poko Camp were the primary bait. If a shark was hooked, it was pulled over to the terrace, shot with a 45–70 hexagonal-barreled elephant gun and then hoisted on the terrace with the boom. The shark hunters dug the steps and the two

caves in the claylike earth of the cliffs that are still visible today. They also constructed a shack for sleeping and storage and named their camp Hale Pukamanō, their version of Shark Hole in Hawaiian.

(16)
Honomanū Bay

Honomanū is a lush, verdant, tree-blanketed valley. A stream runs the length of the narrow valley and crosses the narrow boulder beach at the head of Honomanū Bay. Occasionally during the summer months, small amounts of beach sand accrete on the otherwise rocky beach. Sometimes boats are launched across the beach when the ocean is calm. Directly offshore from the beach, the bottom is very rocky, making poor conditions for recreational swimming. Diving or snorkeling is possible, but only on calm days. During heavy surf the entire bay is turbulent and strong rip currents run seaward from the inshore areas. The waves are sometimes good enough for surfing, but the rocky bottom makes it a risky venture.

Honomanū is an undeveloped beach park. A secondary dirt road from the Hāna Highway leads to the beach

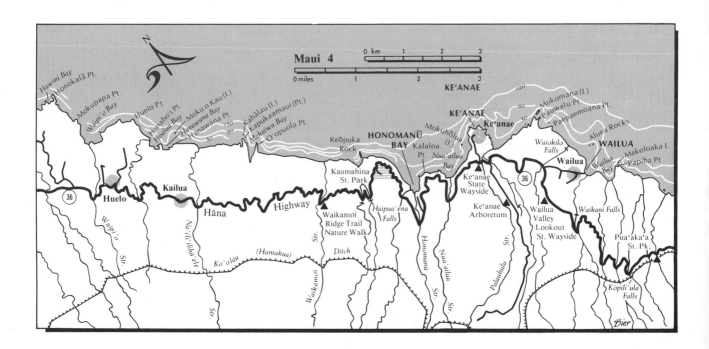

18

HONOMANŪ BAY. The waters of Honomanū Stream flow into the ocean after crossing the rocky beach at the head of Honomanū Bay. The surf offshore is dangerous, breaking over numerous submerged boulders, but it still draws many surfers as surfing opportunities are very limited along this coastline. A secondary public road leads to the beach from the Hāna Highway.

on the Keʻanae side of the valley. There are no facilities, but the open area in the backshore provides a nice picnic ground and is a good place to watch the surfers. Wading and limited swimming are possible in the stream to the rear of the beach. The area is frequented primarily by fishermen and surfers.

(17)
Keʻanae

Keʻanae is a low fan of lava that extends about a half mile into the ocean from the sea cliffs on the shoreline. In former times Keʻanae was famed for its taro patches, and the name Keʻanae, "the mullet," is said to have been originally the name of a royal taro patch. There is no beach on the Keʻanae headland, as the entire peninsula is edged by low sea cliffs composed of jagged black pinnacles of lava. Keʻanae Park is located on the windward side of the peninsula next to historic Lanakila ʻIhiʻihi o Iēhowa Ona Kaua Church, a Congregational church that was built in 1860. The park is simply a grassy area with no facilities. It is a nice picnic area in pleasant, picturesque surroundings, and also provides opportunities for shoreline fishing.

In 1961 the County of Maui with the help of local residents constructed a 12-foot-wide boat ramp on a small parcel of state-owned land. The concrete ramp is located on the leeward side of the peninsula near the site of the old Keʻanae Landing. It is used primarily by boaters from Keʻanae from April to September, when ocean conditions are favorable. Even on calm days, however, launching a boat at this ramp is a tricky operation. The exit and entry channel is very narrow and is bordered by large rocks.

A small pocket of shingle can be found at the mouth

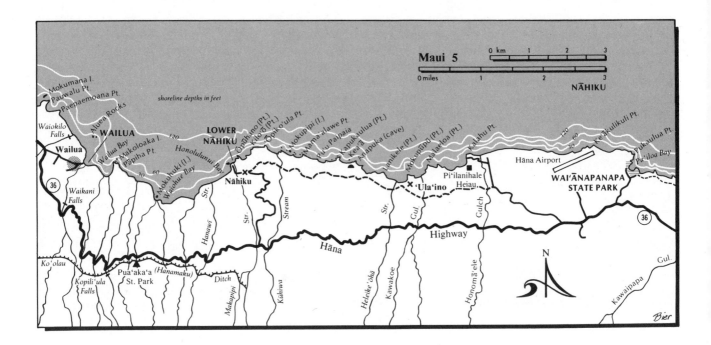

of Palauhulu Stream on the east side of Keʻanae Peninsula. The bottom offshore is rocky and the beach is exposed to the open ocean. There is no public access.

(18)
Wailua

Wailua means "two waters" and is the name of one of the most famous taro-producing areas on Maui. The large patches under cultivation can best be seen from the Hāna Highway where it passes inland and above the village of Wailua. This area is part of the Koʻolau district and is actually made up of two land divisions, Wailuanui and Wailuaiki. This Wailua in Koʻolau is sometimes confused with the Wailua of the Kīpahulu district, an entirely different place.

Wailua Beach is composed of boulders and is unprotected from the open ocean. The alongshore currents are very strong throughout the year, no matter what the ocean conditions are. Swimming is very dangerous. Occasionally the waves are good enough for surfing, but heavy surf makes the currents worse, increasing the dangers in the ocean. The area is frequented primarily by fishermen. Keep Out signs have been posted by the County of Maui near the bottom of the access road to keep visitors from driving all the way to the shoreline, as their cars invariably get stuck at the bottom of the steep hill and there is no help available for miles. Anyone not familiar with the area should park above the signs and walk the remaining distance.

(19)
Lower Nāhiku

Nāhiku means "the seven (districts of the area)" and it is the wettest place on Maui. This fact undoubtedly influenced Harry P. Baldwin, who started the Hāmākua Ditch in 1876 to carry water from the mountains of Nāhiku to Pāʻia to irrigate his sugar cane.

On January 24, 1905, the Nāhiku Rubber Plantation, the first rubber plantation on American soil, was incorporated. High-quality rubber trees had been planted in the area as early as 1899 to determine if they would grow well and also be commercially productive. By 1905 the firm was convinced that their rubber trees would thrive and produce a good quality of latex. The Nāhiku Rubber Plantation had purchased nearly 900 acres of fee simple property, and began planting on a large scale.

20

Planting and tapping operations continued until 1916, when high labor costs finally forced the company to close. The three-mile winding road from the Hāna Highway to the shoreline in Lower Nāhiku passes many groves of rubber trees and the crumbling remains of a coral flume, and ends at the ruins of Nāhiku Landing. The landing was constructed in 1903 and abandoned when the plantation closed.

The cove in Lower Nāhiku is located at the east end of Honolulunui Bay. This Honolulu, situated between Hanawī and Makapipi streams, and the one on the island of Hawai'i are the only two places in the islands that bear the same name as the state capital on O'ahu.

The shoreline of Lower Nāhiku is composed of low sea cliffs with boulder beaches at their bases. The entire area is exposed to the open ocean and is subject to heavy surf and strong inshore currents. The access road from Hāna Highway near the Makapipi Stream Bridge ends at a small unimproved park of *hau* and *kamani* trees, a pleasant picnic area with a beautiful view of the coast to Moku Mana. The ruins of the old landing are nearby on the rocks.

(20)
Wai'ānapanapa State Park

Wai'ānapanapa means "glistening water" and is the name of a large water-filled cave located on the park grounds. The cave is actually a collapsed section of a lava tube that has filled with fresh water. The legend of Wai'ānapanapa Cave says that a cruel chief, Ka'akea,

WAI'ĀNAPANAPA STATE PARK. With the exception of Pa'iloa Beach, this pocket beach composed of small, smooth, water-rounded pebbles, the entire shoreline of Wai'ānapanapa State Park is lined with low sea cliffs such as those visible on the left and right points of the bay. Heavy surf funnels unchecked directly into the bay, creating a powerful shorebreak and dangerous rip currents. Many of the drownings and near-drownings that have occurred here have been caused by these dangerous water conditions.

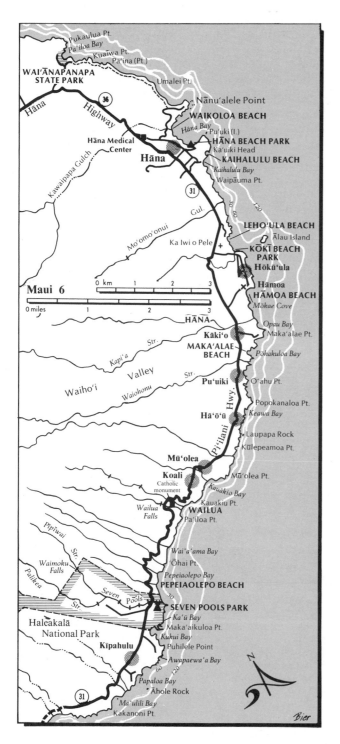

suspected his wife, Pōpō'alaea, of having an affair with another man. Pōpō'alaea fled and took refuge in a hidden chamber of the cave that could be reached by swimming a short distance under water. She and her attendant came out at night for food. One day Ka'akea was passing the pool when he saw the shadow of the servant holding a *kāhili*, a royal standard. Their hiding place was exposed and Ka'akea killed them both. The water in the pool is said to turn red on certain nights, commemorating their deaths.

Wai'ānapanapa State Park encompasses 120 acres which include many historical sites, 12 lodging units, a caretaker's residence, a beach park, picnic tables and barbecue grills, restrooms and showers, paved parking lots, a shoreline hiking trail, and a black shingle beach. This pocket beach—called Pa'iloa, "always splashing" —is located below the improved portion of the park and is situated at the head of a rather narrow bay that is open to the ocean. Waves breaking offshore come into the beach unchecked by any reef or rocks. Strong rip currents are common, originating at the edge of the often pounding shorebreak where the ocean bottom drops off sharply to overhead depths. Pa'iloa Beach is not a safe beach for nonswimmers, poor swimmers, or little children. People overconfident of their abilities or unfamiliar with the ocean and careless of its power have lost their lives here. Pa'iloa has a nice pocket of black shingle for sunbathing.

Pa'iloa Beach is the only shingle beach in Wai'ānapanapa State Park. Pokohulu and Keawaiki, the two coves to the north of Pa'iloa, contain only narrow boulder beaches. To the south of Pa'iloa is an unusually shaped inland rock that resembles two fingers forming a victory or peace sign. It was called Haili, "loving memory," and the rocks behind it form Moku Popolo, "*popolo* (plant) island." The remainder of the park's shoreline on either side of Pa'iloa Bay is composed of low, rough lava sea cliffs backed by *hala* trees and *naupaka* bushes. A shoreline trail passes through this beautiful but rugged country. The black lava sea cliffs are continually eroded by the ocean, and many small inlets, caves, rock bridges, and deep holes border the sides of the trail. Hikers, especially young ones, should not stray from the main path, and the trail should never be crossed at night. The area is frequented by shoreline fishermen.

22

Waikoloa Beach

One day a chief from a foreign place came to ride the surf at Keaniani in Kapueokahi, the old name of Hāna Bay. While he was riding a wave to shore, two young girls on the beach tried to get his attention with enticing movements. They succeeded, but he was so startled to see them that he ended his ride before reaching the beach. From that time on the waves of Keaniani never rolled all the way to shore. Today two points of land on the shoreline bear the names of the girls, Popolana and Poku'olae. Waikoloa Beach is located between these two points.

Waikoloa Beach is a cobblestone beach on the west side of Hāna Bay. Kawaipapa and Holināwāwae streams meet here and form a *muliwai* in the backshore. A large grove of *kamani* trees dominates the area. These trees are not the true Hawaiian *kamani* and are frequently called false *kamani* or *kamani haole*. Their English name, tropical almond, refers to the appearance and taste of the edible kernels inside the mature fruit. The fallen fruit, or "nuts," can be found scattered over the ground throughout the grove. This variety of *kamani* is widespread in Hawai'i and thrives near the ocean.

Waikoloa offers poor conditions for swimmers. The offshore bottom is extremely shallow and is as rocky as the adjoining beach. The area is frequented primarily by surfers who consider the site to be one of the best places to surf in Hāna. Public access to this small, undeveloped park is from Waikoloa Road which turns *makai* from the Hāna Highway.

Hāna Beach Park

Hāna is one of the most beautiful and famous districts on the island of Maui. The area abounds in legends and is replete with important historical sites. In times past Hāna was a coveted place not only for residence but for its strategic military position as well. Hāna was the ideal place for the warring chiefs of Maui to launch an attack against the island of Hawai'i and, conversely, the ideal place for the chiefs of Hawai'i to begin an assault on Maui and the island beyond. Its extensive use as a center of war raids is shown by the comparatively large number of important *heiau* not only in Hāna but also in the neighboring districts of Kīpahulu and Kaupō. Kamehameha I, for example, touched here in 1802 with his vast *peleleu* war fleet and is said to have repaired and dedicated four *heiau* to his war god, Kūkā'ilimoku. Kamehameha I was the last chief to use the Hāna area for such purposes, however, ending a long tradition. During his rise to power all the Hawaiian Islands were united under his rule, and wars between the islands ceased. One person who in later years recalled some of the fierce fighting in Hāna prior to the consolidation of the islands was Queen Ka'ahumanu, Kamehameha I's favorite wife. In 1830 she led the Reverend William Richards to Ka'uiki at Hāna Bay. There she showed him the cave where she was hidden as a child during the battles between Kalaniopu'u of Hawai'i and Kahekili of Maui during the late 1770s. Ka'ahumanu, the daughter of Ke'eaumoku and Namahana, was born in Hāna.

Sugar cane was first planted in Hāna about 1860 by Kelk and Needham, who also constructed a bullock-powered grinding mill. Out of these early beginnings came the Ka'elekū Sugar Company, which formed the economic foundation for Hāna until the 1930s when it closed. Some of the resulting unemployment was offset when Paul I. Fagan purchased the plantation.

Fagan, a member by marriage of the locally prominent Irwin family, was a millionaire sportsman, rancher, and part-owner of a professional baseball team, the San Francisco Seals. He formed the Hāna Ranch Company and built the Hotel Hāna Ranch, one of Hāna's famous landmarks. Originally, the hotel was an exclusive resort for his millionaire friends. It was officially opened to the public on June 15, 1947, but still remained predominantly a resort for the rich. The present name, Hotel Hāna Maui, was adopted in 1948.

At the opposite end of the socioeconomic spectrum is Hāna's other famous contemporary landmark, the Hasegawa General Store, where shoppers can find bargain items to suit any price range. Hasegawa General Store is a family business that takes seriously the word "general." The store has everything.

Hāna Beach Park is located on the shoreline of Hāna Bay, or Kapueokahi as it was formerly known. Kapueokahi, "the single owl," is said in one legend to have been a *kupua*, a supernatural being who could take the form

HĀNA BEACH PARK. Kapueokahi Beach, the sandy beach in Hāna Beach Park, is the safest swimming beach on East Maui and a favorite gathering place for local residents and visitors alike. The ruins of a former landing are still visible at the left end of the beach.

of an animal or a human. Kapueokahi wanted to marry a woman named Kapoulakinau, so he changed himself from an owl to a man. This incident took place in Kawaipapa, a district in Hāna that has its seaward edge on the bay. From that time on, the bay as well as its lone sand beach were called Kapueokahi.

At the south end of Hāna Beach Park is a large T-shaped pier that provides about three hundred feet of berthing space for small craft and commercial tugs and barges. The wharf is not used today for interisland shipping, however. The site is unprotected from the open ocean and the waters are generally much too rough for the commercial vessels now serving the neighbor islands. In addition, Hāna is now connected by a paved highway to the deep-draft harbor in Kahului. Traversing this highway, which was opened as a dirt road in 1927, is a major undertaking, especially for commercial vehicles, but it is an established land route nonetheless.

To the south of the pier is an island called Pu'u Ki'i, "image hill." It is said to have been named after the great chief Umi erected on the island an immense wooden statue of a warrior to deter invaders. Ka'uiki Light was established on Pu'u Ki'i in 1908. The automatic light can be easily reached for servicing from the mainland but is off-limits to the general public.

The beach at Hāna Beach Park is about seven hundred feet long and one hundred feet wide and is bordered on the north by a lava point and the pilings of the

24

old Hāna Landing and on the south by the wharf. A sea-wall along the coast protects the park behind it from erosion. Offshore, the sand slopes very gently to the outer reefs in the bay. This brown detrital sand beach is the safest swimming beach, especially for children, in the district of Hāna. Even during periods of heavy surf, usually only a gentle shorebreak forms inshore, with negligible alongshore currents. On calm days snorkelers can find interesting grounds between the pier and the lighthouse; staying inshore is a must, however. The currents outside the lighthouse are very powerful and flow out to sea.

Facilities in Hāna Beach Park include one pavilion with picnic tables, restrooms, and showers, and a boat ramp. The abandoned boat ramp in the park grounds is the former site of the Hāna Ranch Company's boat-house. The enclosed pavilion *mauka* of the beach road was donated to the County of Maui by the Hāna Ranch Company in 1977 and is used by the Hāna Community Association.

Beyond the T-pier on the side of Ka'uiki Hill is a small cove called Papaāloa. This area is exposed to strong alongshore currents and is not a safe place to swim. Papaāloa, as well as the entire seaward side of Ka'uiki, is also dangerous because of falling rocks. Ka'uiki Hill is a volcanic cinder cone composed of very loosely packed material. The cinder erodes easily and evidence of landslides and falling boulders is common. Warning signs are posted near the base of the hill.

(23)
Kaihalulu Beach

Kaihalulu means "roaring sea" and it is said to have been a famous landing place for canoes. Kaihalulu Beach is located in a small cove on the *makai* side of Ka'uiki Hill. The cove is enclosed by high cliffs inland and by a natural lava pinnacle barrier across its mouth. The lava barricade helps to form a somewhat protected inshore pool. A channel through the rocks at the north end of the beach is the primary drain for the pool's waters. The alongshore currents flow into the channel and often form fast-moving rip currents into the deep, unprotected waters outside the cove. Swimmers should exercise caution, particularly at the north end of the beach.

Kaihalulu Beach is a true volcanic cinder beach. The

KAIHALULU BEACH. Heavy surf washes over the natural lava barrier protecting Kaihalulu Beach from the open ocean. This secluded cove is situated on the *makai* side of Ka'uiki Head, a large cinder cone bordering the town of Hāna. The beach is composed almost entirely of cinder eroded from the surrounding cliffs.

cinder originates from the erosion of Ka'uiki and is both black and red. The red cinder dominates the mixture and gives the beach its alternate name, Red Sand Beach. Kaihalulu is not visible from the shoreline bordering either side of Ka'uiki Hill. A narrow, precarious trail leads to the cove over a landslide area of loose cinders and then past a steep drop to the ocean. The sea cliffs at the beginning of the trail have suffered serious erosion from the assaults of heavy surf, wind, and rain. The trail passes under the Hāna Japanese cemetery, and a number of heavy concrete grave markers rest in the ocean below the trail where they have fallen. There is no public access to Kaihalulu.

(24)
Leho‘ula Beach

Kū‘ula, the god of Hawaiian fishermen, made his home in Hāna. ‘Ai‘ai, Kū‘ula's son, was given the task of traveling throughout the islands to teach the people all the ceremonies, skills, and techniques of fishing. When ‘Ai‘ai was ready to leave Hāna, one of the gifts from his father was a red cowrie shell, a *leho‘ula*. Leho‘ula Beach was named for this gift.

Leho‘ula is located on the north side of Ka Iwi o Pele, a large cinder hill very similar to Ka‘uiki Hill. Ka Iwi o Pele means "the bones of Pele," and was named when the bones of the volcano goddess were left here after she lost a battle with her older sister, Nā Maka o Kaha‘i. Leho‘ula Beach is a small, flat pocket of white sand between Ka Iwi o Pele and a rocky point. The inshore waters are shallow, but beyond the small sand bar the bottom drops quickly to overhead depths. The beach is unprotected from the open ocean and is subject to some very strong rip currents, especially during heavy surf. "No Swimming—Bad Undertow" signs are posted. Additional signs are posted on Ka Iwi o Pele Hill, warning of the possibility of landslides and falling boulders.

Hotel Hāna Maui maintains private beach park facilities for its guests at Leho‘ula, including three pavilions with picnic tables and barbecue grills. There is no public access.

(25)
Kōkī Beach Park

Kōkī means the "very top," as in the peak of a career or the culmination of a great achievement. Kōkī Beach Park is a small grassy park on the right side of Ka Iwi o Pele, a large red cinder hill. The roadside park is lined with ironwood trees and *naupaka* bushes. Facilities in the park are limited to picnic tables and barbecue grills. The landscaped area and facilities were provided during the late 1960s as a community service project by Hāna Post 3860 of the Veterans of Foreign Wars and their women's auxiliary. The V.F.W. members received permission to create the picnic area from the Department of Land and Natural Resources and continue to furnish regular maintenance.

During the summer months a wide, flat pocket of white sand fronts Kōkī Beach Park. A shorebreak usually provides waves adequate for bodysurfing. Strong alongshore currents generally run from right to left and then out past the rocks. During the winter and spring months, heavy surf claims the beach, leaving only a narrow strip of sand at the water's edge. Many large boulders are exposed offshore, making the area very dangerous for swimmers. The surf also creates powerful rip currents, and warning signs have been posted by the County of Maui. Occasionally the waves are good enough for surfing, but the rocky bottom makes it a hazardous venture.

Beachcombers may be tempted to follow the shoreline to the north of Kōkī Beach Park along the base of Ka Iwi o Pele, but this is a dangerous walk. The cinder hill is composed of very loose volcanic material that breaks away and falls onto the shoreline below. The jagged edges of many of the huge boulders on the beach attest to the fact that they have only recently come down; the erosive force of the ocean has not yet begun to round them. Looking up on the hill's steep slope will also disclose many paths through the shrubbery which these boulders have bulldozed. An accident in this area could easily be fatal.

Directly offshore from the park is ‘Ālau ("many rocks") Island, with its two coconut trees. On clear days the island of Hawai‘i can be seen in the distance. To the right of the park are two ponds on the ocean that were once used for keeping fish. The larger one is Haneo‘o; the smaller one, Kuamaka. They are jointly owned by a group of local residents and are private property. Between the ponds and Mōkae Cove is a beautiful stretch of tidal pools that should be visited only when the ocean is calm.

(26)
Hāmoa Beach

Hāmoa, the name of a small *ahupua‘a,* is generally thought to be a shortened form of Ha‘amoa, an old name for Samoa, but the actual origin of the name of this district is not known. The name began to be associated with the beach in the 1930s, with the construction

26

KŌKĪ BEACH PARK. The shorebreak at the edge of this wide and flat beach is a popular surfing and bodysurfing site. During the winter months, however, the beach loses most of its sand, leaving only boulders, like those in the foreground, exposed along its entire length. The same winter surf that erodes the sand also creates dangerous rip currents that have caused a number of drownings in this area.

of the Hotel Hāna Ranch (now Hotel Hāna Maui), and has been used since. The former name of the beach area was Mōkae, which was also the name of a landing built there by the Reciprocity Plantation. The landing and a warehouse were situated on the outer point of the cove. The surf that comes into the cove was a favorite surfing and swimming area in ancient times, as it is today.

Hāmoa Beach at the head of Mōkae Cove is one of several pocket beaches in this area. The 1,000-foot-long and 100-foot-wide white sand beach is surrounded by 30-foot-high sea cliffs. It is unprotected from the open ocean, and surf breaking offshore rolls straight into the beach. The surf makes Hāmoa a popular surfing and bodysurfing area, but also creates powerful alongshore and rip currents.

Hāmoa Beach and its facilities are used almost exclusively by guests of the Hotel Hāna Maui. The access road and trail to the beach are all on private property owned by the Hāna Ranch Company, the owner of the Hotel Hāna Maui. Surfers and bodysurfers reach the surfing area by jumping off the rocks on the outside point. The hotel provides a private lifeguard.

(27)
Maka‘alae Beach

Maka‘alae means "mud hen's eyes" and is the name of a district, a point, and a beach. Maka‘alae Beach is a narrow dark detrital sand beach located at the head of Pōhakuloa Bay. The entire bay is surrounded by high sea cliffs and is not easily accessible by land. The bay is completely exposed to the open ocean and thus is hit hard by heavy surf. There is no public access.

(28)
Wailua

Wailua means "two waters" and the valley was named for the two streams that flow through it. At one time the valley was extensively cultivated in taro from the in-

27

land areas to the shoreline. Today the long-abandoned patches and crumbling terraces are lost in a lush cover of heavy brush and trees. The area was used by Metro-Goldwyn-Mayer for background shots in the movie *Mutiny on the Bounty.*

In the center of the valley is a wooden cross that was erected on March 12, 1906. It is a memorial to Helio Koaʻeloa, the lay apostle of Maui. Helio was living in Hāna when he heard of a new religion, Catholicism. He paddled a canoe to Honolulu to be personally instructed in the faith and to join the church. Then he returned to Maui and converted over four thousand people for the Catholic Mission. His boundless enthusiasm in the promotion of the Catholic faith earned him the title "The Apostle of Maui." Helio died in 1848 and was buried in Wailua, the valley of his birth.

The beach at Wailua is composed of boulders. There is no swimming at all in these dangerous waters. The area is frequented primarily by picnickers, hikers, and shoreline fishermen. There is no public access.

(29)
Pepeiaolepo Beach

Pepeiaolepo is the only sand beach among the rugged sea cliffs that make up the shoreline of Kīpahulu district. Pepeiaolepo means "dirty ear" and it is said to have been named for an incident involving the *kupua* Kamapuaʻa, who could take the form of either a man or a pig and who apparently got mud in his ear while diving in a stream in this area. Pepeiaolepo Beach is a long, wide dark detrital sand beach located at the base of a reach of steep, high sea cliffs. Heavy surf comes inshore unchecked and covers the beach as it sweeps into the cliffs. This is an extremely dangerous area and is not easily accessible by land. Pepeiaolepo Beach can be seen by following the trail to the top of the cliffs above the lowest of the Seven Pools.

(30)
Seven Pools Park

Seven Pools Park in Kīpahulu is part of Haleakalā National Park. The pools are a series of plunge-pools in the natural course of ʻOheʻo Stream, which runs through ʻOheʻo Gulch. Swimmers should be very cautious. The rocks edging the pools are slippery when wet,

and there are submerged boulders in the pools. Throw rings and long bamboo poles are left permanently in the area in case of emergencies.

Prior to 1960, a small, seasonal sand beach accreted every summer below the lowest of the seven pools. In the early 1960s the beach disappeared and has never returned. With or without the beach, however, the ocean fronting the Seven Pools Park is extremely dangerous and unsafe for swimming. The powerful rip currents and alongshore currents have contributed to a substantial number of drownings over the years. Local fishermen also report many sharks in these waters. Seven Pools Park is a beautiful area with a large grove of *kamani* trees along Hono a Piʻilani Highway, opening into wide grassy pastures perched on the lava sea cliffs. Facilities are limited to portable toilets in several locations and roadside parking.

Kīpahulu, the mountainous district that includes the Seven Pools Park, means "fetch (from) exhausted gardens." The district has many important historical sites and has been the source of many legends. In June 1922 the Hawaiian-language newspaper *Ka Nūpepa Kūʻoko-ʻa* carried a story entitled "Makani Kaʻilialoha o Kīpahulu" (The love-carrying wind of Kīpahulu), undoubtedly one of the most beautiful Hawaiian legends.

"The Makani Kaʻilialoha o Kīpahulu blows from *mauka* to *makai* and this is the story of its naming. Long ago two men had one woman and lived happily together for many years. One was married to the woman. One day the woman and the other man went to visit Oʻahu and ended up living in Mākiki, where the woman forgot about her husband in Kīpahulu. He finally went to a *kahuna*, Hāipu, to ask for help.

"Hāipu and the deserted husband went down to a point called Mākaʻikūloa, 'the alert watcher of the sea coast.' The man brought a polished calabash. The *kahuna* played love songs into it with an *ipuhoehoe* [a gourd whistle]. Then he began to pray while holding a deep breath, and then exhaled and closed the calabash. He put the calabash into the sea and immediately a strong wind, the Kūlepe, blew it to Oʻahu.

"The woman, the same day, got a craving for *limu līpoa* [a seaweed] from Waikīkī. The next day she could not resist her desire, and while she was gathering *līpoa* the calabash surfed up on a little wave right in front of her. She looked at it closely and recognized it. When she opened it, her love for her husband grew strong once more.

"She left Waikīkī and went to Hanauma, where she got a ride in a canoe to Lā'au Point [on Moloka'i]. She went by foot to Kalua'aha and there got a ride in another canoe to Lahaina and then traveled by land to Kīpahulu, where she was reunited with her husband and never left him again." (Translated by Thomas K. Maunupau)

Beyond the Seven Pools Park, the mountainous shoreline of Kīpahulu continues. Hono a Pi'ilani Highway follows the coast fairly closely and touches several of the boulder beaches, such as Hanawī and Kālepa, that are typical of the beaches in this district. These boulder beaches occasionally contain pockets of dark detrital sand and offer opportunities for shoreline fishing, beachcombing, and picnicking. The ocean is much too dangerous for swimming or diving. The districts of Kīpahulu and Kaupō are divided by Kālepa Gulch.

(31)
Mokulau Beach

Mokulau is typical of the boulder beaches that characterize the district of Kaupō, which begins on the coast at Kālepa and ends at Wai'ōpae. Kaupō, the "landing (of canoes) at night," is wide and mountainous, with many important historical sites, a number of which are located on the high, steep cliffs that make up most of its shoreline. There are several places along the shoreline where detrital sand beaches are found, in addition to the typically rocky beaches such as Mokulau.

Mokulau is easily recognizable by the numerous rock islands in the ocean for which it is named. Mokulau means "many islands." The ocean here is not safe for swimming. Powerful currents sweep the shoreline

MOKULAU BEACH. This rocky, driftwood-strewn beach is located in the district of Kaupō. Huialoha Church, standing alone on the barren, windswept point, was constructed in 1857 and still has an active congregation. Mokulau means "many islands" and was probably named for the small rocky islets just offshore from the church.

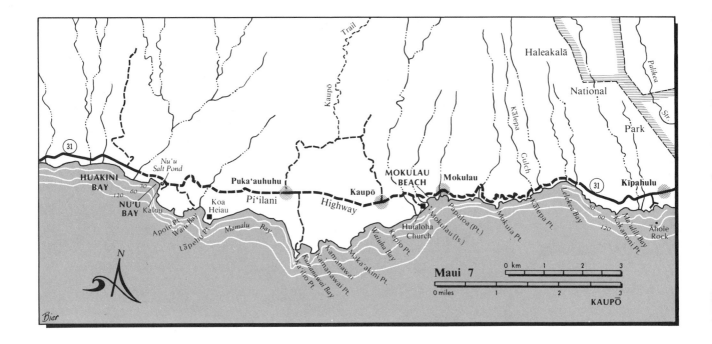

throughout the year and heavy surf often pounds the rocks.

Mokulau is probably best known as the site of Hui-aloha Church. Built in 1859, the small church stands alone on a windswept sea cliff. During the 1970s efforts were made by many people of Kaupō, including Judith and Carl Bredhoff of Kaupō Ranch, to preserve and restore the deteriorating structure. After most of its renovation was completed, a worship service to rededicate Huialoha Church was held on Easter Sunday, March 26, 1978.

Another historical site in the area is the old Mokulau Landing, situated near Halekiʻi Point across the bay from Huialoha Church. Constructed primarily of concrete, the landing was formerly used in cattle shipping operations.

(32)
Nuʻu Bay

The best-known sand beach in the Kaupō district is Nuʻu, a wide pocket of dark detrital sand lined by boulders at the water's edge. Apole Point to the east of the beach offers some protection to the shoreline from

strong trade wind swells, but these leeward waters are only a fair swimming area. The ocean is deep directly offshore, with persistent alongshore currents. The area is frequented by beachcombers and shoreline fishermen.

Nuʻu means "height" and is said by some to have also been the name of a god whose dwelling place was the projecting and inaccessible ledges of steep mountainsides. Nuʻu, an *ahupuaʻa* in Kaupō, was once a large fishing village, and its ruins can be found throughout the area. Fresh water was obtained from Waiū, a spring at the base of Puʻu Maneʻoneʻo. The beach at Nuʻu was a well-used canoe landing for the fishermen of the village and for others as well. During the late 1800s a pier was constructed at Kalou, the name of that particular place on the shoreline. The deep natural harbor became a seaport, and cattle from Kaupō Ranch were shipped from the landing. Remnants of the landing and an old bunkhouse can still be seen.

The fifteen miles of road from Kanaio to Nuʻu was the last section of the Haleakalā belt road to be completed. The construction laborers, all territorial prisoners from Olinda Prison Camp, were paid between eight cents and twenty cents a day depending upon their clas-

LĀPEHU POINT. Scattered throughout the shoreline regions of the districts of Kīpahulu, Kaupō, Kahikinui, and Honua'ula are the remains of numerous precontact archaeological sites.

This picture of Lāpehu Point in Kaupō, taken from the top of Pu'u Mane'one'o, reveals several large symmetrical man-made formations on the 'a'ā flow below.

NU'U BAY. The glare from the mid-day sun whitens the inshore waters fronting the beach at Nu'u. The bay offers fairly good protection to boats from the prevailing trade winds and was formerly a canoe landing and a cattle shipping point. The ruins of the old landing can still be located near the left end of the beach.

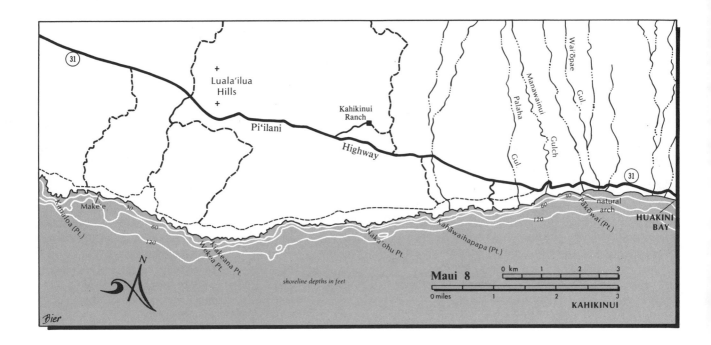

sification. Temporary quarters were erected for them in Kanaio. The project was completed in 1957 and Governor Oren E. Long dedicated the new road.

(33)
Huakini Bay

Beyond Nuʻu is Huakini, another primarily rocky beach with dark detrital sand in the backshore. Huakini and the rest of the boulder beaches near Manawainui are completely unprotected from the open ocean and are too dangerous for swimming or diving. These open, unshielded shoreline areas are frequented primarily by fishermen and beachcombers. They are located alongside Hono a Piʻilani Highway.

(34)
Kanaio Beach

Kahikinui and Honuaʻula are two large *kalana* or land divisions that together cover a vast expanse of desolate, arid, and uninhabited shoreline. Kahikinui begins at Waiʻōpae and ends at Kanaloa. Honuaʻula begins at Kanaloa and ends at Keawakapu. Fishing is good along the coast and in former times Hawaiians lived in isolated communities near the ocean wherever fresh water

could be found. The populations were migratory, living on the ocean during the summer months when they caught and dried fish and moving upland during the wet winter months. The ruins of a number of villages are located throughout the area.

An old shoreline trail that runs fairly close to the ocean begins at Manawainui and ends at Keoneʻōʻio. Where it crosses grassy stretches, it is marked by lines of stones on either side. Where it crosses the ʻaʻā flows, curbs have been built up. The best place to see these details of the trail's construction is La Pérouse Bay. The shoreline trail crosses two wide, desolate lava flows. Between the two flows is an older, more eroded flow covered with sparse shoreline vegetation. It is about a mile long and its shoreline is generally known as Kanaio Beach, Kanaio being an *ahupuaʻa* of Honuaʻula.

Kanaio Beach is actually a series of beaches that are primarily scattered pockets of black sediment-sand, white sand, coral rubble, shingle, cobblestone, or various combinations of all these sediments. These remote pocket beaches, almost invariably fronted by basaltic rock and fairly deep water, are subject to strong alongshore currents and are visited primarily by fishermen in four-wheel drive vehicles. Hiking through this barren,

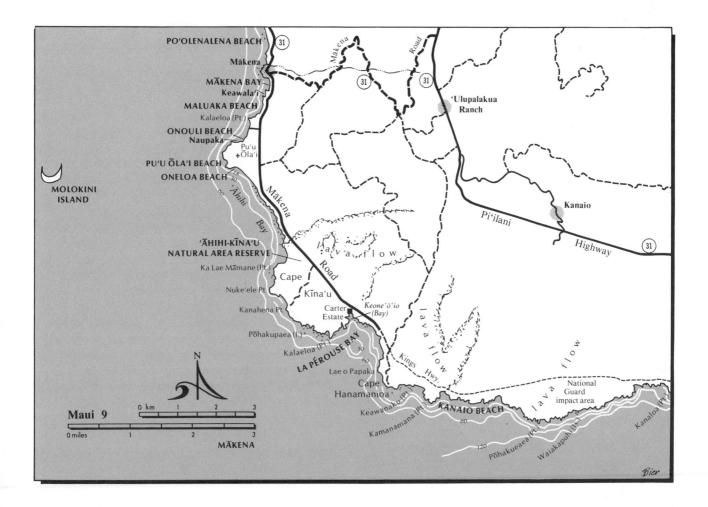

MĀKENA

unshaded desert of lava flows is extremely demanding and is not to be taken lightly.

The state owns a large section of shoreline at Kanaio, so access there is not a problem. Hikers, however, should be alert to the National Guard impact area located on the Pīmoe lava flow between Kanaio and Make'e. The targets are old cars which can be seen in various places on the lava. The shoreline areas surrounding Kanaio are owned by private ranches, but the public is allowed access.

(35)
La Pérouse Bay

When Captain James Cook's third expedition returned to England after circumnavigating the earth, news of the voyage's many discoveries, including the location of the Sandwich Islands, spread throughout Europe. The French government outfitted their own scientific expedition to verify Cook's findings and to explore new lands. In August 1785 two ships, *La Boussole* and *L'Astrolabe,* left France under the command of Captain Jean François de Galaup, Comte de La Pérouse, one of France's finest navigators. In May 1786 the expedition was in Hawaiian waters, and on the twenty-ninth day of that month they were off Honua'ula on Maui, looking for an anchorage. They finally found shelter from severe trade winds in a bay protected by a wide lava flow, and anchored for the night. The following day Captain La Pérouse and a landing party went ashore, becoming the first non-Hawaiians to set foot on Maui. The anchorage became known as La Pérouse Bay and is still best known today by that name. Many Hawaiian families lived in the area well into the twentieth century. In addition to the scores of homes, structures on the bay's shore included a slaughterhouse for Ulupalakua Ranch, a dock, and a Protestant church. The ruins of a number of these old sites can still be found in the *kiawe* forest that lines the shoreline. Today the most prominent landmark at La Pérouse is the seventeen-acre George R. Carter estate on the north side of the bay. The privately owned residential estate has a tiny pocket beach of imported sand.

The Hawaiian name of the bay is Keoneʻoʻio, "the sandy (place with) bonefish." This name comes from the *ʻoʻio,* a popular food fish, that regularly congregate around certain sandy pockets in the ocean bottom offshore.

A road that is passable by an ordinary passenger car ends just beyond the Carter Estate. The remainder of the La Pérouse shoreline is accessible only in vehicles with four-wheel drive or on foot. The rugged, rutted jeep road ends at the Hanamanioa lighthouse. There a narrow fishermen's trail begins, following the edge of low sea cliffs to Keawanaku, a small pocket of dark detrital sand, and then continuing on to the shoreline of Kanaio. This one-mile stretch of coastline between the two wide lava flows is sometimes called Kanaio Beach. There are many small coves with shingle and coral-rubble beaches. This remote area attracts primarily shoreline fishermen. The rocky unprotected beaches are subject to very strong currents. Kanaio can also be reached by the "King's Highway," a two-mile trail that begins at La Pérouse and heads straight across the lava flow.

The shoreline of La Pérouse Bay is composed of a number of small coves between rough, rocky points that are often covered with tidal pools. These coves contain several small white sand beaches, but the majority of them have shingle or coral-rubble beaches. Swimming is generally safe, but the primarily rocky shoreline and the rocky bottom offshore are of greater interest to fishermen and divers than to swimmers. Fishermen and divers should be aware, however, that a small portion of La Pérouse Bay adjoining Cape Kīnaʻu is part of the ʻĀhihi-Kīnaʻu Natural Area Reserve and all consumptive activities are prohibited in that section. The bay is protected from the prevailing currents and generally

safe for inshore water activities. During *kona* storms or periods of heavy surf the inner waters of the bay become very turbulent. Occasionally surfers ride the breaks offshore. La Pérouse Bay is located at the end of Mākena Road.

(36)
ʻĀhihi-Kīnaʻu Natural Area Reserve

In 1973 the State Board of Land and Natural Resources established the ʻĀhihi-Kīnaʻu Natural Area Reserve. The reserve comprises all submerged and emerged lands, as well as inshore ponded and subterranean waters, of Cape Kīnaʻu, including parts of adjoining ʻĀhihi and La Pérouse bays. The three-component system constituting the reserve is made up of (1) the lava flows forming Cape Kīnaʻu and their developing dryland vegetation, (2) an inshore marine ecosystem, and (3) the mixohaline ponds. The purpose and intent of the reserve are officially defined as follows:

> The Legislature has found that the State of Hawaii possesses unique natural resources such as geological features and distinctive marine and terrestrial plants and animals, many of which occur nowhere else in the world, that are highly vulnerable to loss by the growth of population and technology; that these unique natural assets should be protected and preserved for present and future generations of man to provide viable illustrations of an original natural heritage, to act as base lines against which changes made in environments of Hawaii can be measured, to serve as reservoirs of natural genetic materials, and to be used, as feasible, for research in natural sciences and outdoor teaching laboratories. In keeping with these findings, the Legislature has authorized the establishment of a statewide Natural Area Reserves System to preserve in perpetuity endangered species, important geological sites, and specific land and water areas which support native flora and fauna in their natural communities.

The lands and waters of the reserve are off-limits to any activity not consistent with the preservation and protection of the area, such as fishing, hunting, removing coral or lava, and so on. Signs are posted noting some of the restrictions and a complete list plus a map of the restricted area can be obtained from any State Fish and Game office.

In the heart of the reserve is an unpaved parking area on the *makai* side of Mākena Road. A trail leads from there to a series of boulder beaches backed by *kiawe*. While it is a good snorkeling area on calm days, entry and exit from the ocean can be hazardous during heavy surf. Beyond the boulder beaches the trail continues out to Cape Kīna‘u, offering a beautiful view of Pu‘u Ōla‘i and Oneloa Beach. Other than the unpaved parking lot, there are no facilities at all in the reserve.

The State Board of Land and Natural Resources plans eventually to develop a Mākena-La Pérouse State Park which will include the ‘Āhihi-Kīna‘u reserve. The State Legislature has appropriated money for the park, for which planning was completed in 1977, but land acquisition, particularly in the vicinity of Pu‘u Ōla‘i, is necessary before its development can begin. The present plans call for the preservation of all ancient Hawaiian archaeological sites in the proposed park area. To help preserve its natural state, access to most of the park will be by foot or on jeep trails.

(37)
Oneloa Beach

Oneloa means "long sand," an appropriate name for this long, wide stretch of white sand beach. Oneloa Beach, 3,300 feet long and over 100 feet wide, is one of the most popular undeveloped beaches on Maui. The coastline consists of a dusty forest of *kiawe, pānini,* and

ONELOA BEACH. Oneloa literally means the "long sands" and is a fitting name for this very long stretch of white sand that abuts Pu‘u Ōla‘i near Makena. The *kiawe* forest to the rear of the beach covers some extremely valuable undeveloped shoreline property.

koa haole. Amid this arid-area vegetation are several shallow stagnant ponds. These ponds form a natural settling basin, trapping runoff from heavy rains and preventing it from reaching the ocean. This is one reason the ocean fronting Oneloa is almost invariably clear, providing excellent conditions for snorkeling and diving. There is no protective reef offshore, so the beach is exposed to heavy surf and *kona* storms. These particular water conditions often create dangerous rip currents and a powerful, hard-hitting shorebreak, as evidenced by the steep foreshore. The offshore bottom drops quickly to overhead depths. Occasionally the surf is good enough for board surfing as well as bodysurfing.

The outstanding landmark on the shoreline at Oneloa is Pu'u Ōla'i, a large cinder cone that rises 360 feet above sea level. Pu'u Ōla'i, "earthquake hill," is said to have been one of the last volcanically active cones on Maui. Oneloa Beach adjoins the base of Pu'u Ōla'i and stretches well over a half mile to the east. It is sometimes also referred to as Long Sands Beach and Hippie Beach. The former name describes the beach, whereas the latter is descriptive of a semipermanent colony of squatters who once made Pu'u Ōla'i and its surrounding beaches their home. During the 1960s the word "hippie" was coined to describe a wide spectrum of America's youth who rebelled against the norms of established society. This rebellion expressed itself in many ways, some of the most apparent being longer hair styles, colorful and unusual clothing, and radically alternative styles of living. One of the prevalent themes that emerged was an urge to return to the unspoiled land and a simple way of life, so as to shed the trappings of society and regain a spiritual peace in the serenity and harmony of nature. With these ideas in mind many hippies made their way to Maui as well as to the other Hawaiian islands in an effort to return to paradise. Remote and deserted areas such as those surrounding Pu'u Ōla'i attracted the seekers until large communities developed. At Oneloa, or Mākena Beach as the transients preferred to call the area, a hippie community was established about 1968. By 1970 about one hundred people had settled there and were living in tents and shanties. Among local residents the name Hippie Beach was a natural outcome of this activity.

In March 1970, after several previous warnings, police served eviction notices to the transient community, but the notices listed only a few parcels of land. Not all of the land owners had participated, so the hippies checked the tax map keys and moved into the areas not listed. By 1972 the situation had gotten out of hand, and serious problems had developed. Besides squatting on private land, the Mākena community had no toilet or water facilities. Thus diseases caused by a lack of personal hygiene, and by unsanitary waste disposal and contaminated water, were prevalent, in addition to venereal disease. There was also illegal trafficking in marijuana and a wide variety of drugs, which occasionally resulted in violence and other crimes. Finally, the situation became intolerable. Armed with notices from all the private land owners involved, police and health officials evicted all of the transients in April 1972. Today the only reminders of the former hippie community at Pu'u Ōla'i are the still popular names they coined for Oneloa, Big Beach and Mākena Beach.

(38)
Pu'u Ōla'i Beach

On the seaward side of the cinder cone Pu'u Ōla'i is a flat white sand beach in a secluded cove. In former times Pu'u Ōla'i Beach was one of the favorite fishing areas of the Mākena community. During the 1970s the beach was named Little Beach by the transient community that lived in this area. Still a popular name, Little Beach is probably best known as the foremost nudist beach on Maui. In Hawai'i nudists are subject to arrest under the state "open lewdness" statute, and at Little Beach under the Department of Land and Natural Resources' regulation prohibiting nudity in a state park. The statute and the regulation are enforced periodically by unannounced police raids, but nudists still gravitate to the area, oblivious of those who choose to remain clothed. Anyone visiting the site should be prepared to encounter nude sunbathers and swimmers.

Pu'u Ōla'i Beach is an excellent swimming beach with a shallow sandy bottom. The cove almost always has a gentle shorebreak that attracts bodysurfers, bodyboarders, and surfers. On calm days snorkeling is excellent around the point separating Oneloa and Pu'u Ōla'i. A trail leads from the large beach over the rocky point to the secluded smaller one. Both Oneloa, Big Beach, and Pu'u Ōla'i, Little Beach, are part of an undeveloped state park.

PUʻU ŌLAʻI BEACH. The island of Kahoʻolawe is framed between two *kiawe* trees looking out to sea across Puʻu Ōlaʻi Beach. The smaller island of Molokini is also visible to the right. This sandy, secluded cove, located on the *makai* side of Puʻu Ōlaʻi cinder cone, is a popular although illegal nudist beach.

(39)
Oneuli Beach

Oneuli Beach, also known as Black Sand Beach, is located on the north side of Puʻu Ōlaʻi and extends to Kalaeloa, a low, rocky lava point. The name Oneuli means "dark sands" in Hawaiian. The name is commonly pronounced Onouli by many local residents. Puʻu Ōlaʻi, the outstanding feature of the shoreline in the Mākena area, is also known as Millers Hill for an English whaler who made his home in the area. Little is known about Miller, but his son, Alexander, and Alexander's daughter, Sara Miller Makaiwa, made their home at Paʻakō near Puʻu Ōlaʻi and are buried there in a family graveyard. The Makaiwa family still owns the old homestead site. Puʻu Ōlaʻi is also called Round Mountain for its two dome-shaped peaks, and Red Hill because the volcanic cone is composed largely of red as well as black cinder.

Oneuli Beach is made up of eroded material from Puʻu Ōlaʻi as well as of soil from the coastline, giving the beach a dark color. The detrital sand is very fine and sticks tightly to wet bodies. The entire length of the beach at the water's edge is lined by exposed reef, making entries and exits from the ocean precarious. These two features are probably the reasons most people bypass Oneuli for the white sands of Oneloa on the other side of Puʻu Ōlaʻi. Oneuli is safe for swimming and snorkeling, except during heavy surf or *kona* storms. The offshore bottom is primarily rocky and drops quickly to overhead depths.

Although there is no evidence of it now, a small patch

of *naupaka* once stood on the coastline near the south end of the beach. For this reason this particular area was called Naupaka by local fishermen. This name was picked up in several shoreline studies and as a result the entire beach has sometimes been called Naupaka Beach. *Kiawe, pānini,* and *koa haole* now make up the vegetation on the coastline. In this area of Pu'u Ōla'i is also the foot of a trail that leads up the slope of the mountain. It is a much harder hike than it appears to be to the eye. The moderately steep trail is composed entirely of loose cinder that continually slides underfoot, making climbing rather strenuous. However, unless a short portion of Pu'u Ōla'i's seaward edge adjoining Oneuli is traversed by swimming, the trail is the only easy way to reach Pu'u Ōla'i Beach from the dark detrital sand beach. Public access to Oneuli Beach is provided on a state-owned dirt road.

(40)
Maluaka Beach Park

Maluaka is the name of a small *ahupua'a* that touches the shoreline in Mākena and includes the best swimming beach in Mākena Bay. Maluaka Beach is a small but wide crescent of white sand separated from Oneuli Beach by Kalaeloa, a low rocky point. The north end of the beach is also bordered by a lava point. Historic Keawala'i Congregational Church and several private residences occupy the point.

The nearshore bottom is sandy and slopes gently to the deeper and rockier areas offshore. Swimmers should be alert to submerged boulders in the shorebreak at either end of the beach. The boulders are not always visible during periods of high seas when the ocean is turbulent and murky. Vegetated sand dunes and *kiawe* trees make up the backshore. Because of the dunes the beach is sometimes called Pu'u One or "sand hills."

A small landscaped park at the north end of the beach provides public access to the Maluaka shoreline. Roadside parking is available. The Maui Prince Hotel is located inland of the beach.

Immediately north of Maluaka Beach is Keawala'i Congregational Church, founded in 1832. The church building, constructed primarily from coral blocks cut from nearby reefs, was completed in 1855. Seaward of the church is a beautiful cove with a tiny pebble, coral rubble, and white sand beach. The cove is protected by two concave lava points that shelter its inner waters during most adverse ocean conditions. The cove's name is Keawala'i, which means "the calm bay." The north point of the cove is actually a small rock islet with three *kiawe* trees growing on it.

(41)
Mākena Landing Beach Park

Mākena Bay was once one of the busiest ports on Maui. In the late 1850s L. L. Torbert started a sugar plantation at Ulupalakua, *mauka* of Mākena. He subsequently sold it to Captain James Makee, a retired sea captain. Makee is said to have invested close to one million dollars in the plantation, and by 1866 the Makee Sugar Mill ranked third in tonnage among the ten mills then operating in Hawai'i. Mākena Landing served as the port for the plantation.

After Makee's death in 1879, a prolonged drought forced the closing of the mill and the plantation. Makee's Rose Ranch, famed for its beauty and hospitality, became a cattle ranch and was renamed Ulupalakua Ranch. Mākena's prominence as a landing increased substantially with the regular shipping of cattle on the old interisland steamers.

With over one hundred families living in the area, Mākena was a thriving community until the mid-1920s. At that time the interisland steamers stopped calling at the landing. Major improvements made to Kahului Harbor had focused shipping and commerce in Maui on Kahului, eliminating the need for many of the landings scattered around the island, including Mākena Landing.

The calling of the interisland steamers had provided Mākena with its major source of income. They had also been the primary means of transportation to the area. The only accesses by land were the *makai* trail from Kīhei and the *mauka* trail from Ulupalakua. When the steamers stopped visiting, the population on the bay quickly declined.

During World War II the U.S. Army occupied Mākena as a training area, building barracks and bunkers and the shoreline road from Kama'ole. They also tore down the historic pier at Mākena Landing. After the war, few of the former residents returned to the area, as it had little to offer them other than a secluded place to live.

Mākena Landing today is bordered by a small, land-scaped beach park. Facilities include restrooms, showers, and a paved parking lot. South of the landing are two small pockets of white sand, Pāpipi and Papakuewa, that are popular with weekend picnickers. Pāpipi, the "cattle fence," fronts one of the old holding pens that was used when cattle were shipped out of Mākena. The corral, with its gates and loading chute, is still intact. Papakuewa is the next small pebble-and-sand pocket between Pāpipi and the homes near Keawala'i Congregational Church. The nearshore bottom at both of these pocket beaches slopes very gently offshore, making ideal swimming areas for little children.

(42)
Po'olenalena Beach Park

Po'olenalena, "yellow head," is the name of a large rock located on the fairway of the 5th hole of the Wailea Blue Golf Course. The large, dark, and somewhat rounded rock has natural yellow streaks on its sides. Po'olenalena, visible from the public road as well as from the golf course, has long been a local landmark for residents in the Mākena area.

Po'olenalena Beach is a long, wide, flat white sand beach that is interrupted along its length by three small rocky points. The point directly *makai* of Po'olenalena is Pepeiaolepo, while the point to the south is Kapua-'ikea. The Chang family, part of an old Mākena family, has long farmed the land just *mauka* of this section of beach. After World War II, fishermen from other areas on Maui began finding their way to this part of the island. They referred to it as Chang's Beach and the name is still used by many local residents. Eddie Chang's home is located *mauka* of the beach at Pāipu, his family property.

Po'olenalena Beach is a good swimming beach with a gentle slope to the deeper waters offshore. The bottom is generally sandy with a few large rocks exposed in several places along the shoreline. Alongshore currents are usually not strong unless the wind is blowing exceptionally hard or the surf is up. Other dangerous water conditions usually occur only with heavy surf or severe *kona* storms. High sand dunes and *kiawe* make up the backshore. The Chang home is the only residence in the area. Po'olenalena Beach Park itself remains undeveloped,

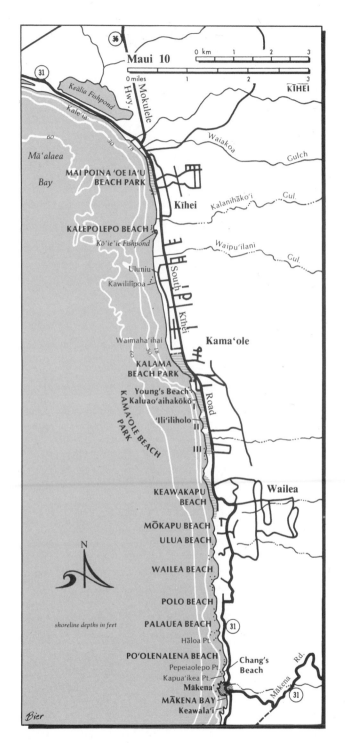

39

PALAUEA BEACH. *Pōhuehue,* the beach morning glory, covers the low sand dunes between Palauea's flat sand beach and the inland *kiawe* forest. The gentle shorebreak is often good enough for bodysurfing, but is infrequently ridden because of inconvenient public access to the area. A portion of the West Maui Mountains is visible in the distance.

but parking is available at several unpaved sites within the park.

To the south of Poʻolenalena Beach is a long, wide lava point with many inlets that continues along the ocean to Mākena Landing. At Pāmōlepo is a small family graveyard where several members of the Kukahiko family, the old Mākena family to which the Changs belong, are buried. Between the graveyard and Poʻolenalena Beach, just *makai* of the end of the golf course, is Ulupikunui, the "large fig tree." Ulupikunui was named for a large fig tree that formerly stood on the low sea cliffs above this small cove of white sand. The secluded beach is an excellent protected swimming area for little children, and it also offers good snorkeling and fishing. Adverse ocean conditions occur only with heavy surf and *kona* storms.

To the north of Poʻolenalena Beach is Hāloa Point.

Prior to World War II it extended much farther into the ocean. The point was shortened considerably when military personnel used it as a demolition training site during maneuvers. Hāloa is a fairly wide point that separates Poʻolenalena Beach from Palauea Beach. There is one small secluded pocket of dark detrital sand on the point. The coastline is primarily *kiawe* with a handful of new residential homes.

(43)
Palauea Beach

Palauea, "lazy," is an *ahupuaʻa* in the *kalana* of Honuaʻula that includes this secluded beach of the same name. Palauea Beach is a flat, wide crescent of white sand situated on the north side of Hāloa Point. The coastline is made up of sand dunes covered with strand vegetation, primarily *kiawe.* One concrete pillbox remains in the center of the beach, a reminder of the military maneuvers conducted here during World War II. Several large residential beach homes are located on the north point of the beach, but otherwise the area is undeveloped.

Palauea Beach is an attractive bodysurfing beach as well as a good place to swim. The surf is normally a small, gentle shorebreak, over a shallow, sandy bottom. The inshore bottom slopes gently to the deeper offshore waters. The entire beach is somewhat recessed into the surrounding shoreline, so the prevailing winds are not as strong here as at other beaches nearby. Dangerous water conditions occur during heavy surf or severe *kona* storms. Palauea Beach is not visible from the public road and is accessible to the public only by following the shoreline from either Poʻolenalena Beach or Polo Beach. Although most of the coastline between the beach and road is undeveloped, it is replete with fences and No Trespassing signs.

(44)
Polo Beach

Polo Beach is the first of five beaches that are part of Wailea, an extensive resort complex that covers two miles of shoreline and includes residential properties as well as a few select hotels. The name Polo was introduced with the building of Wailea and comes from a pamphlet titled "Ke Alaloa o Maui." It is an abbreviated version of Ke One o Polo, the name listed for this beach. However, Polo (or Ke One o Polo) is apparently a new name for this area and it is not recognized by any of the longtime residents of the surrounding communities. Most of these older individuals say that the local name Wailea, which was primarily associated with the wide rocky point to the north of the beach, also included this beach as well.

In more recent times Polo Beach was known as Dead Horse Beach. Formerly, cattle as well as horses from Ulupalakua Ranch roamed this region. They frequented the beach because of the freshwater springs that surfaced near the rocks below the present walkway. The animals were often observed pawing in the sand for the spring water on calm, low-tide days. However, the connection between the horses who frequented the shoreline and the name Dead Horse Beach is now only a matter of surmise.

Polo Beach is probably best known to local residents as Ferkany Beach. In 1950 Judge Cable Wirtz, who owned several acres of land adjoining the beach, sold a portion of it to Dr. Joseph Ferkany. Dr. Ferkany's property had two beach houses on it with peaked roofs. These houses became landmarks to fishermen, especially those passing offshore in their boats. They began calling the area Ferkany Beach. In 1959 the doctor changed his name from Ferkany to Andrews, but Ferkany Beach remained the commonly used name until Wailea introduced the name Polo Beach.

Polo Beach is a long, wide white sand beach backed by low sand dunes. The south half of the beach has a generous amount of beach rock exposed at the water's edge. The sand ends at a shingle, cobblestone, and detrital sand beach fronting a row of private beach homes. The north end of the beach is contained by a wide lava point covered with *kiawe*. Snorkeling is excellent on calm days around these rocks. The offshore bottom of this beach slopes gently to overhead depths, providing a good area for swimming as well as bodysurfing. Dangerous water conditions usually occur only during periods of large surf or severe *kona* storms. During these conditions a heavy shorebreak pounds the beach, creating strong rip currents. Heavy surf also erodes the beach sand in some places, temporarily exposing beach rock that is ordinarily hidden. This situation created unexpected hazards for those who do not visit the area regularly.

Polo Beach has a landscaped minipark, a paved parking lot, a paved walkway to the shoreline, and a sign on the public road indicating its location. The improved areas as well as the beach are open to the public.

(45)
Wailea Beach

Wailea, the "water of Lea," the goddess of Hawaiian canoe makers, is the second of five beaches that are part of the Wailea resort complex. The place name Wailea originates from the wide rocky point to the south of the beach, although the specific feature the name indicated is now unknown. The white sand beach, as well as a portion of its rocky north point, was formerly known as Kahamanini. The extension of the name Wailea to include its present two-mile expanse of shoreline came into widespread public use when the Matson Navigation Company purchased the coastal lands of the districts of Paeahu, Palauea, Keauhou, Kalihi, Waipao, and Pāpaʻanui. Matson named the area Wailea when registering title in the land court, and when Alexander and Baldwin, Inc., acquired Matson in 1969, they retained the name. During the early 1970s Alexander and Baldwin, Inc., announced the construction of a luxury resort community to be called Wailea. The Wailea Development Company, a joint venture between A & B and Northwestern Mutual Life Insurance Company of Milwaukee, is the developer of a complex that includes residential properties, several hotels, and a variety of recreational facilities, shops, and restaurants. A & B is Maui's largest employer and also owner of the Hawaiian Commercial and Sugar Company, with 34,000 acres the largest of the state's fifteen sugar plantations.

An essential aspect of the Wailea development was the guarantee that public rights-of-way to all the beaches would be provided for Maui residents and other visitors to the area. These beaches are Polo, Wailea, Ulua, Mōkapu, and a portion of Keawakapu. The rights-of-way to each one are clearly marked at the public road and paved parking lots and paved walkways are provided as well. The general public is welcomed to all of Wailea's beaches.

Wailea Beach is a long, wide white sand beach backed by high sand dunes at its south end. The inshore waters are usually shallow and slope gently to the deeper areas offshore, providing a good swimming area. Bodysurfing is good in the small shorebreak. which is usually not as hard-hitting here as at the other Wailea beaches. Snorkeling is good around the rocky points when the ocean is calm. Dangerous water conditions usually occur only during periods of large surf or severe *kona* storms. During these times a heavy shorebreak creates hazards similar to those occurring at Polo Beach.

(46)
Ulua Beach

Ulua, named after the "adult crevalle fish," is the third of five beaches in the Wailea resort development. The name Ulua is an abbreviated version of Ke One Ulua, which was introduced in a pamphlet titled "Ke Alaloa o Maui" at the time of the building of Wailea. Like Polo,

it is a new name and is unfamiliar to longtime residents of the surrounding communities. The former name of this sand beach was Kaulaʻuo, by which it was known until World War II. During the early 1940s the Marines stationed on Maui made numerous amphibious landings on many of the island's beaches. Kaulaʻuo was where the Marines practiced maneuvers for the invasion of Tarawa, so they named the beach Little Tarawa. The name stayed with the beach until Wailea was developed and the name Ulua Beach was introduced. One of the few reminders of the war years is a concrete pillbox on the rocky point between Ulua Beach and Mōkapu Beach.

Ulua Beach is a fairly long, wide pocket of white sand between two rocky points. It is the most popular of the five Wailea beaches for several reasons. When a swell is running, the surf here is usually a little bigger than at the surrounding beaches, attracting bodysurfers and people who enjoy playing in the surf. When the ocean is calm, snorkeling in the area is excellent, and many consider the offshore waters to be the clearest of any around. Ulua Beach is also the site of Wailea's water recreation activities desk and is centrally located to both Wailea ʻElua and the Hotel Inter-Continental Maui.

The inshore bottom of Ulua Beach is usually shallow and slopes gently to the deeper waters offshore. Dangerous water conditions usually occur only during periods of large surf or severe *kona* storms. Swimmers, snorkelers, and divers should be alert to the boat traffic at Ulua Beach. Several commercial cruise boats use the north end of the beach as an anchorage and as a base of operations.

To the rear of the beach is a landscaped minipark, a paved parking lot, and a paved walkway. Access to the beach is marked by a sign on the public road, and it is open to the public.

(47)
Mōkapu Beach

Mōkapu Beach is one of five beaches that are part of the Wailea resort complex. The word *mōkapu* is an abbreviated form of *moku kapu* and means "sacred island." Prior to World War II, Mōkapu was a small rock island offshore from the beach. Sea birds such as the *kōlea* gathered on it in the evenings, and on the rocky point nearby. The birds would feed *mauka* in Kula during the day and then return to the shoreline for the night. The flocks were immense, making Mōkapu a popular hunting area. During the war, however, the rock island was almost entirely destroyed by explosives detonated during combat demolition exercises. So little remains of Mōkapu today that it is simply another rock among the others nearby.

Mōkapu Beach is a short, wide pocket of white sand with beach rock exposed in the center of the beach. The sandy inshore bottom has a gentle slope to the deeper waters offshore, providing an excellent swimming area. On calm days snorkeling is good, especially around the rocky areas. When a swell is running, the shorebreak is suitable for bodysurfing and occasionally a small peak forms far enough offshore to accomodate board surfers. Dangerous water conditions occur only during periods of large surf or severe *kona* storms. Like the other beaches of Wailea, Mōkapu Beach has a landscaped minipark, a paved parking lot, and a paved walkway to the shoreline. A sign at the public road marks the access to the beach.

(48)
Keawakapu Beach

Keawakapu means "the sacred (or forbidden) harbor," but the reason the name was given to this area is now unknown. Keawakapu, part of the *ahupua'a* of Kama-'ole, is often but incorrectly pronounced and spelled Keawekapu. Keawakapu Beach is about half a mile long and is bounded by lava points at both ends. The wide white sand beach with its sandy bottom is a popular place for swimmers, snorkelers, and bodysurfers. However, like the Kīhei and Wailea beaches, Keawakapu has no protection from the open ocean. There is no coral fringing reef offshore to dissipate the force of heavy surf, or of severe *kona* storms which periodically devastate the unprotected beaches on this side of Maui. Keawakapu historically has suffered the severest property damage, primarily because a large residential community lines almost the entire sandy coastline. In January 1959 a tropical storm scoured the shoreline at Keawakapu, eroding the entire beach and leaving only exposed beach rock in its wake. Thirty to forty feet of high ground and bluffs fronting the homes were lost to the ocean. Old high-tide stone walls that had been hidden for years were suddenly exposed. After the storm subsided, homeowners went to great effort and expense to restore their property. During the summer the sand slowly began to return, following its natural accretion pattern. Then in the winter of 1962–1963 the beach was again severely eroded by repeated storms from the south, resulting in considerable damage to the private beach homes on the low sandy terrace behind the beach. One of the worst and longest sieges of wind and surf occurred in February, and Keawakapu homeowners watched helpelssly as the ocean carried away what they had only recently restored, and more. The storm and heavy surf, pushed by strong southwesterly winds, joined forces with the February high tides. Property losses were tremendous. The destructive force of the ocean at these times in only too evident and no one should even consider any type of aquatic activity.

Keawakapu Beach is bordered on its south end by the Wailea resort development. Public parking and a public right-of-way to the beach are located there, as well as at the intersection of South Kīhei Road and Kilohana Drive.

In 1957 the Division of Fish and Game of the Department of Land and Natural Resources initiated studies on the effects of artificial reef shelters on standing crops of fish. Early attempts using specially fabricated boxlike concrete structures proved successful in increasing fish populations in areas lacking in natural shelters. The division subsequently constructed four artificial reefs, utilizing primarily car bodies and damaged concrete pipes. Three of these reefs are located on O'ahu, at Maunalua, Wai'anae, and Kualoa, and the fourth is located on Maui at Keawakapu. In August 1962 one hundred fifty car bodies were transported to the reef site from Honolulu by a chartered tug and barge. The reef is located approximately four hundred yards offshore from Keawakapu at depths of eighty to eighty-five feet. The existing bottom is mainly flat sand with a few small, dead coral heads. Fish populations have increased substantially within this area since the introduction of the artificial reef.

In 1983 the state dedicated a new launching ramp for Maui boaters on the shoreline between Keawakapu Beach and Kama'ole III Park. The old ramp at the south end of Kalama Beach Park closed officially on July 1, 1983. Today the Kīhei Boat Ramp is the major launching facility on Maui's southeastern shore. Facilities include a wide, single-lane ramp with a catwalk, a small turning basin protected by two breakwaters, a large paved parking lot for trucks and trailers, and a washdown area. The rocky shoreline adjoining the ramp is popular with shoreline fishermen.

Kama‘ole

Kama‘ole is said to have been a spring from which a land division, a large ranch, a section of Hawaiian homesteads, and three beach parks took their name. Kama‘ole means "childless," but the origin of the name is now unknown. Three separate beach parks carry the name Kama‘ole and are known simply as Kama‘ole I, II, and III. These parks are very popular recreation areas with local residents and visitors alike because each one borders South Kīhei Road, making them easily accessible; each has an excellent swimming beach; and each is equipped with restrooms and showers, picnic tables and barbecue grills, and paved parking lots. On weekends and holidays the three parks are jammed with picnickers, swimmers, sunbathers, and fishermen.

(49)
Kama‘ole III Beach Park

The north point of Kama‘ole III Beach Park was once known as Kalaehuku, and this name included the sand beach as well. The rocky south half of the park's shoreline was called Ana‘iao, for an inlet where large schools of ‘iao, a popular bait fish, congregated. The beach at Kama‘ole III is a short but wide pocket of white sand bordered by rocky points. Large rocks are also exposed in several places along the beach at the water's edge. The sandy offshore bottom slopes quickly to overhead depths—a danger to little or nonswimming children. The waves in the shorebreak attract bodysurfers. The ocean is safe for swimming except during heavy surf or kona storms. During these times strong rip currents and a powerful shorebreak make swimming very dangerous.

Although Kama‘ole III has the smallest beach of the three Kama‘ole parks, it seems to be the most popular.

KAMA‘OLE III BEACH PARK. Only a few scattered sunbathers take advantage of a beautiful sunny day at this popular beach park. On weekends and holidays all three of the Kama‘ole Beach parks are crowded with local residents and tourists. Each of the parks borders South Kīhei Road and offers picnic facilities, showers, restrooms, and paved parking.

This popularity is probably due to certain specific features of the park itself: it is the longest and the widest of the three, it is the only one that has playground apparatus for children, and it has the most parking. Other facilities include restrooms, showers, picnic tables, and barbecue grills. The south half of the park is undeveloped and covered with kiawe.

Kama'ole II Beach Park

Like the rest of the shoreline on this side of Maui, the Kama'ole area is occasionally devastated by *kona* storms. These storms originating from the south often generate high winds, huge waves, and heavy rains, all of which cause considerable damage to shoreline property. They also severely erode any beaches unprotected by a coral reef. When the sand disappears from the beach at Kama'ole II, a large bed of shingle is exposed, and as the waves surge and recede across these rounded beach rocks or *'ili'ili,* an ominous rumbling results. The Hawaiians called this beach 'Ili'iliholo, "running pebbles," for this unpredictable and dramatic phenomenon.

The beach at Kama'ole II is a very wide white sand beach located between two rocky points. The sandy off-shore bottom drops off sharply to overhead depths. Usually a small shorebreak is present, attracting body-surfers. Swimming is safe except during periods of heavy surf or *kona* storms. Facilities in the grassy park include restrooms, showers, picnic tables, barbecue grills, and paved parking. Kama'ole II Beach Park is located in the 2500-area of South Kīhei Road.

Kama'ole I Beach Park

Ka lua o 'Aihakōkō, "the pit of 'Aihakōkō," is a place name that was formerly associated with the shoreline at Kama'ole I Beach Park. In *Ruling Chiefs of Hawaii,* Hawaiian historian Samuel Kamakau gives this brief description of the origin of the name: "Kiha a Pi'ilani killed 'Aihakōkō's personal attendant in the sea. That was why 'Aihakōkō lamented grievously at sea. He landed at Kapa'ahi in Kama'ole, Kula, and that place was given the name Ka lua o 'Aihakōkō ('Aihakōkō's pit)." Today the entire area is known as Kama'ole I Beach Park.

The beach at Kama'ole I is a very wide white sand beach situated between two rocky points. The offshore bottom is sandy, but drops quickly to overhead depths. The shorebreak is often good enough for bodysurfing, but generally not big enough to be of concern to those who wish only to swim. Dangerous water conditions occur during heavy surf or *kona* storms. Facilities in the grassy park include restrooms, showers, picnic tables, barbecue grills, and paved parking. Kama'ole I Beach Park is located in the 2300-area of South Kīhei Road.

The north end of the Kama'ole I beach is known to most local residents as Young's Beach. It was named for the Charley Young family, who have lived on the low sea cliffs above the beach since the 1950s. Charles Clinton Young was born in Minneapolis, Minnesota, on January 30, 1905. When he arrived in Honolulu in 1932, he was a sergeant in the Hawaiian Coast Artillery Brigade. He had been sent to Hawai'i as a military reporter covering the widely publicized Massie Case. In the ensuing years Charley and his wife, Betty, elected to remain in Hawai'i as civilians and made their home on Maui. In February 1940 they purchased property in Kama'ole, but before they had a chance to build, World War II erupted. The military took over their land and other surrounding parcels to build a Combat Demolition Training Station. The training was said to have been the most rigid and intense of any naval training at the time. Over forty teams of one hundred men each were thoroughly schooled in reconnaissance and demolition activities. The beaches of Mā'alaea, Kīhei, Kama'ole, and Wailea were fortified to resemble enemy beachheads and they were assaulted in training exercises. At the south end of the beach at Kama'ole I, an old concrete pillbox is one of the few reminders left of the war years.

After the war the barracks and other buildings were torn down, and in 1950 the Youngs built their home. On November 21, 1958, Resolution 83 was passed by the County Board of Supervisors, officially naming a nearby bridge "Charley Young Bridge." The name is still visible on the concrete bridge located at the south end of nearby Kalama Beach Park. The Youngs had become well-known figures on Maui, especially Charley for his newspaper work with the *Maui News* and the *Honolulu Star Bulletin,* and for his involvement in numerous civic, social, and business organizations. Charley Young died on January 21, 1974.

A public right-of-way at the end of Kaiau Street leads to Young's Beach, a popular gathering place for local youth from the surrounding neighborhoods. The primary attraction is the bodysurfing waves, which are usually better here than at any of the surrounding beaches.

Kalama Beach Park

Kalama Beach Park was named in honor of Samuel E. Kalama, the Maui County chairman and executive officer for the twenty-year period from 1913 to 1933. Born September 1, 1869, Kalama began his public career in 1888, when he was named clerk and tax accessor of the Makawao district. In 1893 he was appointed captain of the Makawao police and also clerk of the road board. In 1899 he began a three-year term as deputy sheriff of the Makawao district. Kalama was elected as a Maui representative to the territorial legislature in 1902, and then again as a senator, serving from 1904 to 1912. In 1912 he was successful in his bid for the chairmanship of the Maui Board of Supervisors, the equivalent of being mayor of Maui County. Kalama took over the position in 1913 and held it until the day of his death, on February 27, 1933. The park was officially dedicated with a public ceremony in May 1953.

Kalama Beach Park covers over thirty-six acres and contains a multitude of facilities, including twelve pavilions, three restrooms and showers, picnic tables, barbecue grills, playground equipment, one soccer field, one baseball field, tennis courts, a volleyball/basketball court, a caretaker's residence, and a paved parking lot. Swimming at Kalama Beach Park is safe, but generally appeals only to children. The offshore bottom is very shallow and rocky, marking the beginning of the coral fringing reef that runs down the coast to Kīhei. The seaward edge of the entire park is lined with a gently sloping boulder wall. Pockets of sand that can accommodate sunbathers exist only in the middle of the wall where a break was left to allow drainage of an intermittent stream, and at the far south end of the wall where a tiny sand beach has accreted.

The building of the revetment fronting Kalama Beach Park created a great deal of controversy. Opponents of the project claimed the wall would permanently obliterate the beach, obstruct access to the water from the park, and create a "child trap" because the huge boulders have openings between them to allow drainage through the wall. Proponents, however, cited that fact that although the beach experiences seasonal erosion and accretion, the net effect has been erosion. Surveys made in 1912 and in 1961 showed that the shoreline had receded three hundred feet during this forty-nine-year period. The erosion impaired the recreational use of the park and threatened the highway embankment at the south end of the beach. In the early 1970s an erosion control project was completed which included construction of a revetment along the threatened highway, construction of a twenty-five foot berm along the *makai* length of the park, and construction of a three-thousand-foot-long revetment seaward of the berm. The sloped revetment was designed to protect the berm from erosion and to encourage accretion of sand on the seaward side.

The south end of Kalama Beach Park is the site of the former Kīhei Boat Ramp. It was officially closed on July 1, 1983, and replaced by the present ramp between Kamaʻole III Beach Park and Keawakapu. A popular surfing site is located directly offshore the old ramp.

To the north of Kalama Beach Park is a fairly long, winding white sand and coral-rubble beach that fronts several residential communities. The ocean bottom is a mixture of sand and rocks and is deep enough for swimming. The beach is well protected by the reef offshore and is often covered with seaweed. There are many marked public rights-of-way from Hālama Street and Uluniu Road. Two sections of this beach are known as Waimāhaʻihaʻi and Kawililīpoa.

Between West Waipuʻilani Road and the office of the National Oceanic and Atmospheric Administration at 726 South Kīhei Road is an unmarked public right-of-way to the beachfront. It is the Waipuʻilani Gulch drainage ditch, located between two of the large hotels in the area. This right-of-way leads not only to the beach but to a state beach reserve, a wide strip of public land located between the beach and the *makai* edge of the hotel's property. The state has given the hotels permission to landscape this area, but under the state's direction and as long as the hotels provide maintenance. Although this land is public property and open to the public, it is not possible to differentiate the private from the public land. The boundaries are indistinguishable because of the continuity of the landscaping. This situation has created some problems between the resorts' guests and nonguests who attempt to utilize the beach reserve.

(53)
Kalepolepo Beach Park

Kalepolepo is not a large shoreline area, but it is a historically colorful place. The name Kalepolepo means "the dirt" and is thought to be a reference to the large clouds of dust that once swept through this area. During the mid-1800s Kalepolepo was a thriving Hawaiian village, not at all the barren and desolate place it later became and remained until recent years. Coconut and *kou* trees grew beside pools of clear water, as well as taro and *'ape*. On the shoreline was Kō'ie'ie fishpond, the only pond of the three in the area that was still in use; it had not yet filled with sand and silt and was kept well stocked with fish. The Hawaiian newspaper *Ke Au 'Oko'a* reported in December 1869 that Kamehameha I had ordered the pond rebuilt during his reign, as was Haneo'o pond at Hāmoa. From the 1840s to the 1860s a small whaling station was maintained at Kalepolepo. Whale boats plied their trade among the mating and calving whales who came to the waters of Ma'alaea during the winter and spring months.

Two churches, one Mormon and one Protestant, offered their services for those of religious persuasion. The Protestant church is known today as the David Malo Memorial Church. David Malo, a scholar as well as a minister, moved to Kalepolepo in 1843 and was noted for calling his congregation to worship with a conch shell. The church was built after his death in November 1853, and services are still held on the original church grounds. The present church is unique because the altar, the pulpit, and the pews are covered only by overhanging branches of the surrounding *kiawe*. It is located in the *kiawe* forest *mauka* of South Kīhei Road in Kalepolepo.

Kalepolepo's most famous resident was probably Captain John Joseph Halstead, who built Kalepolepo's onetime famous landmark, the Koa House. Halstead, the son of a New York colonial family, opted for a career at sea as a whaler. He made Lahaina his home in the 1830s, becoming a carpenter, a cabinet maker, and finally a trader. He married Kauwaikīkīlani, a granddaughter of Isaac Davis, commander of the Royal Artillery during Kamehameha I's conquest of Hawai'i. With the discovery of gold in California in 1848 and the resulting heavy demand for Irish potatoes and other

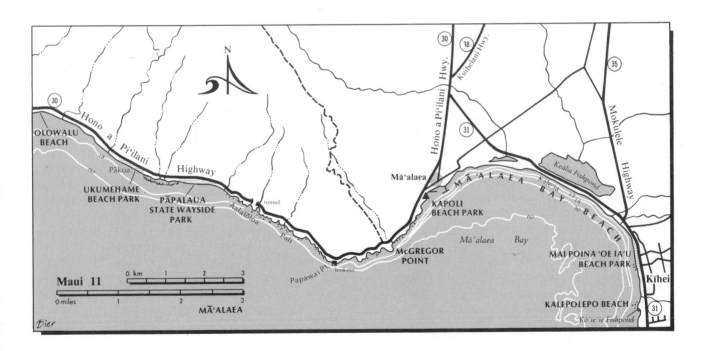

food supplies, Halstead moved his family to the village of Kalepolepo to capitalize on the potato industry that had already been developed in Kula to service the whalers.

In the early 1850s Halstead built a three-story house, patterned after a Pennsylvania Dutch farmhouse, on the shoreline next to the old fishpond. *Koa* wood shelves and counters were installed on the first floor, which was then used as a store. The upper two stories were the family's living quarters. Many of the larger pieces of furniture were made of *koa* by Halstead himself. With its mullet-filled fishpond, the Koa House (the name Halstead chose for his store-home) became a popular retreat for Hawaiian royalty. Kamehameha III, Kamehameha IV, Lunalilo, and Kamehameha V were among the royal dignitaries who visited and stayed at the Koa House.

Halstead finally closed his store in 1876, as demands for his goods had steadily decreased, and moved to Ulupalakua, where he died in May 1887. By this time the once thriving Hawaiian village at Kalepolepo had been almost totally abandoned as well. The slopes of Haleakalā had gradually become denuded of their forests and torrential rains had caused heavy soil runoffs into the Kalepolepo shoreline. Cattle had trampled down the brush and grassy fields, causing sand dunes to drift and fill up the pond. Clouds of dust filled the air instead of cooling winds. Except for a handful of fishing families, Kalepolepo was deserted.

In 1946 the one-hundred-year-old Koa House was declared a menace to public safety. It was condemned and burned to the ground on August 26. Near the site of the Koa House was a building housing the National Bureau of Standards radio station, WWVH. The radio station was relocated to the Barking Sands facility on Kaua'i. Its two-story building is now used as a field office by the National Oceanic and Atmospheric Administration.

Kalepolepo Beach Park centers on the remaining fishpond, which still has its walls intact. The remnants of a larger neighboring pond south of the Kalepolepo pond are visible only from the air. The existing pond is shallow and filled with white sand, a safe and well-protected swimming pool for children. Facilities in the small, grassy park include restrooms, showers, and a paved parking lot. The park is adjacent to the N.O.A.A. station.

The beach that ends on the south side of Kalepolepo pond begins at Waimāha'iha'i and winds through Kawililīpoa to Kalepolepo. The nearshore bottom is rocky with scattered pockets of sand. On the north side of the pond the beach begins again in a series of sand dunes covered with *kiawe*. The dunes flatten out fronting the drainage ditch from Kalanihāko'i Gulch and form a wide, sandy beach. After heavy rains a *muliwai* often forms in the ditch near the road, a danger to little children. The nearshore bottom is the same as on the south side of the pond, rocky with scattered pockets of sand.

(54)
Mai Poina 'Oe Ia'u Beach Park

Mai poina 'oe ia'u is a gentle command in Hawaiian that means "Forget me not." A sign in this park reads:

IN MEMORIAM

Mai Poina 'Oe Ia'u Park

Dedicated to all those who sacrificed their lives to preserve our freedom for all humanity.

When the land was first set aside for use as a public park in May 1951, it was called Kīhei Memorial Park. The name Mai Poina 'Oe Ia'u was introduced at the park's dedication on August 3, 1952. Both names have been used interchangeably over the years, occasionally leading people to believe that there are two different beach parks. Instrumental in the park's creation were the Kīhei Community Association and Louis Ambrose, its president. The memorial plaque in the pavilion was unveiled on December 18, 1955, after the end of the Korean War. Rededication ceremonies were held, to include all war dead. Today the phrase *Mai poina 'oe ia'u* embraces those who died in the Vietnam War as well. Locally, the park is often simply called Memorial Park or Veterans Park.

Mai Poina 'Oe Ia'u Beach Park is located in Kīhei—a name now synonymous with luxurious shoreline resorts, beautiful beaches, and Canadian investors and visitors. The real estate and construction boom did not begin in Kīhei until the late 1950s, when a steady stream of investors began buying the prized beachfront. Kīhei's previous growth as a residential area had only really begun in 1952 when the Maui County Waterworks Board built

MAI POINA 'OE IA'U BEACH PARK. *Mai poina 'oe ia'u* is a gentle command in Hawaiian that means "forget me not." The park is dedicated to the memory of Maui veterans who died in com- bat and is located in the town of Kīhei. The crumbling remains of the old Kīhei Landing are still standing at the water's edge.

delivery mains from Wailuku. With the introduction of a dependable water supply, Kīhei grew with amazing speed, as did its land values. In light of today's real estate prices in the area, it is interesting to note that in 1940 the Territorial Land Commission auctioned one-half-acre beach lots in Kīhei and Kama'ole for an upset price of three hundred dollars, less than two cents a square foot.

The name Kīhei, "cape (or cloak)," originally was applied to only a small area, basically the shoreline surrounding the old landing. However, with the tremendous surge of tourist activity and interest in this area of Maui, Kīhei has become as well known a name as Lahaina or Kā'anapali. For this reason many developers have capitalized on the magic of the name, so that Kīhei

Beach today is anywhere along South Kīhei Road from the town of Kīhei to Keawakapu, a distance of some six miles.

At the north end of Mai Poina 'Oe Ia'u Beach Park are the remnants of the old Kīhei Landing. About 1890, at the request of Maui plantation owners and farmers, this site was selected for a landing in Mā'alaea Bay. The 200-foot-long wharf that was constructed was used for many years by interisland boats for landing freight and shipping produce. About 1915 the interisland steamers stopped calling at Kīhei because the sand accretion in the area had become so severe that the vessels could not reach the wharf. However, the landing was still used extensively by Maui's fishing fleet and many pleasure craft until 1952, when it was abandoned following the construction of Māʻalaea Boat Harbor. The aging and deteriorating wharf was finally condemned by the Harbors Board in the interest of public safety and in light of the harbor improvements at Māʻalaea. In December 1959 the wooden wharf was destroyed by fire. Today only a few pilings and a rubblemound remain. Pleasure craft still use the waters offshore as an anchorage.

At the south end of Mai Poina ʻOe Iaʻu Beach Park is a monument to Captain George Vancouver. In March 1792, with his expedition becalmed in the bay, Vancouver went ashore with his men for water and briefly explored the island. To commemorate this visit, a monument was designed and erected by J. Gordon Gibson, the original owner of the Maui Lu, located directly across the street. The shoreline around the monument has suffered severe erosion from the ocean, and in 1964 the County of Maui constructed a 200-foot-long revetment to protect the highway in this area.

The beach fronting Mai Poina ʻOe Iaʻu Beach Park is a part of the long white sand beach that follows Māʻalaea Bay through Kīhei. The inshore bottom is generally sandy with scattered patches of rock—a good swimming area. Offshore is the end of the shallow protective reef that begins up the coast at Kalama Beach Park. Facilities in the narrow roadside beach park include a pavilion with restrooms, showers, picnic tables, and a paved parking lot.

During the winter and spring months the park provides a good vantage point for watching the whales offshore in Māʻalaea Bay. The waters off Māʻalaea and Kīhei are the favorite calving, nursing, and mating grounds of the humpbacks, and they can frequently be seen spouting and breeching. Residents of the shoreline from Kīhei to Keawakapu report that on very still nights the water-slapping antics as well as the calls of the whales can be heard very clearly.

(55)
Māʻalaea Beach

The name Māʻalaea is thought to be a contraction of Mākaʻalaea, which means "ocherous earth beginnings." ʻAlaea ("ocherous earth") is an edible, water-soluble red clay used for medicine, for dye, for certain purification ceremonies, and most commonly for coloring paʻakai (salt). ʻAlaea salt can still be found in most local stores.

The curving three-mile reach of shoreline that follows the head of Māʻalaea Bay between Kīhei and Māʻalaea Boat Harbor is a barrier beach of white sand with an average width of seventy-five feet. Outcrops of beach rock are found along the beach, which is backed by low sand dunes. The inshore bottom is generally sandy and slopes quickly to overhead depths along most of the beach—a danger to little children or poor swimmers. The shorebreak is normally small enough to pose no problems for swimmers, while attracting bodysurfers. Occasionally small rip currents form when a large swell is running, but they are usually of short duration and of little concern to the average swimmer familiar with the ocean. The inshore waters of the entire bay are generally free of strong currents during most prevailing ocean conditions. The waters offshore are often murky, but are seasonally clear and calm enough for diving and snorkeling. Māʻalaea Bay has a very rich and varied molluscan population, possibly containing the greatest number of species found in any Hawaiian locality.

For surfers there are two periodically good surfing areas: Mudflats, situated roughly off the middle of the beach, and Māʻalaea, outside the breakwater at Māʻalaea Boat Harbor. Both of these spots break best on a large south swell. The extremely fast right slide at Māʻalaea is considered by most surfers to be the best break on Maui's south shore and also one of the best on the island.

In recent years the beach at Māʻalaea has also become a favorite walking and jogging path for exercise-conscious individuals. The sand near the water is usually packed hard, providing a long, continuous, and solid shoreline track. The only natural deterrent to a prolonged visit to the area is the wind. The prevailing winds usually begin to blow across the isthmus from Kahului toward Māʻalaea about mid-morning. By noon they are often howling across the beach toward Molokini and Kahoʻolawe. Although the wind abates in the evening, its severity during the day is enough to discourage most casual picnickers.

The beach at Māʻalaea Bay is known to most local residents simply as Māʻalaea; however, other names are occasionally found on maps and in scientific literature. These names include Kaleʻia, Palalau, and Kanaio—all old shoreline names from this area.

Just inland of the east half of Māʻalaea Beach, on the

far side of North Kīhei Road, is Keālia Pond, an important breeding and nesting refuge for indigenous waterfowl. This salt-water marsh supports major populations of *āe'o* (Hawaiian stilts), *'alae ke'oke'o* (Hawaiian coots), and *'auku'u* (black-crowned night herons), as well as many migratory birds. In 1953 three hundred acres of the pond were designated as a wildlife refuge and set aside for this use. Between Keālia Pond and the hotels and condominiums at Mā'alaea on the near side of North Kīhei Road is another important but shallow intermittently ponded area. The birds utilize it during the winter and spring when it is flooded, and move to Keālia Pond during the summer if it dries out. This particular tidal flat was once the runway of Mā'alaea Airport, one of the first airports on Maui.

At the west end of Mā'alaea Bay is Mā'alaea Boat Harbor. Constructed in 1952 as a recreational boat harbor by the State of Hawai'i, it includes a wide entrance channel, two breakwaters, a paved wharf, berthing facilities, a launching ramp, a Coast Guard Station, restrooms, and several parking areas. On July 15, 1975, Mā'alaea Boat Harbor became one of the terminals for an interisland hydrofoil service called Seaflite. The 95-foot-long, hydrofoil-borne, water-jet-propelled vessels had a cruising speed of 50 miles per hour and were thought to be the answer to the long-discussed need for an interisland ferry system. The company was beset with problems from the beginning, however, and eventually, because of the heavy financial costs of maintaining the vessels, closed down the operation. The last commercial run made by a Seaflite hydrofoil was on January 15, 1978.

(56)
Kapoli Beach Park

Kapoli, "the bosom," is the name of a spring that is said to have been located behind Buzz's Wharf Restaurant in Mā'alaea Boat Harbor. Also to the rear of Buzz's are two large boulders that are of historical interest. One of them was used as a grinding stone, and the other is said to have been a *pōhaku piko,* a stone used for hiding umbilical cords. These stones were brought to Mā'alaea from a Hawaiian village situated above McGregor Point. In 1952 the contractor who was building the Mā'alaea Boat Harbor breakwaters was getting his boulder material from this village. When the destruction

of this historical site was discovered, these two stones were saved.

Kapoli Beach Park is a small unimproved parcel of land covered with *kiawe* to the rear of Mā'alaea Boat Harbor. In its present state it is of no recreational value to anyone. The shoreline edge of the park is a severely eroded soil bluff. The ocean below is shallow and rocky.

(57)
McGregor Point

Daniel McGregor was born on May 4, 1857, in Leith, Scotland. He put to sea as a young man and arrived in Hawai'i about 1875. He then became involved in the Ko'olau trade. Ko'olau is a name for the windward side of any Hawaiian island, and Ko'olau trade was the term coined for the pick-up and delivery of supplies at windward landings by interisland vessels. Sometime during the period between 1875 and McGregor's death on April 4, 1887, he was captain of a ship that was caught in a storm while passing the sea cliffs between Olowalu and Mā'alaea. It was there that he made his famous landing. This account of the incident was told to McGregor's granddaughter by Paika Kanakaole, who had been a crewman aboard the ship.

The ship had been bound for Mā'alaea on an extremely stormy night. The captain knew that his intended landing was much too open and rough to offer any shelter from the weather, but he was determined to make a safe landing for the night. In the pouring rain he lined his crew on both sides of the deck and had them take continuous soundings as the ship edged its way along the rugged coastline. Finally, about two or three o'clock in the early morning, the ship found its way into a sheltered spot, just barely clearing the bottom. The weary and rain-soaked crew dropped anchor and slept the few remaining hours until dawn. With the coming of the day everyone on board was surprised to find that they had landed only a stone's throw away from a high sea cliff.

Of course, news of the incident spread and the emergency anchorage was named McGregor Point. Other ships began to use the same spot, taking advantage ot its protection from the powerful winds of Mā'alaea. Eventually, a wharf was constructed there and McGregor Point became an official government landing. The wharf was a frequent port of call for the steamers of the

Inter-island Steam Navigation Company as well as for other vessels.

The protected waters at McGregor Point were not exempt from tsunami, however. In August 1906 seismic waves severely damaged the wharf, in addition to destroying Māʻalaea wharf farther up the coast. The ensuing surf was said to be the heaviest ever known in these waters. The McGregor superstructure was repaired and the landing continued its service for a number of years. Today, however, only a few sections of the wharf's concrete foundations and a cleat embedded in the rock remain as remnants of the old landing. A lighthouse and a Federal Aviation Agency blockhouse now occupy McGregor Point.

McGregor Point is situated along an extensive range of hills and rocky sea cliffs between Māʻalaea and Pāpalaua. This *pali* was known to the Hawaiians as ʻĀalalō-loa, the "long path (of) rough lava." When a road was eventually constructed through the area, the four-mile stretch contained 115 sharp curves. It was often called Maui's Amalfi Drive because of its resemblance to a highway skirting the edge of the Mediterranean Sea in Italy. Finally, in 1950, work on the *pali* tunnel and a new highway was started, to eliminate the many dangerous curves. The 315-foot-long tunnel, the first public vehicular tunnel constructed in the Hawaiian Islands, was completed in July 1951. Today many sections of the old road can still be seen, primarily on the *mauka* side of the present highway. Many older Maui residents also know this area as Lahaina Pali.

The shoreline on either side of McGregor Point has a number of small unimproved beach parks situated at the base of the sea cliffs. Most of these *kiawe*-shaded areas are accessible by dirt roads that turn off the main highway. These roads are badly eroded, however, and are usually not passable in an ordinary passenger car. Roadside parking is available to some extent off the highway on the *makai* side of the guardrail. All pedestrians and drivers in this area should be alert to the flow of traffic, which generally moves at much faster speeds than the posted forty miles per hour. There is very little room to maneuver alongside the highway—a very dangerous situation for anyone getting off or back on the highway.

To the east of McGregor Point, between the last shoreline houses at Māʻalaea and the lighthouse, are three small pockets of white sand. The offshore bottoms are shallow and a mixture of sand and rock—fine swimming areas for children on calm days. The lava shelves between these sandy areas contain many small tidal pools. To the west of McGregor Point are several similar beach areas, except that the shoreline is shingle and cobblestone, not sand, and the waters offshore tend to be a little deeper. All of these small beach parks are excellent areas for snorkeling, fishing, and picnicking. They are completely unimproved and unmarked by signs.

Beyond McGregor Point toward the *pali* tunnel, the sea cliffs begin to rise higher above the ocean. On the *makai* side of this stretch of highway is the scenic Papawai Point Lookout, offering a beautiful view of Haleakalā and its coastline as far as Puʻu Ōlaʻi near Mākena, as well as of the islands of Molokini, Kahoʻolawe, and Lānaʻi. The lookout is also a good spot to watch the boat traffic coming in and out of Māʻalaea Boat Harbor, and an excellent place for whale watching.

The humpback whale, Hawaiʻi's official state marine mammal, winters in Hawaiian waters and summers in Alaskan and Siberian waters. The first whales begin arriving in October. The population peaks with approximately six hundred animals in mid-February, most of whom leave before summer. The humpbacks are seen in various areas around the island chain, but concentrate particularly in the waters between the four islands of Kahoʻolawe, Lānaʻi, Molokaʻi, and Maui, where calving, nursing, and mating occur. Proposals to make this particular area a National Marine Sanctuary are strongly supported by many groups and individuals concerned with the survival of this endangered species. Humpbacks are protected from harassment from aircraft, boats, divers, and swimmers under the Marine Mammal Protection Act of 1972 and the Endangered Species Act of 1973; violators are subject to prosecution.

(58)

Pāpalaua State Wayside Park

Pāpalaua, "rain fog," is the name of the gulch across the park on the *mauka* side of Hono a Piʻilani Highway. Two different articles in the Hawaiian newspaper *Ka Nūpepa Kūʻokoʻa* give the spelling of this name as Papaláʻau. The earlier article, by W. N. Pualewa, dated September 5, 1863, says, "Thus they ran until they passed Wailuku, Kamaʻalaea, the cliff of ʻĀalalōloa, and down the incline of Papalāʻau." The second article, by S. W. Kepano, dated September 2, 1921, says, "It didn't take long ere we roared up the incline to Papalāʻau to the pali of ʻĀalalōloa."

Although the official name of this long, narrow beach is Pāpalaua State Wayside Park, it is popularly known to Maui residents as Thousand Peaks. The name refers to the numerous surfing breaks or peaks that form on the shallow offshore patches of reef. When a swell strikes the area, dozens of peaks develop along the beach, attracting many surfers and bodyboarders. Swimming and snorkeling are also popular activities.

The narrow roadside park is undeveloped and covered with *kiawe*. Beachgoers park and picnic under the larger trees. This shoreline offers an excellent view of Kahoʻolawe's western shore across Kealaikahiki Channel.

(59)
Ukumehame Beach Park

Ukumehame is the name of the land division that includes this beach park as well as the narrow canyon *mauka* of the park. Ukumehame means "(to) pay (in) *mehame* wood," a prized native hardwood formerly used for anvils for preparing *olona* fiber and in later years for making cabinets. The old shoreline name for this place was Pākoa.

Ukumehame Beach Park is a narrow roadside park. The widest portion of the park is landscaped with a small grassy field and some ironwood trees. There is a paved parking lot, but no other facilities. A narrow detrital sand beach fronts the park. The offshore bottom is shallow and rocky with scattered patches of sand. The area is frequented primarily by fishermen.

Between Ukumehame Beach Park and Olowalu is a long, straight stretch of highway bordered primarily by cobblestone. Punahoa is the area where a lone ironwood tree stands next to Ukumehame Bridge. Occasionally the waves offshore are good enough for board surfing. Surfers refer to the break as Pine Tree or Lone Pine. Beyond Punahoa is a long shingle beach that was simply called Kaʻiliʻili. Pākalā is the area where the sand beach begins again.

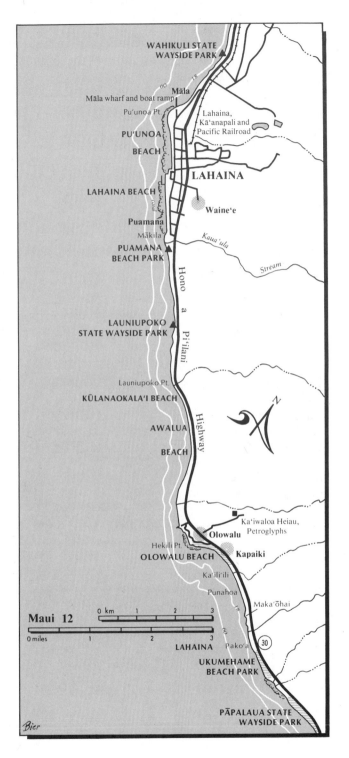

(60)

Olowalu Beach

Olowalu, "many hills," is probably best known as the site of a terrible slaughter now called the Olowalu Massacre. In 1790 two Americans, Captain Simon Metcalf and his son Thomas, anchored their ships, the *Fair American* and the *Elinor,* off Honua'ula. One night some Hawaiians stole a longboat that was tied to the stern of one of the ships and killed a sailor in the process. The boat was taken ashore and stripped for its nails and metal fittings, metal at that time being an extremely prized possession for any Hawaiian. Captain Metcalf fired several cannon rounds in to the village inshore, killing several people and wounding others. This retaliation did not satisfy Metcalf, however, who set sail for Olowalu when he discovered that the men who had taken the boat were natives of that area. Anchoring offshore from Olowalu, Metcalf encouraged the Hawaiians to approach his ship to trade, but only on one side. When a large group had gathered, Metcalf's crew opened fire with their cannons, killing over eighty and wounding many more. The Olowalu chief, incensed by the massacre, captured the *Fair American* and killed the entire crew except for one man, Isaac Davis. Kamehameha I captured John Young, the boatswain of the

OLOWALU. *Kiawe* trees overhang the narrow detrital sand beach at Olowalu. The tiny pocket of white sand alongside the remains of Olowalu Landing is a popular entry point for snorkelers and skin divers who frequent the shallow reefs offshore. The huge pass in the West Maui Mountains is called Olowalu Gorge.

Elinor. Both of these men eventually became advisors to Kamehameha I, took Hawaiian wives, and became chiefs in their own right.

In 1876 Olowalu Plantation was started by Philip Milton and Goodale Armstrong. This sugar venture surprised many skeptics, who felt the land was much too rocky for profitable cultivation. A mill was constructed, however, and planting progressed satisfactorily. Sugar cane is still grown in the area today. Directly *makai* of Olowalu General Store are the rubblemound ruins of the former Olowalu Landing and crumbling associated structures. The landing has not been in use for many years.

The beach at Olowalu begins at Kapaiki, where the Teen Challenge building is located, and continues around the wide stream delta *makai* of Hono a Pi'ilani Highway to Awalua. To the south of the old landing is a long, narrow brown detrital–white sand beach covered along its entire length by *kiawe.* The trees fall across the beach as the ocean undermines the shoreline under them. The bottom offshore is shallow and rocky with patches of sand, providing only fair swimming conditions. The deeper areas away from the beach are popular snorkeling and diving areas when the water is not murky. To the north of the old landing is a long cobblestone beach fronted by a shallow reef. Occasionally the waves are good enough for board surfing. Public access to the outer areas of Olowalu is gained only by following the shoreline from either Kapaiki or Awalua. The bulk of the land between the highway and the landing is private property.

Inland at Olowalu are two frequently visited sites, Ka'iwaloa *heiau* and the Olowalu petroglyphs. In 1964 the Lahaina Restoration Foundation acquired a lease to the petroglyph site as well as a public right-of-way to it. Wooden stairs and a platform were constructed to facilitate viewing. The access road to the area is marked with a sign on the main highway.

(61)
Awalua Beach

Awalua, "double channel," is the name of a popular roadside detrital sand beach near Olowalu. Awalua is mentioned in the legend of 'Ele'io told by W. N. Pualewa in the September 5, 1863, issue of the Hawaiian newspaper *Ka Nūpepa Kū'oko'a:* "Thus they ran until they passed Wailuku, Kama'alaea, the cliff of 'Āalalōloa, and down the incline of Papalā'au. He ('Ele'io) exerted himself and ran past Ukumehame, on to and past Olowalu, on to and past Awalua, on to and past Kūlanaokala'i, on to and past Launiupoko, and on to Waianukole. There 'A'ahuali'i (the ghost chasing 'Ele'io) almost caught up with him."

Awalua Beach is bordered by shingle to the south and Cut Mountain to the north. Cut Mountain is the local name for the low escarpment that separates Awalua from Kūlanaokala'i. The name was coined when the highway was cut through the mountain. Awalua Beach has a sandy inshore bottom with a gentle slope to the deeper waters offshore. It is a very popular swimming area, and its waves are often good enough for board surfing, attracting many novice surfers. The narrow roadside beach is unimproved.

(62)
Launiupoko State Wayside Park

Launiupoko, "short coconut leaf," is the name of the land division in which the park is located. Local fishermen say that this area is a shark breeding ground. During certain times of the year net fishermen have to be careful or else the numerous sharks in the area become entangled in their nets, causing much damage. The May 16, 1902, issue of the Hawaiian newspaper *Ka Nūpepa Kū'oko'a* offered this information, in A. D. Kahaulilio's "Fishing Lore" column, about deliberately fishing for sharks:

> Ho'omoemoe fishing for sharks was much practiced by the old timers of this land division of Mākila and also by the people of the upland Kaua'ula since we were children. [Mākila is the shoreline area where the present Puamana complex is located, and Kaua'ula is directly *mauka* of Mākila. Mākila and Kaua'ula are two of the numerous small *ahupua'a,* some as small as three acres, in the ancient *kalana* of Lahaina.] The kind of sharks caught by the ho'omoemoe method were the lālākea and hammerheads. . . . The place where ho'omoemoe fishing was done was at Pāhe'e in Launiupoko.

Although it is not widely known, the Hawaiians did eat certain kinds of shark as well as use their skins and teeth. The families that abstained were primarily those whose family guardian was the shark.

Launiupoko State Wayside Park is fronted by a large, man-made wading pool for children. The pond is formed by a boulder retaining wall and has a shallow detrital sand bottom. To the left of the pond is a short but wide detrital sand beach. The inshore bottom is shallow with pockets of sand and rock. Offshore the waves are occasionally good enough for surfing. The park offers an excellent vantage point to view all three offshore islands—Kahoʻolawe, Lānaʻi, and Molokaʻi—as well as all the vessels anchored in the Lahaina roadstead. It is a popular picnic area. Facilities include restrooms, showers, picnic tables, barbecue grills, and a paved parking lot.

(63)
Puamana Beach Park

Puamana was the family home of Annie Kahalepouli Shaw Farden and Charles Kekua Farden. Their large two-story house, built in 1915, was located on Front Street in Lahaina. The property was originally awarded to Anna Keohokalole, a Hawaiian chiefess, as Land Court Award 5874 and entitled Puamana. After her death her remaining lands were partioned among her surviving children, David (later King David Kalākaua), Liliʻu (later Queen Liliʻuokalani, and Miriam (Princess Miriam Likelike), and William (Prince William Pitt Leleiohoku II). David received Puamana along with other lands, and upon his death, title went to his widow, Kapiʻolani. She in turn deeded the land to her nephews Jonah Kalanianaʻole and David Kawananakoa, who incorporated as the Kapiʻolani Estate. When Charles Farden purchased the half-acre lot from the Kapiʻolani Estate, Puamana was still the name of the property. He felt it would be a fitting name for his home and retained it. The word *pua* can mean "flower or blossom"; "to issue or emerge"; or "children or descendants." The word *mana* means "supernatural or divine power." The combination of the two words obviously holds more than one meaning, but to the Farden family Puamana means the "home that holds its members close," an expression of the love that has always been shared among the members of the family.

Puamana is probably best known to residents of Hawaiʻi through the song of the same name. It was composed about 1935 by Irmgard Farden Aluli, one of Annie and Charles Farden's twelve children. Irmgard was teaching on Molokaʻi at that time and had returned to Puamana for a visit. One morning she sat down at the family piano and found herself playing a new tune. She liked it and decided it would be a song for their home. The composition of the verses was a united effort of Irmgard and the rest of the family. The translation of the verses into Hawaiian was done by Charles Farden. Today the song "Puamana" is a Hawaiian classic.

Puamana

1. *Puamana, kuʻu home i Lahaina*
   Puamana, my home in Lahaina
   Me na pua ala onaona
   With the fragrant flowers
   Kuʻu home i aloha ʻia.
   My home that I love.
2. *Home nani, home i ka ʻae kai*
   Beautiful home, home at the water's edge
   Ke kū nani a ka mahina
   Standing beautifully in the moonlight
   I ke kai hāwanawana
   By the whispering waves
3. *Kuʻu home, i ka ulu o ka niu*
   My home, in the grove of coconut trees
   ʻO ka niu kū kilakila
   The coconut trees standing so majestically
   E napenape mālie
   Their leaves gently fluttering
4. *Haʻina ʻia mai ka puana*
   Tell the refrain
   Kuʻu home i Lahaina
   About my home in Lahaina
   Ua piha me ka hauʻoli
   That filled us completely with happiness

© 1946 Criterion Music Corporation.
© Renewed 1974 Criterion Music Corporation.

After the death of the elder Fardens, Puamana was leased and eventually sold. The original house was dismantled for its lumber and a new two-story house took its place. The only visible reminder of the former home is the row of coconut trees lining the rear of the seawall. Under their parents' direction, each of the twelve children had planted and cared for his or her own coconut tree. Other trees were planted in the same area, but the children of course knew their special trees and delighted in comparing growth and productivity as the years passed. The entire family often gathered in the yard under these trees to play music and sing on quiet moonlit nights, as the song "Puamana" tells us. All the Farden children became musically adept in composing, teaching, and performing. Their accomplishments were recognized in 1977 by the Hawaiian Music Foundation's Hawaii Aloha Award for outstanding contribution to the development of Hawaiian music—the first time the award was ever presented to an entire family.

Puamana Beach Park is located next to the Puamana resort complex at the south end of Front Street. The old name of the park area was Waianukole, and the shoreline fronting the resort complex was known as Mākila. In May 1902 A. D. Kahaulelio gave this account in *Ka Nūpepa Kū'oko'a:* "You remember . . . that large sandy spot on the southeast side of the writer's residence [at Mākila] running toward the cape over which one looks down to Launiupoko. That spot was named Waianukole and directly seaward my father and uncles caught *uhukai.*"

During the 1960s surfers who began to frequent the area called the beach and its offshore break Hot Sands, because often the heat of the sand was so intense that they ended up running with their surfboards. Nevertheless, since the construction of Puamana, the shoreline has most commonly been known as Puamana Beach.

Puamana Beach Park is fronted by a narrow white sand beach. The ocean bottom is a mixture of rock and sand and it is fairly shallow—a safe area for swimmers. The waves offshore are occasionally good enough for surfing, but most surfers prefer the summer breaks fronting the Puamana complex. Facilities in this grassy, tree-lined park include picnic tables and a paved parking lot.

(64)
Lahaina

Lahaina. For local residents and visitors alike, the name suggests a variety of pleasant and enticing images. It has the same magical attractiveness that once was exclusive to Waikīkī.

The old pronunciation of Lahaina is Lāhainā, mean-

ing "cruel (or merciless) sun." A chief who lived *mauka* in Kaua'ula is said one day to have cursed at the hot sun: *"He keu hoi keia o ka lā hainā"*—"What an unmerciful sun." The people of the area remembered his words and as the story was retold, the place became known as Lāhainā. Prior to this incident, Lāhainā was known as Lele and was renowned for its large, shady breadfruit trees. Ka malu 'ulu o Lele, "the shady breadfruit trees of Lele," is still a well-known poetic epithet that refers specifically to the Lahaina area. The phrase appears in the song "He Aloha no o Honolulu" as well as in the name of Malu 'Ulu o Lele Park on Front Street in Lahaina. Other interpretations of the name Lahaina have been offered by various individuals. One is that the name is Lāhaina, "day (of) sacrifice," because of sacrifices and other related events held in the area. Another interpretation is based on the pronunciation Lāha'ina, "day (of) explanation," because it was supposedly the custom of the chiefs to tell the people the schedule of work at daily gatherings.

The village of Lahaina served historically as a royal residence and as a seat of government for many Maui chiefs and kings. The famous Kahekili maintained his home and his royal court there until his death in 1794. In the early 1800s Kamehameha I, the first king to rule all the Hawaiian Islands, established Lahaina as his home and his capital. Lahaina became a popular resort for Hawaiian royalty and many of their homes lined the beach. The ocean fronting these residences was the favored place for swimming and surfing on either a surfboard or a canoe. The surf was called 'Uo and the canoe landing, the site of the present boat harbor, was called Keawaiki, "the little harbor." In 1820 Kamehameha II officially designated Lahaina as the capital of the Hawaiian Kingdom. The town continued in its capacity as the official seat of government until 1845. In that year Honolulu was made the capital of the islands.

Beginning about 1820 the newly discovered whaling grounds off the northwest coast of America, south of Alaska in the Okhotsk, Bering, and Anadyr seas, and in the Arctic Ocean north of the Bering Straits brought numerous whalers to the Hawaiian Islands, to be outfitted, repaired, and provisioned. The hell-raising exploits of the seamen in Lahaina are legendary. Rowdy crews from the whalers, continually in search of women

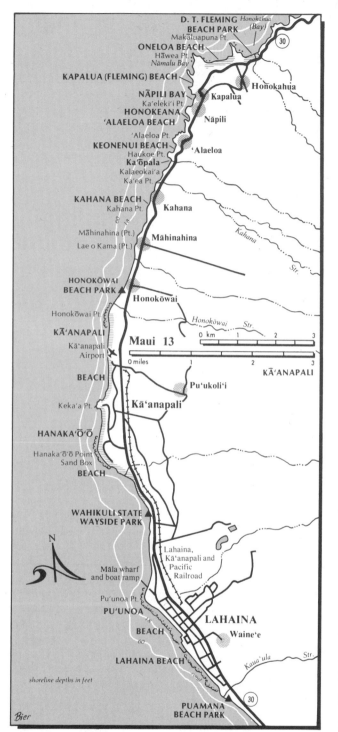

and alcohol, provided a booming business for stores, saloons, and innkeepers. The peak period for whalers in Hawai'i was from 1843 to 1860. The year 1846 saw 395 whalers drop anchor in the Lahaina Roadstead. The census for that year listed 3,445 Hawaiians, 112 foreigners, 882 grass houses, 155 adobe houses, 59 stone and wooden houses, 528 dogs, and 600 seamen.

The first Christian missionaries arrived in Lahaina on May 31, 1823, and were welcomed by Keopuolani, the highest-born wife of Kamehameha I. The impact of the missionaries on Lahaina is also legendary. Among their many contributions, the missionaries established Lahainaluna, the first school west of the Rockies, and three years later, in 1834, they printed *Ka Lama Hawaii,* the first Hawaiian newspaper. The Catholic church also established itself in Lahaina, after a long period of conflict with the previously settled Protestants. Maria Lanakila ("Mary [Our Lady of] Victory") Church was erected in 1858.

By the 1870s the entire whaling enterprise had ceased in Hawai'i. The decline of the industry was attributed to a number of causes, the most important one probably being competition from the petroleum industry, which had started in 1859 in Pennsylvania. Kerosene, produced from petroleum, began replacing whale oil as a lantern fuel, and petroleum oil began replacing whale oil as a lubricant. The end of Hawai'i-based whaling, however, came with the great Arctic disaster of September 1871, when thirty-three out of forty-two whaling ships operating out of Honolulu were crushed in the ice near Point Barrow in the Arctic Ocean. The ships had stayed too late into the fall and had been trapped in the ice floes.

By the late 1800s most of Lahaina's populace, including the missionaries, had left for other areas of Hawai'i. Lahaina reverted back to a quiet country village, but not completely. James Campbell, an Irish sailor, had arrived in Lahaina in 1852 and had established himself as a carpenter, building ships and homes. In 1861 he started a small sugar cane plantation and took on Henry Turton as a partner. In 1865 Campbell and Turton bought Pioneer Mill, a plantation that had been started by Benjamin Pittman in 1862. From these early beginnings, Pioneer Mill eventually emerged as the largest sugar plantation in West Maui, creating jobs for many people.

In 1895, when the company was incorporated, Pioneer Mill began a period of rapid expansion and growth. During this same decade Henry P. Baldwin established Honolua Ranch. Interested in using his extensive West Maui lands for pineapple, Baldwin brought David T. Fleming to Honolua as the ranch manager. Fleming had been with the original Maui pineapple pioneers at Ha'ikū and, within a few years, established pineapple as a commercial crop in West Maui. Baldwin Packers, the fruit-packing branch of the new industry, opened a cannery in Lahaina in December 1919, which provided employment for many local residents.

Sugar cane and pineapple sustained Lahaina until the sugar industry began mechanizing its field labor. The cannery finally closed down in the early 1960s, forcing many residents to leave the town and the surrounding villages for other parts of Hawai'i. Lahaina remained a friendly but very quiet plantation town. During this same period, however, American Factors, the owner of Pioneer Mill Co., had begun developing an eight-hundred-acre site as a resort complex called Kā'anapali. By early 1963, two hotels, the Royal Lahaina and the Sheraton Maui, were in operation. This development marked the beginning of a new period of expansion and commercial growth for Lahaina, which peaked in the 1970s. Today numerous bars, restaurants, shops, and other businesses cater to the thousands of tourists who daily throng through the town. Lahaina is no longer a sleepy residential community. It is a full-fledged tourist resort second only to Waikīkī.

The beach in Lahaina begins at the edge of the Lahaina Boat Harbor breakwater and continues toward the end of Front Street near Puamana where the sand gives way to cobblestones. The shoreline is well protected by the offshore reef, but the shallow rocky bottom between the reef and the beach is not attractive to most adults as a swimming area. Snorkelers and divers make good use of the area, however, as do many surfers who congregate at the offshore breaks. There is public access from the harbor area and a marked public right-of-way on the south side of the Hotel Lahaina Shores on Front Street.

Lahaina Boat Harbor, located in the heart of town, was built before the growth of Lahaina as a popular tourist center. Today there is a tremendous demand for mooring space and the small harbor is continually crowded. It is not uncommon to find up to one hundred vessels that cannot be accommodated inshore anchoring offshore in the Lahaina roadstead and near Mala Wharf. The concrete boat ramp in the harbor, constructed in 1963, compounded the congestion until 1979. In that year, a new double ramp with ample parking was completed next to Mala Wharf and the Lahaina Ramp was closed.

(65)
Pu'unoa Beach

Pu'unoa, "hill freed of taboo," is the name of the beach and residential area bordering the north end of Lahaina town. Pu'unoa is the site of two well-known landmarks, the Lahaina Jodo Mission Buddhist Cultural Park and Mala Wharf. The cultural park is one of Lahaina's busiest tourist attractions, while its neighbor on the shoreline sits in ruins.

Mala, "garden," is the name of the residential area to the north of the wharf. Mala Wharf was dedicated on April 5, 1922. Governor Wallace R. Farrington was the chief guest of honor, with many other territorial officials and dignitaries attending the opening ceremonies. Most of them left Honolulu in the morning on the steamer *Mauna Kea* and disembarked that afternoon as the first passengers at the new wharf. Mala Wharf was expected to eliminate the customary landings at Lahaina, which involved passengers and freight going ashore on lighters while the interisland steamer waited at anchor offshore. It was built at a cost of $220,000 and constructed of reinforced concrete with ornamental light posts and concrete railings extending almost its entire length. It was deliberately built high above the water because of the occasionally heavy surf that hits the Pu'unoa-Mala shoreline. A built-in landing area with stairs leading up to the top of the wharf was constructed for passengers.

After the dedication, marked by the landing of the *Mauna Kea,* only one other steamer ever tied up there successfully. The strong currents and heavy surf sweeping into the wharf made mooring a dangerous endeavor. After several steamers were damaged while attempting to tie up, the old practice of anchoring offshore and using lighters from ship to shore was resumed. Mala

Wharf was then used only by fishing boats, yachts, and other small craft, its intended function as a major interisland cargo and passenger terminal having been almost completely abandoned. The terminal was finally closed in 1950.

Pu'unoa Beach is a narrow detrital sand beach that begins near the old seawall *makai* of the businesses on Front Street and ends at Mala Wharf. The shallow offshore bottom extends out to the edge of the reef. The area is frequented primarily by fishermen and surfers. On the north side of Mala Wharf the shoreline is entirely rocky, with many seawalls protecting the residential property inshore. Many vessels use the waters offshore as a mooring area. In 1979 a new double boat ramp was constructed next to Mala Wharf to relieve some of the congestion at Lahaina Boat Harbor. Public rights-of-way to the area are clearly marked and there is ample parking for automobiles and boat trailers.

(66)
Wahikuli State Wayside Park

Wahikuli means "noisy place" and is an alternate name of the *ahupua'a* of Mala which includes this park. Wahikuli State Wayside Park is one of the most popular beach parks in West Maui. It is usually crowded with picnickers, swimmers, and sunbathers, especially on weekends and holidays. Wahikuli's popularity is undoubtedly due to its size, its good swimming conditions, its excellent facilities, and its proximity to Lahaina. Facilities include four restrooms with showers, many small pavilions with picnic tables, barbecue grills, and paved parking lots. Almost the entire shoreline of this long roadside park is lined with a retaining wall composed of large boulders. There is one small sandy beach that provides good swimming and snorkeling. The inshore bottom is a combination of sand and rock and slopes gently to the deeper areas offshore.

(67)
Hanaka'ō'ō Beach Park

Hanaka'ō'ō means the "digging stick bay," but the origin of the name is now unknown. The beach fronting the park was once known to Maui residents as Sand Box Beach. Sand Box was also the name of a still-popular surfing break fronting the neighboring Hyatt Regency Maui. During the early 1900s Pioneer Mill constructed a

rock crusher near Hanaka'ō'ō Cemetery, now situated within the park. The rock crusher had several large storage bins to hold the crushed material, including a box for sand. The sand box was kept filled with beach sand, which was bagged as needed for various construction projects. The rock crusher shut down operations in the 1920s, but the sand box remained on the beach for many years, giving the beach its once-popular name.

Hanaka'ō'ō Beach Park is located between Wahikuli State Wayside Park and the Hyatt Regency Maui. The beach fronting the park is the beginning of the long stretch of sand that runs for a mile to Pu'u Keka'a or Black Rock in the center of Kā'anapali. The park is heavily used by swimmers, snorkelers, and picnickers. The shorebreak that forms on the beach attracts bodysurfers and bodyboarders. The nearshore waters offshore the beach also provide boaters with a popular summer anchorage. Facilities in the park include picnic pavilions, restrooms, showers, paved parking, and a canoe storage shed for the outrigger canoe clubs who use the park as a practice site.

(68)
Kā'anapali Beach

Kā'anapali is the name of an ancient *kalana* that was obliterated by the Hawaiian Legislature in 1859 by combining its lands in a new Lahaina district. The name was preserved by American Factors, Ltd., the developer of the Kā'anapali resort complex. The outstanding geographical feature in the resort area is Pu'u Keka'a, "the rumbling hill," a volcanic cinder and spatter cone. Pu'u Keka'a is most commonly known to local residents as Black Rock, a reference to the color of the cone.

According to legend, the lands surrounding Pu'u Keka'a were once an area of intense cultivation and the home of the Maui chief Kaka'alaneo when he ruled West Maui. Kaka'alaneo's son, Ka'ululā'au, was born there and became famous in his own right. An extremely mischievous youngster, he vandalized many of the shady breadfruit trees of Lele (Lahaina), for which the village was renowned. He was finally banished to Lāna'i, an island then inhabited only by spirits. Using his mental and physical agility, Ka'ululā'au outwitted the spirits and made Lāna'i safe for human habitation.

Pu'u Keka'a, according to tradition, is a *leina a ka 'uhane*, a "soul's leap." When a person lay on his death-bed, his soul would leave his body and wander about. If all earthly obligations had been fulfilled, the soul found its way to Puʻu Kekaʻa. There it was taken by minor gods and at that moment physical death came to the individual's body. Every island had at least one if not several locations designated as a *leina a ka ʻuhane.*

In more recent times the Kāʻanapali area was acquired by Pioneer Mill Company for cultivation in sugar cane. A landing was built on the north side of Black Rock to ship out the sugar that was processed and bagged at the mill in Lahaina and hauled to the landing by train. The Lahaina, Kāʻanapali, and Pacific Railroad that today offers train rides primarily to tourists is a revival of the former Lahaina to Kāʻanapali connection. The bagged sugar was stored in a warehouse to the rear of Black Rock. When the sugar boats called, the bags were run out to the end of the landing on flatcars. Many laborers were temporarily brought into the area from the fields to facilitate the operation. Other buildings in the area included oil and molasses tanks and, on the beach, a pavilion and beach cottages reserved for the use of Pioneer Mill Company's supervisors. There was also a quarter-mile track on the tidal flats to the rear of Hanakaʻōʻō Point, used for racing horses on special occasions and holidays. The ruins of Kāʻanapali Landing, abandoned just prior to World War II, can still be seen on the north side of Black Rock. The old bagging, hauling by rail, and shipping operation was replaced by a more efficient, mechanized operation based at Kahului Harbor.

In December 1957 American Factors, Ltd., the owner of Pioneer Mill Company, announced plans for a multi-million dollar resort to be built around Puʻu Kekaʻa and its two long white sand beaches. The complex was to be called Kāʻanapali, thus preserving an old Hawaiian name. Title clearance delayed the project for several years, and construction on the first hotels commenced in the early 1960s. The Royal Lahaina was the first to open, in December 1962, followed closely by the Sheraton Maui in January 1963. The Hyatt Regency Maui, the resort's largest hotel, opened in 1980 and the Maui Marriott, the chain's first Hawaiʻi hotel, opened in 1981. In addition to its two other major hotels, the Maui Surf and the Kāʻanapali Beach Hotel, Kāʻanapali today includes five condominium complexes, an 18-hole golf course, the Sugar Cane Train that transports passengers between Kāʻanapali and Lahaina, and the Whalers Village, a marketplace with more than one hundred shops and an open-air museum featuring whaling and nautical artifacts.

Kāʻanapali Beach fronts the entire Kāʻanapali resort complex. It begins at Hanakaʻōʻō Beach Park and ends three miles up the coast at Honokōwai Beach Park. This magnificent beach is divided into two distinct sections by Puʻu Kekaʻa, Black Rock, which sits almost in its center. The southern section of the beach is moderately steep, a result of the surf that periodically strikes this shoreline. The nearshore bottom drops abruptly to overhead depths, a point of caution for children and non-swimmers. During periods of high surf, strollers should be alert to powerful waves sweeping inland over the sand. Periods of calm seas offer excellent swimming conditions. The only reef offshore the beach is located at Hanakaʻōʻō Point fronting the Hyatt Regency Maui. This reef provides good snorkeling conditions in its numerous sand pockets and channels. Surfers and body-boarders frequent the site during periods of high surf. During these periods rip currents form here and along the beach.

The northern section of Kāʻanapali Beach begins at Puʻu Kekaʻa and ends at Honokōwai Beach Park. During periods of calm seas snorkeling opportunities around Black Rock are excellent and considered to be among the best on the island. The beach is moderately steep, a result of the surf that periodically strikes this shoreline. The nearshore bottom drops quickly to overhead depths, a point of caution for children and non-swimmers. Periods of high surf generate dangerous water conditions, including a strong shorebreak and powerful rip currents. As the beach rounds the point and approaches Honokōwai, the inshore waters become rocky as a nearshore reef makes its first appearance.

Conspicuously marked public rights-of-way are located throughout the Kāʻanapali resort complex. Each right-of-way is accompanied by a limited number of public parking spaces.

(69)
Honokōwai Beach Park
Honokōwai is the first of six famous bays of West Maui whose names being with the word *hono* or "bay." Collectively they are known as Hono a Piʻilani, the "bays

61

(acquired) by (Chief) Pi'ilani." Besides Honokōwai, the bays are Honokeana, Honokahua, Honolua, Honokō-hau, and Hononana. The county highway that circles West Maui is named Hono a Pi'ilani Highway. Honokō-wai means the "bay (for) drawing water," and it is said to have been a canoe landing. Freshwater springs were found at the water's edge.

Honokōwai Beach Park is fronted by a narrow white sand beach lined along its *makai* edge by a wide shelf of beach rock. On the south side of the park the beach rock splits, forming a double shelf. Between the two sections of rock is a narrow, shallow pool with a sandy bottom, an ideal swimming area for children. Offshore from the beach rock, the ocean bottom is fairly shallow and rocky—good conditions for snorkeling but only fair for swimming. Facilities in the park include restrooms, showers, picnic tables, and a paved parking lot. To the north of the beach park is Māhinahina, where the sand beach ends. The Māhinahina shoreline is primarily rocky with seawalls at the water's edge.

(70)
Kahana Beach

Kahana, the site of a former plantation camp, is now a busy and expanding resort community. Most of the former residential housing has been replaced by a variety of accommodations catering to the needs of tourists. Similar resort communities have been developed at Honokō-wai, Māhinahina, 'Alaeloa, and Nāpili.

The winding white sand beach at Kahana begins at the S-curve on Hono a Pi'ilani Highway just past Māhina-hina and continues past the row of shoreline hotels. The offshore bottom is a shallow combination of sand and rock, providing a safe swimming area. Strong currents are infrequent because of the protective reef offshore. Public access is available near the S-curve.

Just beyond Kahana Beach is a private estate called Kalaeokai'a, located on the small point of the same name. The shoreline estate is owned by the Robinson family, and the waters offshore are known to many local residents as Robinson Bay. On the *makai* side of Kalae-okai'a is a small secluded cove of white sand. A shallow and safe swimming area, it is not easily accessible or visible to the public because of its rather isolated location.

To the north of Kalaeokai'a is a slightly larger cove,

but with a much smaller pocket of white sand. This is Ka'ōpala and it is not highly regarded for water activities because the ocean is usually very murky. Roadside parking is available.

(71)
Keonenui Beach

Keonenui, "the big sand," is the former name of the white sand beach fronting the Kahana Sunset. The land on which the resort was developed was formerly the residence of the Yabui family, so the beach is also known to many local residents as Yabui Beach. Keonenui has a moderately steep foreshore as evidence of the surf that comes into the bay. The slope of the beach continues into the ocean, whose bottom drops off fairly quickly to overhead depths. This is a danger to little children and poor swimmers. Snorkeling and swimming are best during the summer months. During the winter, heavy surf can produce a strong shorebreak and a rip current running seaward, although swimming is safe during periods of calm. Public access is available by following the shoreline from Hui E Road.

(72)
'Alaeloa Beach

'Alaeloa, the "distant mud hen," is the name of the land division that includes the shoreline from Haukoe Point to Honokeana. The shoreline is composed primarily of low sea cliffs. Besides the sandy beach at Keonenui, there is only one other pocket of sand in this district. 'Alaeloa Beach is a small cove of white sand with a gentle slope to the sandy and rocky offshore bottom. Swimming and snorkeling are good, except during periods of heavy winter surf. This surf often attracts many surfers, who call the offshore break Little Mākaha because of the waves' similarity to that of Mākaha on O'ahu. There is no convenient public access to the area, which is surrounded by the 'Alaeloa resort development.

(73)
Honokeana

Honokeana, "the cave bay," is the second of six famous bays that comprise the Hono a Pi'ilani, the "bays (acquired) by (Chief) Pi'ilani." The other five at Hono-kōwai, Honokahua, Honolua, Honokōhau, and Hononana. Honokeana played a small part in the development of the pine industry on Lāna'i. In his book *True Stories of Lanai* Lawrence Gay related that his father was the first person to grow pineapples on Lāna'i, under a contract from the Ha'ikū Pineapple Company. The original plants were from Honolua and were supplied by David T. Fleming, the manager of Honolua Ranch. The tops were collected from the fields at Honolua and then trucked to Honokeana, where the Lāna'i boats were anchored. Gay said he spent many weeks hauling pineapple tops between Honokeana and Mānele.

The north point of Honokeana is called Ka'eleki'i, "the image blackness," which was the name of the beach as well. The shoreline of Honokeana is composed primarily of cobblestone with a few scattered sand patches. The entire backshore of the beach is lined with a retaining wall protecting the property to the rear from erosion. The bottom of the bay is a combination of sand and rock with a gentle slope to the deeper waters offshore. Swimming and snorkeling are good, except during periods of heavy surf. During these times the bay is turbulent with strong currents. There is no convenient public access to Honokeana. The Honokeana Cove Apartments occupy the entire backshore of the bay.

(74)
Nāpili Bay

Nāpili means either "the joinings" or "the pili grass," but the reason the name was given to this area is now unknown. Nāpili Bay today is a highly concentrated area of tourist-oriented facilities, primarily hotels. All of the former residential homes *makai* of Hono a Pi'ilani Highway in the bay's backshore have been replaced by accommodations for visitors. The main attraction of this beautiful bay is its long and wide white sand beach that curves between two rocky points—an excellent swimming area. The beach is moderately steep and suffers some erosion, especially during the winter months when large surf occasionally finds its way into the bay, creating good surfing and bodysurfing waves, but a strong rip current as well. The rip generally runs out to sea along the north point of the bay. Former homeowners on the point often threw the rubbish from their yards into the ocean there because they knew the

rip current would carry it out to sea. The moderately steep slope of the beach continues into the ocean, where the sandy bottom drops quickly to overhead depths. This presents a danger to little children and poor swimmers, especially when the shorebreak is sweeping across the beach. Just offshore from the middle of the beach is a small rock island. On calm days, especially during the summer months, the inner waters of Nāpili Bay are an excellent setting for all types of water activity. Public rights-of-way can be found at several locations, including Nāpili Place and Hui Drive.

Sitting inconspicuously on the north point of the bay is one of Nāpili's well-known local landmarks. It is simply called the Drydock. During the early 1920s David T. Fleming, the manager of Honolua Ranch, decided to build a drydock at Nāpili that could service one vessel at a time. A large cut was made into the rocky point, and concrete posts to support a raised boat were constructed. After its completion, a boat was maneuvered into the drydock and chain-hoisted out of the water. A gate of wooden posts was dropped to keep the ocean from surging into the working area. This first drydocking, however, was also the last. Working conditions in the hole were wet, cramped, and uncomfortable. Moreover, a boat could only be guided in on a very calm day, and once the work was completed, another calm day was needed to get it out. The entire operation proved to be so inconvenient and time-consuming that the drydock was never used again after its trial run. The ruins of the project can still be seen on the point.

(75)
Kapalua Beach

Kapalua, "two borders," is one of the most picturesque beaches on Maui and has long been a favorite picnic and swimming area among local residents. The crescent white sand beach is bordered on both ends by rocky points, while a large stand of coconut trees lines the backshore. Beyond Hōkūanui, the south point, a coral reef arcs into the bay, acting as a barrier against the strong offshore currents, as does Ka'ekaha, the long north point. Occasionally a small shorebreak forms inshore at the right end of the beach. With its gentle slope to the deeper waters offshore and its lack of strong inshore currents, Kapalua is the safest swimming beach on this side of Maui, especially during the winter months. The inshore waters of the bay are almost invariably clear enough for snorkeling and diving. A public right-of-way and a paved parking lot are located at the left end of the beach.

Prior to the development of the shoreline surrounding the beach as a resort complex, Kapalua Beach was known to local residents as Fleming Beach. David T. Fleming, one of the early managers of Honolua Ranch and Baldwin Packers, developed the coast of Kapalua Beach as a park, complete with restrooms and a coconut grove, and then opened the area to the public. Local residents began calling Kapalua Fleming Beach and the name was used until development of the area as a resort in the mid-1970s, when the name Kapalua was reintroduced. Fleming's generosity and contributions to Maui were not forgotten, however. The public beach park a short distance away at Honokahua was named D. T. Fleming Beach Park when it was completed in 1975.

(76)
Oneloa Beach

Oneloa, "long sand," is a wide, straight white sand beach situated between Hāwea and Makāluapuna points. The ocean bottom inshore is a shallow sandbar that extends out to the edge of the surfline. When a swell is running, especially during the winter months, a shorebreak with waves good enough for bodysurfing builds up along the outer edge of the sandbar. Rip currents also form at various places along the beach and can prove dangerous if there is any sizable surf. The beach suffers some seasonal erosion and accretion of sand, which occasionally exposes a shallow reef shelf along the shoreline.

Oneloa is a popular windsurfing site. On calm days swimming is safe close to the beach, as are snorkeling and diving in the lee of Makāluapuna Point. The beach profile and water conditions found at Oneloa are very similar to those at D. T. Fleming Beach Park. The rocky bluff above the west end of Oneloa is occupied by the Kapalua Bay Villas, but the rest of the backshore is composed of sand dunes covered with strand vegetation, primarily *kiawe.* A public right-of-way and a public parking lot are located at the north end of the beach.

(77)
D. T. Fleming Beach Park

D. T. Fleming Beach Park is located in Honokahua, the third of six famous bays of West Maui collectively called Hono a Pi'ilani, the "bays (acquired) by (Chief) Pi'i-lani." Honokahua literally means "sites bay," while the name of the beach park honors the memory of David Thomas Fleming (1881–1955).

Fleming was born in Scotland and came to Maui as a child. In 1912 he became manager of Honolua Ranch, the Baldwin estate on West Maui. Henry P. Baldwin was interested in raising pineapples commercially and under Fleming's guidance the cattle ranch was converted to a pineapple plantation. This was the beginning of Baldwin Packers, Maui Land and Pineapple Co., Inc., and an industry on West Maui that still continues today. Fleming's home, Maka'oi'oi, completed in 1915, is now called Pineapple Hill Restaurant. The original seedlings that became the double row of Norfolk pine trees leading up to the former residence were brought to Honokahua from the Baldwin Estate in Ha'ikū. The seedlings that George C. Munro used to reforest Lāna'ihale on Lāna'i also came from the same nursery. Fleming was noted as an agricultural experimenter and established a nursery at Pu'u Māhoe on Haleakalā for indigenous trees and other plants of special interest and value. He was also a community leader, serving as a member and chairman of the Maui County Board of Supervisors, as a member and chairman of the Maui County Board of Waterworks, and as a member of the Board of Trustees of Mauna'olu Community College.

D. T. Fleming Beach Park, not to be confused with Fleming Beach, an alternate name for Kapalua Beach, is an improved park with restrooms, showers, picnic tables, barbecue grills, and a paved parking lot. The park is situated on low sand dunes that build considerably near Makāluapuna Point, showing the direction of the prevailing wind. The long, wide white sand beach begins at Makāluapuna Point, the site of the 16th hole of Kapalua's golf course, and ends at the low sea cliffs forming the east end of the park. A shallow sandbar fronts most of the park's shoreline and extends offshore to the edge of the surf. The shorebreak that builds up on heavy swells is often good enough for bodysurfing. The

D. T. FLEMING BEACH PARK. This popular beach park was named in honor of David Thomas Fleming, the second manager of Honolua Ranch. Among Fleming's many contributions to the island of Maui was his successful introduction of pineapple as a commercial crop to West Maui early in the twentieth century. The beach park is situated on Honokahua Bay, one of the six famous bays of West Maui that are collectively known as Hono a Pi'ilani.

east end of the beach near the rocks is fronted by a shallow reef. Board surfers sometimes ride the surf there. When a swell hits the beach, dangerous rip currents develop in various places depending on the size and direction of the waves. The beach itself is steep, occasionally creating a backwash across the sandbar. The combination of these adverse water conditions has caused a number of drownings and necessitated many rescues at this well-used beach park. D. T. Fleming Beach Park is popular with local residents and visitors alike. It was set aside for public use by Maui Land and Pineapple Co., Inc., in 1975.

(78)
Mokulē'ia Beach

Mokulē'ia, often misspelled Makuleia on maps, means "district (of) abundance." Mokulē'ia is a rarely used name for this beach, which most local residents know as Slaughterhouse. At some time during the existence of Honolua Ranch, two sheds were constructed on the cliffs above Mokulē'ia. One was a slaughterhouse and the other was a storage shed for hides. They were built on the edge of the sea cliffs apparently for convenient disposition of unwanted remains, which were simply dumped into the ocean below. Even though the slaughterhouse was torn down in the mid-1960s, the beach is still called Slaughterhouse.

Mokulē'ia, or Slaughterhouse, is a large pocket of white sand nestled against the base of moderately high sea cliffs. The beach sand is subject to erosion during the winter and accretion during the summer. Heavy surf often pounds the beach during the winter, washing sand offshore and exposing large boulders in the shorebreak. These are dangerous conditions even for experienced watermen. During the summer, when the sand returns and forms a shallow sandbar offshore, the shorebreak is much safer and attracts many bodysurfers. The beach can be reached by hiking down any number of trails leading *makai* from Hono a Pi'ilani Highway.

Fishermen and divers should be aware that Mokulē'ia Bay is part of the Honolua—Mokulē'ia Bay Marine Life Conservation District, established in 1978. Possession of fishing gear and the taking of any marine life are unlawful within the district. Details of prohibited activities, exceptions, and a map of the conservation areas can be obtained from any state office of the Division of Fish and Game.

(79)
Honolua Bay

Honolua is the fourth of six famous bays of West Maui, collectively called Hono a Pi'ilani, the "bays (acquired) by (Chief) Pi'ilani." Honolua means "two harbors." Honolua Bay was once the site of the original headquar-

MOKULĒ'IA BEACH. Mokulē'ia Beach is best known by its popular name, Slaughterhouse Beach. At one time a slaughterhouse constructed and used by Honolua Ranch stood on the sea cliffs above the beach. During the winter months this beach suffers a substantial loss of sand during its seasonal erosion. Many boulders are exposed in the shorebreak, such as those just barely visible offshore of the left end of the beach.

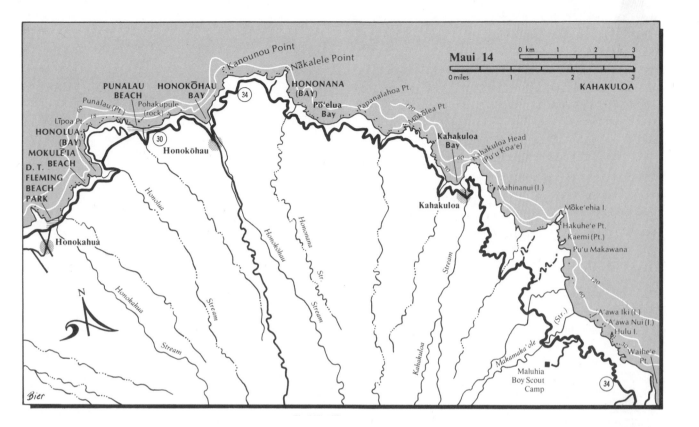

ters of Honolua Ranch. The ranch was started in the early 1890s by Henry P. Baldwin to raise cattle. The first manager of Honolua Ranch was Richard Cooper Searle, Sr., and he assumed control of the ranch operations in 1892. Searle's father was the Reverend Cooper Searle, an Episcopal minister who had come to Hawaii from London by way of Australia. During Richard C. Searle, Sr.'s tenure as ranch manager, the interisland steamers called once a month at Honolua to deliver supplies and to pick up cattle hides, coffee, and other marketable items the ranch produced. The pier that the lighters tied up to was located close to the present boat ramp. Honokōhau, a nearby valley, supported a large taro-growing community that supplied taro to Honolua and points beyond. A horse-drawn taro wagon made a daily trip from Honokōhau to Lahaina. *Akule* were netted in the bay and in true Hawaiian tradition everyone who helped was given a *ka'au* of fish (a portion of for-

ty). The coastline inland of the bay was grassy and open with a scattered variety of ornamental, fruit, and shade trees. In addition to the main ranch house, there were several other homes, a machine shop, a saddle shop, a nursery, a coffee warehouse, and a company store.

In 1912 Richard C. Searle, Sr., retired after serving for twenty years as manager of Honolua Ranch. Searle left the island and moved to Honolulu. About this time H. P. Baldwin had decided that the ranch operations should include pineapple cultivation, then in its infancy on Maui. Searle's successor was David T. Fleming, who had been with the original pineapple growers on Maui at Ha'ikū. The cattle-ranching operation was slowly phased out, and by 1914 the first crop of pineapple had been planted, the pine tops having been shipped from Maliko Bay near Ha'ikū to Honolua Bay. About this time the name of the pineapple-growing operation was changed to Baldwin Packers.

In 1915 Fleming and his family moved into their newly constructed home, Maka'oi'oi, at the top of a hill in Honokahua. This move also marked the relocation of the entire Honolua Ranch complex to Honokahua village. When the company store made its move from Honolua, it retained its original name; this is why there is a Honolua Store until this day in Honokahua. During this period of transition the population of Honokahua began to grow substantially, and the post office that was located in Honokōhau was moved to Honokahua. The post office also retained its former name and even brought its old sign along. Finding both Honolua Store and Honokōhau Post Office in Honokahua proved very confusing to visitors passing through, who were never sure exactly where they were. The same confusion has also caused many map errors over the years, both in place name locations and spellings. A pineapple cannery was built near the present location of Honolua Store, but an adequate labor force could not be attracted there during the peak harvest season. A new cannery was built in Lahaina, which opened in December 1919. Today little remains of the former ranch headquarters at Honolua Bay besides a variety of trees and other plants usually associated with residential areas. The old landing was completely demolished by the tsunami of 1946.

During the late 1950s and early 1960s, surfing again became a popular sport in Hawai'i. As the surfing population grew, many surfers began looking for new, uncrowded spots. At about this time the surf at Honolua Bay was discovered. During the winter the same storms in the northern Pacific that bring huge waves to O'ahu's famous North Shore beaches also bring excellent big waves to Honolua Bay. Honolua on a good day is regarded by many surfers as the best break on Maui and one of the best surfing spots in the world. On a big winter day the cliffs above the bay are lined with surfers and spectators watching the often crowded action in the surf below. The first surfing contest held at Honolua, in 1965, was organized and run by Dick Brewer, a well-known surfer and surfboard manufacturer.

On May 1, 1976, a canoe voyage began at Honolua Bay that captured the attention of the entire world. The canoe was the double-hulled Polynesian voyaging canoe Hōkūle'a, "happy star," and the voyage was her unassisted crossing of the Pacific between Hawai'i and Tahiti. This was the climax of three years of hard work by Tommy Holmes, Herb Kane, and Ben Finney. In 1973 these three men had formed the Polynesian Voyaging Society. They knew that the Polynesian people who had populated Hawai'i had come to these islands from the south on large double-hulled canoes. Following the discovery and settlement of Hawai'i, a period of voyaging between the island groups had also occurred—amazing feats of navigation and seamanship, considering the tremendous distances and the adversity of the open ocean between Hawai'i and the islands to the south.

Holmes, Kane, and Finney founded the Polynesian Voyaging Society to build a replica of a double-hulled voyaging canoe that would make the monumental crossing from Hawai'i to Tahiti, simulating in every way possible the original conditions under which these voyages were made. The Hōkūle'a left Honolua Bay on May 1, 1976. When first land was sighted on June 1, the canoe's course was altered and at 6:30 A.M. that morning a landing was made on Mataiwa, an island 168 miles north of Tahiti in the Tuamotu Archipelago. On Friday, June 4, 1976, the Hōkūle'a sailed into Papeete Harbor on Tahiti, climaxing 34 days at sea. The canoe's arrival was met by a tremendous crowd of over 10,000 people. After the official ceremonies were concluded, three days of festivities followed. After a brief stay in Tahiti, the Hōkūle'a sailed home to Hawai'i on July 4, 1976, arriving on July 26.

In March 1978 the State Board of Land and Natural Resources established the Honolua–Mokulē'ia Bay Marine Life Conservation District. The district was created to preserve, protect, and conserve marine resources and geological features, and to foster recreational, nonconsumptive public use of the area. The possession of fishing gear and the taking of any marine life are unlawful within the conservation area. Details of prohibited activities, exceptions, and a map of the district can be obtained from any state office of the Division of Fish and Game. One of the provisions of particular interest permits the bagging of akule within the conservation area if they are netted outside of the district. Akule, migratory schooling fish, traditionally have been bagged in the calm waters of Honolua Bay after being netted in the often rough open ocean.

The beach at the head of Honolua Bay is made up primarily of boulders with several scattered patches of sand. The amounts of sand that are present vary according to the time of year, with the summer months showing the most accretion. A badly deteriorated concrete boat ramp crosses the beach and provides primary access to the water from this area of the bay. The inner bay waters are usually murky, but the cleaner areas offshore are very popular with snorkelers. A good snorkeling tour consists of following the rocks and reef along the west side of Honolua Bay, rounding Kalaepiha Point, and then landing on Mokulēʻia Beach for a rest before returning. On the east side of the bay is another reef, a large one, that is also the popular Honolua surfing area. This area of the bay can be reached from the edge of Kulaokaʻeʻa, the large plateau above the bay that is cultivated in pineapple. A number of trails lead down the cliffs to the three small pockets of cobblestones and white sand below, to the reef offshore, and to the surfing area.

Kulaokaʻeʻa is known to many local residents as Golf Links. During the early 1920s David Fleming built a rugged nine-hole golf course on Kulaokaʻeʻa, which was then in use as a cattle pasture. The course was named the West Maui Golf Course and remained in use until World War II. The sturdy clubhouse with its beautiful lava-rock walls still stands, covered with underbrush, in a small grove of Norfolk pine trees near Līpoa Point. A small stand of coconut trees in the cove at Kāʻohoʻoulu marks the former picnic grounds of the golfers and their families.

(80)
Punalau Beach

Punalau means "many springs" and refers to the freshwater springs that once were found at the water's edge in this area. Punalau is the name by which this beach is most widely known, but it also has an English name, Windmill Beach. At the west end of the beach is the bed of an intermittent stream. Honolua Ranch formerly maintained a tall windmill, used to draw water to fill a water trough for cattle, on the stream bank just back from the beach—hence the name Windmill Beach. The name is still commonly used even though the structure is long gone. Punalau has also been called Pōhakupule

Beach. Pōhakupule, "prayer rock," is the large black rock that stands on the shallow reef just offshore from the beach. People who needed to cleanse or purify themselves spiritually came to the beach inshore of this rock to pray for absolution. Another name for the beach is Keonehelelēʻi, "the scattered sand," which is the place name attributed to this area.

Punalau Beach is a white sand, coral-rubble, and shingle beach backed by a grove of ironwood trees at the base of a sea cliff. A long, wide, shallow *papa* runs the length of the entire beach. Snorkeling and swimming are possible in several small channels in the *papa* at the east end of the beach, but are not recommended. The ocean washes across the *papa* very rapidly, creating strong currents, especially when the surf is big during the winter months. The shallow reef and the strong currents make a bad combination for swimmers. Occasionally surfers find their way to Punalau when a big swell is running, but the shallow bottom presents a serious danger as the waves draw near to the shore, especially at low tide. Punalau is frequented primarily by fishermen, picnickers, and beachcombers. People with ordinary passenger cars should attempt the steep dirt road down the cliff only during dry weather.

(81)
Honokōhau Bay

Honokōhau is the fifth of six famous bays of West Maui collectively known as Hono a Piʻilani, the "bays (acquired) by (Chief) Piʻilani." Honokōhau literally means "bay drawing dew." A fishing and taro-farming community until the 1930s, Honokōhau today has very few residents.

The beach at the head of Honokōhau Bay is made up primarily of boulders. Sometimes sand pockets accrete during the summer months, but not with any dependable regularity. Large submerged boulders are found in the deep waters offshore from the beach. During the winter the surf surging through the bay creates very powerful rip currents. Overall, the bay is not particularly safe for water activities at any time of the year. Access to the shoreline is from Hono a Piʻilani Highway, which passes through the backshore of the beach. The large residence on poles built against the side of the cliff to the rear of the beach belongs to Sam K. Kaai,

PUNALAU BEACH. Coral rubble and debris from the ocean cover the sand at Punalau. On the shallow reef offshore are a number of large boulders protruding above the surface of the ocean. The largest and outermost of these rocks was called Pōhakupule, the "prayer rock." In former times people who were distraught or troubled would come inshore of Pōhakupule, to this beach, and pray for guidance.

Jr., a noted woodcarver and the owner of Ka Honu, a shop at Kāʻanapali.

The shoreline from Honokōhau to Waiheʻe is composed entirely of sea cliffs. Where the cliffs are cut by gulches or valleys, boulder beaches can be found at the water's edge. The beach at Kahakuloa, "the tall lord," a fishing and farming community located about midway through this area, is a good example of the typical boulder beach found throughout this stretch of shoreline.

There are no safe swimming areas along this entire shoreline, which is pounded constantly by heavy surf. All of these unprotected rocky beaches are exposed to the fury of the open ocean, as is evidenced by the large amounts of driftwood and debris that are often washed a good distance *mauka* of the water's edge. These beaches are frequented almost exclusively by shoreline fishermen.

70

Island of Moloka'i

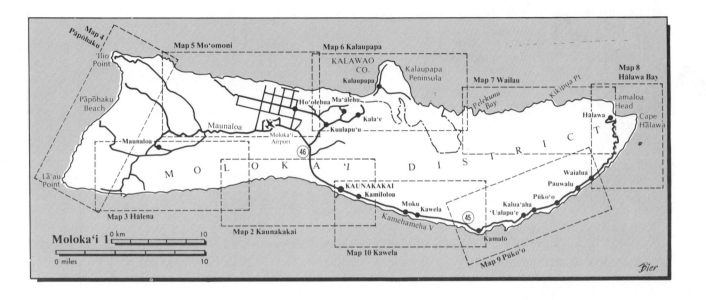

Map 4 Pāpōhaku
'Īlio Point
Pāpōhaku Beach
Lā'au Point
Maunaloa
Maunaloa

Map 5 Mo'omoni
Ho'olehua Ma'alehu
Kala'e
Kualapu'u
Moloka'i Airport
46

Map 6 Kalaupapa
KALAWAO CO.
Kalaupapa
Kalaupapa Peninsula

Map 7 Wailau
Pelekunu Bay
Kikipua Pt.

Map 8 Hālawa Bay
Lamaloa Head
Cape Hālawa
Hālawa

M O L O K A 'I   D I S T R I C T

KAUNAKAKAI
Kamiloloa
Moku Kawela
Kamehameha V
45

Waialua
Pauwalu
Pūko'o
Kalua'aha
'Ualapu'e
Kamalō

Map 3 Hālena

Map 2 Kaunakakai

Map 10 Kawela

Map 9 Pūko'o

Moloka'i 1
0 km   10
0 miles   10

Bier

BEACHES OF MOLOKAI

BEACH & LOCATION	BEACH ACTIVITIES				PUBLIC FACILITIES			BEACH COMPOSITION			ACCESS	
	SWIMMING	SNORKELING	SURFING	BODY-SURFING	COMFORT STATION	PICNIC EQUIPMENT	PAVED PARKING	SAND	DETRITAL SAND	ROCK	PUBLIC	PRIVATE
1) KAUNAKAKAI WHARF, KAUNAKAKAI	✔		✔		✔		✔	✔			✔	
2) KIOWEA PARK, KALAMA'ULA									✔			✔
3) KOLO WHARF, KAUMANAMANA	✔								✔		✔	
4) HĀLENA BEACH, HĀLENA	✔							✔			✔	
5) HALE O LONO BEACH, HALE O LONO	✔		✔					✔				✔
6) KANALUKAHA BEACH, KANALUKAHA	✔		✔					✔				✔
7) KAPUKUWAHINE BEACH, KAPUKUWAHINE	✔							✔				✔
8) KAHALEPŌHAKU BEACH, KAHALEPŌHAKU	✔							✔				✔
9) LIGHTHOUSE BEACH, LĀ'AU POINT								✔				✔
10) KAMĀKA'IPŌ BEACH, KAMĀKA'IPŌ								✔				✔
11) KAUPOA BEACH, KAUPOA	✔	✔						✔				✔
12) KAUNALĀ BEACH, KAUNALĀ	✔	✔						✔				✔
13) KAPUKAHEHU BEACH, KAPUKAHEHU	✔	✔						✔				✔
14) PO'OLAU BEACH, PO'OLAU	✔	✔						✔				✔
15) PĀPŌHAKU BEACH, PĀPŌHAKU	✔			✔			✔	✔			✔	
16) KEPUHI BEACH, KEPUHI	✔		✔	✔			✔	✔			✔	
17) PŌHAKU MĀULIULI BEACH, PŌHAKU MĀULIULI	✔							✔				✔
18) KAWĀKIU BAY, KAWĀKIU	✔							✔			✔	
19) KEONELELE BEACH, MO'OMOMI								✔				✔
20) KAWA'ALOA BAY, MO'OMOMI	✔		✔					✔				✔
21) MO'OMOMI BEACH, MO'OMOMI	✔	✔						✔				✔
22) KALAUPAPA, KALAUPAPA	✔							✔				✔
23) PELEKUNU, PELEKUNU	✔									✔		✔
24) WAILAU, WAILAU	✔									✔		✔
25) PĀPALAUA, PĀPALAUA										✔		✔
26) HĀLAWA BEACH PARK, HĀLAWA	✔		✔	✔	✔	✔		✔			✔	
27) FAGANS BEACH, PŌHAKU PILI	✔	✔						✔				✔
28) SANDY BEACH, LUPEHU	✔	✔						✔			✔	
29) HONOULI MALO'O, HONOULI MALO'O	✔	✔							✔		✔	
30) HONOULI WAI, HONOULI WAI	✔	✔	✔						✔		✔	
31) MURPHY BEACH PARK, MOANUI	✔	✔				✔		✔			✔	
32) PŪKO'O, PŪKO'O									✔		✔	
33) KAKAHAI'A BEACH PARK, KAWELA						✔			✔		✔	
34) ONEALI'I BEACH PARK, MAKAKUPA'IA					✔	✔			✔		✔	

72

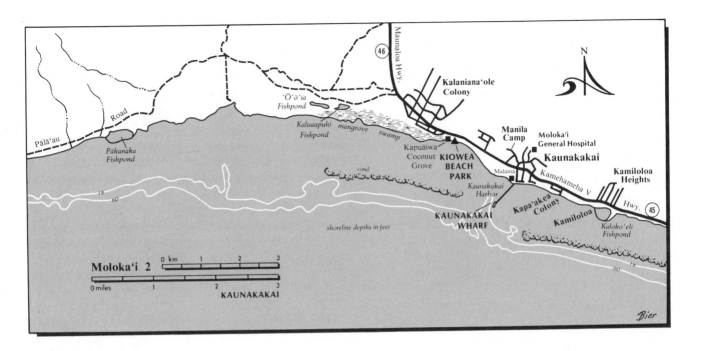

(1)

Kaunakakai Wharf

Kaunakakai is an abbreviated form of Kaunakahakai, which means "beach landing." The outstanding feature along the Kaunakakai shoreline is the large wharf extending out into the ocean. The first major wharf at Kaunakakai was constructed in 1898, just prior to annexation, when the American Sugar Company, the forerunner of Moloka'i Ranch, Ltd., was formed on Moloka'i. A long mole constructed of boulders transversed the inner shallows and ended in deep water a half mile offshore. Piles made of coconut tree trunks were driven for a wooden wharf that was built to adjoin the mole. Ships' passengers rode to town on a flat rail car pulled by a mule, or walked. With the closing of the sugar company, the Territory of Hawai'i took over the facility. In 1929 the wooden wharf was replaced by a concrete one.

The existing Kaunakakai Harbor was completed in 1934 by the Army Corps of Engineers. They dredged a channel 530 feet wide and a large barge basin, creating the principal port on the island. The barge harbor, how-ever, is incapable of handling deep-draft ships, so all goods for local residents are transshipped from Honolulu. The harbor is administered by the State Division of Harbors and also includes restrooms, a marina, and a boat ramp. The 12-foot-wide ramp was constructed in 1963 and is located on the leeward side of the mole. Navigational aids for boats were also provided, along with parking for 15 cars with trailers. This ramp is the only public boat ramp on Moloka'i. Many residents, however, launch directly across the beaches in other areas.

On the shoreline near Kaunakakai Wharf are the remains of a vacation home named Malama that belonged to King Kamehameha V. It was a large grass-thatched house with several big rooms. Also on the seaside estate were several other spacious grass-thatched houses for the king's guests and a number of smaller ones for his retainers and for storage. Fresh water was supplied by a windmill located about one mile inland. The beach in front of Malama was formerly a point of sand called Kala'iakamanu, "the peace (made) by the bird," and it was used exclusively by the king and his guests. Today the only visible evidence of the royal resi-

73

dence is a raised stone platform that was part of Malama's foundation. It can be seen on the shoreline to the west of Kaunakakai wharf.

This foundation is also the former site of Kala'iaka-manuhou Church in Kalama'ula. Originally located at the site of the present police station in 1866, the church was later moved to Malama. In 1924 it was relocated again to Kalama'ula and the word *hou,* "new," was added to the name Kala'iakamanu.

The shoreline to either side of Kaunakakai Wharf is a narrow detrital sand beach. A very shallow and rocky mudflat extends almost the entire distance from the beach to the edge of the offshore reef. The water is usually murky and is unappealing to most swimmers except young children. A more popular swimming area is the deeper waters off the boat ramp. Occasionally the waves on the west side of the entrance channel are good enough for surfing.

(2)

Kiowea Park

Kiowea Park, a beach park located on Maunaloa Highway between Kaunakakai and Kalama'ula, is owned and managed by the Department of Hawaiian Home Lands. Kiowea is a variant spelling of *kioea,* the Hawaiian name for the bristle-thighed curlew, a large brown migratory shoreline bird. The May 9, 1863, edition of the Hawaiian newspaper *Ka Nūpepa Kū'oko'a* described the *kioea* this way:

> This bird is about the size of a wild pigeon with a pointed head, a straight beak, dark feathers, and long legs. When he flies, his legs swiftly point back and whip up under his tail.
>
> He is an expert bird at fishing and his flesh is very delicious. This bird was named because of his cry which is like calling out kioea. There is no other bird-cry like it.

Once commonly seen on the main Hawaiian islands, the *kioea* is now only an occasional visitor, preferring the uninhabited islands in the northwestern part of the island chain during the winter months. A variety of other shoreline birds can be seen in the park area, however, including the *'auku'u,* the black-crowned night heron.

Kiowea Park is located in a famous coconut grove

KIOWEA BEACH PARK. The large coconut grove that covers most of Kiowea Beach Park is said by some authorities to have been planted by High Chief Kapua'iwa, who later became King Kamehameha V. The shoreline of the park has been severely eroded by the ocean as can be seen by the toppling coconut trees at the water's edge. Several freshwater springs that were once in the park itself are now located in the ocean offshore.

known as Kapua'iwa or Kamehameha Coconut Grove. It was named in honor of the high chief Kapua'iwa. One source says that he was given this name by a chief of Moloka'i because he was a statuesque young man with a noble walk. Kapua'iwa means "the young *'iwa,*" and the *'iwa* or frigate bird is a poetic symbol for a hand-

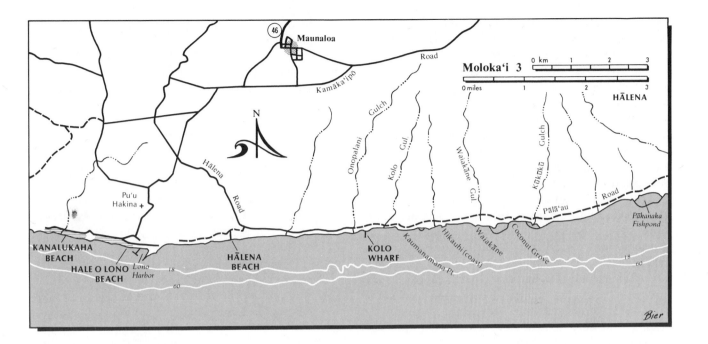

some person. Kapua'iwa is also alternately spelled Ka-
puāiwa, which means "the mysterious taboo." In 1863
Kapua'iwa became King Kamehameha V. Traditional
stories say that the king himself planted the trees in the
grove. Another source says the planting was done by
Rudolph W. Meyer, King Kamehameha V's agent and
ranch manager on Moloka'i.

The beach fronting Kiowea Park is a narrow strip of
detrital sand. To the east of the pavilion in the park and
just offshore from the beach are several springs that can
be seen bubbling up at low tide. During the 1920s these
springs were located at the edge of the park, but since
that time the shoreline has eroded and they are now in
the ocean. Beyond the beach the ocean bottom is very
shallow, rocky, and muddy—a poor swimming area.
Facilities in the park include picnic tables, barbecue
grills, restrooms, and a pavilion. Kalaniana'ole Hall, a
meeting hall for the Hawaiian Home Lands residents, is
located to the left of the park. Visitors to this area
should be alert to the danger of falling coconuts in the
extensive coconut grove surrounding the park. Warning
signs are posted in several places. Kiowea Park has
occasionally also been called Kaunakakai Beach Park.

(3)
Kolo Wharf

The shoreline from Kaunakakai to Kolo Wharf consists
primarily of dense growths of mangrove growing over
the tidal mudflats and brown detrital sand beaches.
Ironically, the mangrove was introduced in an attempt
to mitigate the impact of soil runoff, but instead of
reducing siltation, the plant has often aggravated conditions by creating extensive mudflats. This unfortunate
situation has occurred particularly in the numerous
Hawaiian fishponds that line Moloka'i's southern
shoreline from Honouli Wai to Kolo Wharf. The new
mudflats add to the original land and impede the flow
from the ponds' brackish water sources.

In 1923 Libby, McNeill and Libby leased some land
from Moloka'i Ranch, Ltd., at Maunaloa and began
growing pineapple. The road that now connects Kaunakakai and Maunaloa was then in very poor condition—
an impractical route for transporting pineapple from
Maunaloa and supplies into the area. Libby then established a cable landing at Pu'u Kaiaka at the south end of
Pāpōhaku Beach. All of the materials used to construct

the first camp at Maunaloa were landed there. The Puʻu Kaiaka landing proved unsuitable, however. The shoreline offered no protection from the open ocean and the heavy surf that rolls in during summer and winter months alike. Several years later Kaumanamana on the southern side of the island was selected as an alternate site. A channel was dredged through the reef and a wooden wharf constructed to facilitate the tug and barge operations. The wharf was named Kolo for a nearby gulch because Libby felt Kolo would be easier to pronounce then Kaumanamana.

Kolo Wharf was the major pineapple shipping point on Molokaʻi until the early 1950s. At that time operations were relocated to Kaunakakai Wharf, and the pineapple was barged from Kaunakakai to the Honolulu cannery. In August 1953 half of the abandoned Kolo Wharf and a large heavy duty crane were destroyed by fire. The crane had been used for loading fruit on the barges and was scheduled for transfer to the Kaunakakai Wharf. Today Kolo Wharf is in ruins and is used only by shoreline fishermen.

The shoreline from Kaunakakai to Kolo Wharf is made up primarily of mudflats overgrown with vegetation. Nearing Kolo Wharf, the mudflats give way to short and narrow detrital sand beaches overhung by *kiawe* trees. Located along this reach is Coconut Grove, a fairly wide dark detrital sand beach in Waiakāne. It is marked by a small stand of coconut trees and is easily accessible from the road. Coconut Grove also marks the first meeting of the mountains and the seashore along the Pālāʻau Road. The offshore bottom is murky, rocky, and shallow.

Beginning at the remnants of Kolo Wharf, the beach improved steadily. The soil-runoff deposits that mar the shoreline and inshore waters to the east of the wharf are almost entirely absent to the west. The white sand beach that begins here runs past Hālena to Hale o Lono. The low sand dunes to the rear of the beach are covered with *kiawe* trees. The offshore bottom is shallow and rocky. The beach is frequented primarily by fishermen and can be reached by following Pālāʻau Road, which is marked by a public right-of-way sign where it meets the Maunaloa Highway. Kolo Wharf marks the end of the section of Pālāʻau Road which crosses Molokaʻi Ranch land that is always open to the public. From Kolo to Hālena,

Pālāʻau Road is semipublic. If the gate is open, the public may drive through, but if it is locked, the ranch is running cattle in the area and a permit and a key must be obtained to proceed. The gate to proceed beyond Hālena is always locked.

Hālena Beach

Hālena is probably best known as the site of Camp Hālena, a cluster of small cabins and related buildings. George P. Cooke, the first president of Molokaʻi Ranch, and an enthusiastic scouter, supervised the building of these facilities. Molokaʻi Ranch regulates their use by the public. Hālena, which means "yellowish," is the site of a particular type of beach rock that is gold to cream-colored. This rock splits easily into thin slabs and was formerly a popular paving material for patios and foot paths. It can also be found in several places on Shipwreck Beach on Lānaʻi, but is much more abundant at Hālena.

Except for the camp at Hālena, this entire shoreline area is undeveloped. The backshore is made up of low and wide sand dunes covered with *kiawe* trees. The white sand beach is fronted by beach rock at the water's edge for most of its length. A fair swimming area for children can be found *makai* of the camp, but otherwise the beach rock onshore and the rocky offshore bottom make the beach attractive primarily to fishermen. Hālena is the end of the section of Pālāʻau Road that is accessible to the public. The road is always open up to Kolo Wharf, but from Kolo to Hālena the road is semipublic. If the gate is open, one may drive through, but if it is locked, Molokaʻi Ranch is running cattle in the area and a permit and a key must be obtained to proceed. The gate to proceed beyond Hālena is always locked.

5

Hale o Lono Beach

Hale o Lono means "house of (the god) Lono." The name is found on all the major Hawaiian islands, usually at ancient *heiau* sites for the worship of Lono. Hale o Lono on Molokaʻi, once the location of a large fishing village, is now the site of Hale o Lono Barge Harbor. The harbor was built to provide a storage area and shipping point on the west end of Molokaʻi for sand and cin-

HĀLENA BEACH. The only evidence of habitation at Hālena is the former Boy Scout camp that was built on the beach under the direction of George P. Cooke, the first president of Molo-ka'i Ranch, Ltd. The structure situated just above the beach is the old dining room assembly hall. Swimming is safe in the shallows just offshore from the building.

ders. Construction of the harbor and the shoreline facilities at the base of the Hale o Lono sea cliffs was begun in 1959 by the Honolulu Construction and Draying Company, Ltd., at their own expense, and completed several years later. The complex includes an entrance channel, two breakwaters, a harbor basin, assorted loading equipment, several operations shacks, and a large open lot created from the dredged coral fill. The harbor has had some problems since its completion. During heavy summer and winter surf, the access channel is hazardous for tug and barge traffic, and the harbor itself is subject to heavy internal surges. Major losses so far have included two $100,000 barges.

Hale o Lono Barge Harbor, usually called simply Lono or Lono Harbor, is open to public use for small boats as prescribed by law and will revert to state owner-ship upon expiration of a forty-year lease. During the life of the lease certain designated facilities are for the exclusive use of H. C. & D., Ltd., now Ameron H. C. & D., Ltd.

To the west of the harbor is Hale o Lono Beach, a long, narrow white sand beach that ends at a rocky point. Hale o Lono Beach is probably best known as the starting point of the annual Moloka'i to O'ahu canoe race. The race originally started at Kawākiu Beach in 1952 but was relocated to Hale o Lono Beach in 1963 because of more favorable winter water conditions and because it offered a more suitable location from a logistical standpoint. With large numbers of canoe clubs participating in the race, the small beach area, the lack of fresh water, and the lack of cooking and sanitation facilities had proved a major problem at remote Kawākiu.

The entire length of the beach is fronted by a lowshelf of beach rock. The offshore bottom is rocky. To the east of the harbor and the large coral-fill lot is a small cove of white sand. The bottom is shallow and a mixture of rocks and sand pockets. This is the only protected place for swimming in the harbor area. There is no public access to Hale o Lono Beach, although access is permitted on special occasions—primarily the annual Moloka'i to O'ahu canoe race.

(6)
Kanalukaha Beach

Kanalukaha means "the passing wave." The origin of the name is unknown, but it is interesting to note that of the three large white sand beaches between Hale o Lono Beach and Lā'au Point, Kanalukaha usually has the greatest offshore surf activity. This can be attributed to the scattered patches of shallow reef that are more numerous here than at Kapukuwahine or at Kahalepō-haku.

Beginning in 1962, sand mining operations were instituted at Kanalukaha and vast sections of the beach were completely destroyed. Although much of the beach has returned since termination of the sand mining, jagged beach rock is still exposed in some places, usually after periods of heavy surf.

Kanalukaha is a very long and wide white sand beach, usually with a steep slope to the water's edge as a result of the often heavy surf. The east and west ends of the beach are fronted by exposed beach rock, but the center is open and sandy. Although there are many patches of shallow reef offshore, the beach is unprotected from the open ocean. It experiences rip currents and very swift alongshore currents. The bottom slopes quickly to overhead depths. Kanalukaha is visited primarily by fishermen, and it is good for swimming only on very calm days. There is no public access to the beach. Kanalukaha is also known to many local residents as Pu'u Hakina Beach, for Pu'u Hakina, the major hill to the rear of the beach.

(7)
Kapukuwahine Beach

Kapukuwahine means "the gathering place (of) females," although the origin of the name is now

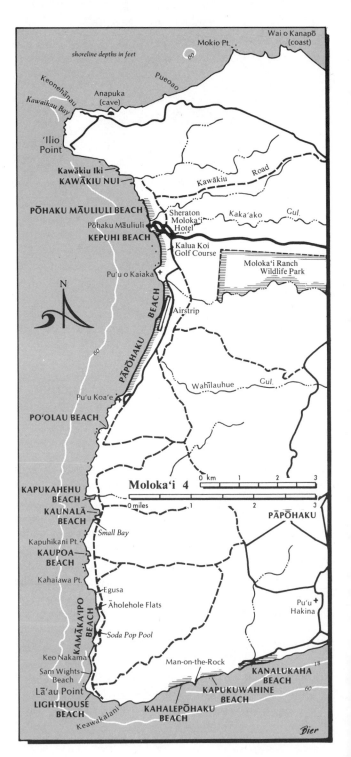

unknown. Kapukuwahine Beach is a very long and wide white sand beach that sits between two rocky points. The backshore of the beach is bordered entirely by a low sea cliff about fifteen to twenty feet high. The foreshore is moderately steep and often displays exposed beach rock at the water's edge. The beach is completely unprotected from the open ocean and experiences strong rip currents and fast alongshore currents. Kapukuwahine is not a safe swimming beach and it is visited primarily by fishermen. Unmarred by any intrusions of man, the isolated beach has no public access.

On the rocky shoreline between Kapukuwahine and Kahalepōhaku, the next sand beach, is a large rock that is called Man-on-the Rock. It stands alone at the edge of the ocean and is a landmark for fishermen passing by. This area is also sometimes called Hale 'Opihi or 'Opihi Road.

(8)
Kahalepōhaku Beach

Kahalepōhaku means "the stone house" and was the name of a former king of Maui. The origin of this name on Moloka'i, however, is not known. Kahalepōhaku Beach is the last of the three long and wide white sand beaches on the southern side of Lā'au Point. The backshore of the beach is bordered entirely by a low escarpment covered with vast expanses of *kiawe* trees. The foreshore is steep and the ocean bottom slopes quickly to overhead depths. Heavy surf exposes large boulders throughout the shorebreak. The currents here are very dangerous and powerful almost all year round because of the beach's proximity to "land's end" at Lā'au Point. The beach is frequented primarily by fishermen and has no public access.

KAHALEPŌHAKU BEACH. The afternoon sun highlights a single set of footprints crossing deserted Kahalepōhaku Beach, near Lā'au Point. This beach and its sister beaches, Kapukuwahine, Kanalukaha, and Hale o Lono, are subject to severe seasonal erosion by the ocean, often causing dramatic changes in their physical appearance throughout the year.

(9)
Lighthouse Beach

Lighthouse Beach is the name of the rocky shoreline composed of low sea cliffs below the lighthouse at Lā'au Point. Interspersed among the high banks of black lava at the water's edge are four secluded coves of white sand. These pocket beaches are subject to seasonal erosion and accretion. They are surrounded by lava terraces covered with tidal pools. There is absolutely no swimming in this area. The currents are very powerful and dangerous, prohibiting any water activities except shoreline fishing and even this must be done with caution. When a heavy swell is running, the surf pounds the shoreline here with devastating force. The area is visited primarily by fishermen and has no public access.

At the north end of Lighthouse Beach near the end of the private, unpaved shoreline access road are the remains of an old landing. Constructed at the *mauka* end of a small, natural inlet, the landing was used to service the lighthouse when it was still a manned station. A boom extended over the inlet to receive the goods that were brought inshore by lighters. Today only several concrete foundation blocks remain.

(10)
Kamāka'ipō Beach

Kamāka'ipō means "the night guard"; however, not all historians agree that this is the correct pronunciation and therefore the correct meaning of the name. The alternate and common pronunciation, "Kamakaipo," lends itself to various other interpretations. Kamāka'ipō Beach is the long storm beach located between Lā'au Point and Kahaiawa Point. The entire length of this steep white sand beach is fronted by beach rock. Storm beaches, large areas of sand deposited inland of the beach rock by storm waves and wind, are common along this shoreline, and Kamāka'ipō is the largest of these beaches. Low sand dunes located to the rear of the beach are covered with *kiawe* trees and other strand vegetation. Offshore, the ocean is deep with strong and powerful currents. The area attracts primarily fishermen. There is no public access.

Five specific places within the one-mile length of Kamāka'ipō Beach are better known by popular names. The first is Sam Wight's located at the left end of the beach near the end of the private access road to Lā'au Point. Sam Wight was one of two assistant managers of Moloka'i Ranch from 1923 to 1932 under George P. Cooke, the first president of the ranch. Wight built a fishing shack on the rise above this rocky beach and the area has since been known by his name. The beach at Sam Wight's is a small, steep pocket of sand and coral rubble fronted by beach rock.

The next well-known place on Kamāka'ipō Beach is called Keo Nakama. A narrow channel that leads out through the beach rock into the open ocean provided the entry point for Keo Nakama when he made his successful swim from Moloka'i to O'ahu. He left early on the morning of September 29, 1961, and landed fifteen and a half hours later at Hanauma Bay. This was the first successful crossing of the Moloka'i Channel by a swimmer. One of the main reasons for selecting this site was to seek the assistance of the powerful current that sweeps around Lā'au Point and runs out into the open ocean toward O'ahu.

Midway down the beach is Soda Pop Pool, a natural pool that fills when waves spill over the beach rock. The foam and bubbles formed by the washing of the white water give the pool its name. Soda Pop Pool is the only safe swimming spot on Kamāka'ipō Beach.

Āholehole Flats was named for the *āholehole* fish, once very abundant in the rough waters offshore. These silver fish love the turmoil of waves breaking on rocks and large schools of them can often be seen flashing through the swirling white water. *Āholehole* are good eating and a favorite target of throw-net fishermen.

Egusa's is the name of the last portion of Kamāka'ipō Beach. It was named for Kimi and Takujiro Egusa, who formerly lived in a house above the beach. They first lived at Hālena near the present campsite, where Takujiro was one of four head beekeepers in Moloka'i Ranch's first honey-producing venture. When the bees suffered from American foul brood, a bacterial disease of the larvae, before World War II, the Egusas moved to Kamāka'ipō. Their original home was in the area now called Keo Nakama, but when a tsunami destroyed that house, they relocated to the bluff at the right end of the beach. While they lived at Kamāka'ipō, Takujiro was the poison man responsible for killing *kiawe* trees in the cattle pastures, and both he and his wife also maintained the Kaupoa beach house for the Cooke family.

(11)
Kaupoa Beach

Kaupoa is the name of the beach that fronts a beach house of the same name. The Kaupoa house, built by George P. Cooke, the first president of Moloka'i Ranch, Ltd., was completed by the end of 1933. He and his family used the house as their beach home while their main residence was at Kala'e. When Cooke died, the house reverted to Moloka'i Ranch, Ltd., and is now used by the ranch shareholders.

The Kaupoa house sits on a knoll overlooking the ocean. Directly below is a long, wide, and moderately steep white sand beach fronted by lava rock and tidal pools. A large natural opening in the rocky shoreline at the north end of the beach provides a good swimming area. Except for one rock just offshore from the middle of the beach, the inshore bottom is sandy. Kaupoa is a good swimming area on calm days, but can be turbulent and rough when a heavy swell is running. The beach has a moderately steep foreshore, and the inshore bottom drops quickly to overhead depths. A wide channel that comes directly into the beach allows easy inshore access for small boats. There is no public access to the area.

Over the years numerous shipwrecks have occurred on the west end of Moloka'i, especially around Lā'au Point. One of the most interesting wrecks was that of the *Carrier Dove,* an American four-masted schooner freighting an 800-ton cargo of copra from Tonga to Canada. She hit the rocky coast near Kaupoa at night on November 4, 1921, and broke up within a few hours. This made the third and final time she had gone aground. The *Carrier Dove*'s history of hard luck was astounding. She had weathered storms, shipboard deaths, pirate attacks, and two former groundings before her final disaster.

(12)
Kaunalā Beach

Kaunalā means "placing (the) sun," but the origin of the name is unknown. Kaunalā Beach is a small pocket of white sand in a protected bay, with a moderately steep slope to the ocean. The inshore bottom is shallow and sandy with scattered rocks, providing a fair swimming area. The inshore waters are often murky after heavy rains because of soil runoffs from Kaunalā Gulch. The backshore of the beach is a large mudflat surrounded by strand vegetation, primarily *kiawe.* On the side of the mudflat are the white and orange remains of the *Kinan Maru,* a Hilo *ahi* boat that was wrecked offshore in the early 1970s. Heavy surf washed a portion of her stern ashore at Kaunalā. Other portions of the wreck can be found at Small Bay, just to the south of Kaunalā. The wreckage of the *Kinan Maru* has created some confusion between Kaunalā and its neighboring beach, Kapukahehu. Kapukahehu is popularly known as Dixie Maru for a sampan that wrecked there, so people unfamiliar with the area occasionally confuse the Kaunalā wreckage for that of the Dixie Maru.

In September 1961 Keo Nakama became the first swimmer to cross the Moloka'i Channel to O'ahu. Shortly before his feat, a young woman named Greta Anderson attempted the crossing. She selected Kaunalā as her starting point, but was unsuccessful in reaching O'ahu.

Kaunalā is frequented primarily by fishermen. The water can be very rough with strong rip currents, especially when the surf is big. There is no public access to the area.

(13)
Kapukahehu Beach

Kapukahehu Beach is a small but wide crescent of white sand at the head of a little bay. The beach bars an intermittent stream that is active only after heavy rains. The foreshore along most of the beach rises steadily to a flat and grassy backshore area spotted with *kiawe* trees. Although the offshore bottom is rocky, the waters fronting Kapukahehu are usually safe for swimming, as the bay is fairly well protected by its outer points. Heavy surf, however, will break across the entire mouth of the bay and create strong rip currents inshore. The waters are also occasionally murky from the stream runoff. The beach is used primarily by fishermen and has no public access.

Kapukahehu is best known to Moloka'i residents as Dixie Maru. The *Dixie Maru* was a Japanese fishing

KAUNALĀ. The beach at Kaunalā is a small pocket of white sand bordered by *kiawe* trees along its *mauka* edge. Like many of the other small bays and coves found between Lā'au Point and 'Ilio Point on West Moloka'i, Kaunalā is occa- sionally cut by an intermittent stream that flows during and shortly after heavy rains. The stream deposits large amounts of mud in the backshore.

sampan that was wrecked off this rocky shoreline area in the early 1920s. One of the cowboys employed by Moloka'i Ranch found her nameplate washed ashore at Kapukahehu and hung it on a nearby gate. Since that time, the bay and the beach have been known as Dixie Maru, although no wreckage of the *Dixie Maru* or her nameplate can be found in the area today.

(14)
Po'olau Beach

Po'olau Beach is a small pocket of white sand at the mouth of Po'olau Gulch. The shoreward edge of the beach is lined entirely by boulders. The offshore bottom is rocky, sloping quickly to overhead depths. It is not a particularly good swimming beach because of the rocks and the drop. Heavy surf closes the entire mouth of the bay, creating dangerous rip currents inshore. The area is visited primarily by fishermen and has no public access.

Po'olau is more popularly known as Bomb Bay. The pasture lands to the rear of the bay were utilized by the military during and after World War II for target prac- tice. A large, unexploded bomb was found by a member of the Cooke family in this area, hence its popular name. Other target areas on Moloka'i were 'Ilio Point and Moku Ho'oniki, an island offshore of East Moloka'i.

(15)
Pāpōhaku Beach

Pāpōhaku means "stone fence," but the origin of the name is now unknown. Pāpōhaku Beach is the largest beach on Moloka'i and one of the largest white sand beaches in the State of Hawai'i. Pāpōhaku lies between Pu'u Koa'e, a lava and sand headland at the south end

82

of the beach, and Puʻu o Kaiaka, a cinder cone headland at the north end. This fairly straight beach is over two miles long and averages one hundred yards wide. The backshore is lined by low sand dunes topped by strand vegetation, primarily *kiawe* trees, but otherwise the beach is a vast expanse of flat white sand. The sand extends offshore almost a quarter of a mile, and high dunes have formed near Puʻu Koaʻe.

This massive natural cache of sand was for many years the site of the largest sand mining operation in the state. Honolulu Construction and Draying Company, Ltd., better known as H. C. & D., began removing sand in the early 1960s and shipping it from Hale o Lono Barge Harbor. The bulk of the sand went to Oʻahu for use by the construction industry. In 1972 the state legislature passed a law that banned sand mining operations below the upper reaches of the wash of waves as evidenced by the vegetation line. All affected companies were given until 1975 to comply with the law. In 1975 H. C. & D. terminated its shoreline operations at Pāpōhaku below the high water mark. The firm then built an eleven-million-dollar sand manufacturing plant at their Kapaʻa Quarry on Oʻahu. There the bulk of Oʻahu's construction sand is now made by crushing basaltic rock quarried in the Kawaewae Hills. The large concrete tunnel at the south end of Pāpōhaku Beach is all that remains of the former sand mining operation. Today H. C. & D. is called Ameron H. C. & D., a division of Ameron, Inc., the multinational corporation that purchased the local firm in 1968.

PĀPŌHAKU BEACH. One of the longest and widest sand beaches in the Hawaiian Islands, Pāpōhaku Beach is located on the west end of the island near the Sheraton Molokaʻi. The concrete tunnel on the beach is what remains of a former sand mining operation in the area. In the distance is ʻIlio Point, which points across Kaiwi Channel to the island of Oʻahu.

Pāpōhaku Beach is not a safe swimming beach. It is subject to rip currents and strong alongshore currents throughout the year. It is also without any reef or point protection against the open ocean and thus is subject to large surf during both the summer and winter months. The unrestrained waves create a devastating, crushing shorebreak. These waves also wash forcefully inland over the wide but very flat beach, creating a danger for anyone walking near the water's edge and especially for children who may be swept off their feet by the backwash and carried seaward into the pounding shorebreak. On calmer days experienced bodysurfers sometimes will go out at Pāpōhaku, but in general this beach should be avoided for swimming. During and after World War II the military practiced beach landings on this shoreline. Still partially buried in the center of the beach at the water's edge are rolls of wire, large pieces of metal runners, and several abandoned vehicles. Heavy surf occasionally exposes these objects, providing another serious hazard to water activities at Pāpōhaku.

(16)
Kepuhi Beach

Kepuhi Beach is a long, wide white sand beach that fronts the Sheraton Moloka'i Hotel. The 292-room hotel, the largest on the island, opened on March 15, 1977, and was completed at an estimated cost of $15.5 million. The resort complex also includes an 18-hole golf course which stretches from Pōhaku Māuliuli to Pāpōhaku Beach. Prior to construction of the hotel, only a lone house occupied the site. It was the longtime home of Joe Joao, a ranch hand employed by Moloka'i Ranch, Ltd., who tended to the cattle fences and water troughs in this remote and desolate end of the island.

Kepuhi Beach is safe for swimming only on very calm days, and even at such time persistent alongshore currents often sweep the length of the beach. The foreshore has a moderately steep slope, and the offshore bottom drops quickly to overhead depths. During periods of heavy surf the entire length of the beach is inundated by waves, creating dangerous shorebreaks and powerful rip currents. Prolonged periods of surf often erode most of the sand beach, exposing large expanses of beach rock that are barely visible at other times. Signs posted below

the Sheraton Moloka'i Hotel state: "Public Beach—Swim At Your Own Risk." Occasionally the waves are good enough for surfing and bodysurfing, but only for those experienced enough to handle the adverse water conditions that accompany the surf. The public right-of-way to the beach is located on the north side of Pu'u o Kaiaka, the large hill that separates Pāpōhaku and Kepuhi beaches. Just beyond the hotel's tennis courts, the paved road ends in a large parking lot provided for the public's use.

In the hills *mauka* of Kepuhi Beach is the Moloka'i Ranch Wildlife Park, a seven-hundred-acre reserve of exotic animals from Africa and India. The animals include Barbary sheep, Indian black buck, eland, sable antelope, oryx, impala, ibex, greater kudu, axis deer, and giraffes. The park was established in 1974 through the efforts of Aka Hodgins, the manager of Moloka'i Ranch, who selected rare and endangered species with the idea of breeding and selling surplus animals. Tours through the wildlife area originate from the Sheraton Moloka'i. Eventually, the park will include a tree-house restaurant for viewing the animals that are now at home on West Moloka'i.

(17)
Pōhaku Māuliuli Beach

Just beyond the north point of Kepuhi Beach is a large cinder cone called Pōhaku Māuliuli, the "black rock." The *makai* end of this hill as been eroded by the ocean and forms a high rocky headland. At the base of the headland are two large coves of white sand with several large tidal pools. These isolated beaches are nice areas for sunbathing, but poor areas for swimming. The offshore waters are deep and often have strong alongshore currents. The sand is subject to seasonal erosion and accretion, and during heavy surf large boulders are exposed at the water's edge. Large waves can also wash across the width of the beach, so anyone in the area should be very cautious when a large swell is running. Another danger is from the hill itself. Pōhaku Māuliuli is composed of very loose cinder rock which occasionally breaks away and falls into the sand below. The base of the hill is not a safe place to walk or sunbathe.

Pōhaku Māuliuli Beach is also known as Make Horse Beach. Apparently, when the entire west end of Moloka'i was still a ranch, an old horse fell off the cliff here and died on the beach below. *Make* is the Hawaiian word for dead. There is no convenient public access to this beach.

(18)
Kawākiu Bay

Kawākiu means "the spy place" or "the spy time," but how the name originated is not known. The name of the bay is acutally Kawākiunui, while the smaller bay to the north is Kawākiuiki; however, Kawākiunui is usually called simply Kawākiu.

Kawākiu Beach is probably best known as the starting point of the first Moloka'i to O'ahu canoe race and many of the early races that followed. The first race in 1952 represented the culmination of one man's determined efforts to establish a canoe race across the Moloka'i Channel. A. E. "Toots" Minvielle, Jr., a surveyor with a profound interest in improving and expanding the sport of Hawaiian canoe racing, had first proposed a Moloka'i to O'ahu race in the mid-1930s, but could not interest anyone in sponsoring or even participating in the event. Hawaiian canoes were then being raced, but only over calm water in protected areas. Minvielle felt that the boats should be raced in the rough waters of the open ocean, the waters that had determined the design of these canoes. Finally, after World War II, Minvielle interested several members of the Waikiki Surf Club in his race proposal, and in 1952 the Aloha Week committee agreed to sponsor the event if at least three canoes would participate. The first entry was the Waikiki Surf Club, the second was the Kukui o Lanikāula Canoe Club of Moloka'i, and the third and last entry was a nameless crew of paddlers from Ala Moana Beach Park. Kawākiu was selected as the starting point because it is the sand beach on Moloka'i that is closest to O'ahu.

On the morning of October 27, 1952, a huge north swell was running and the surf at Kawākiu was gigantic. To get the three canoes out safely past the waves pouring into the bay and the devastating shorebreak, Minvielle went out on the north point of the bay and signaled each boat out between sets. Finally, the three canoes were lined up beyond the huge surf and the race was started. Eight hours and fifty-five minutes later the Kukui o

Lanikāula Canoe Club of Moloka'i crossed the finish line at the Moana Hotel in Waikīkī. The other two boats came in within twenty minutes of Moloka'i's time.

In 1963 the starting point of the race was changed to Hale o Lono Beach, in favor of the calmer water conditions there during the unpredictable winter months. The move was also precipitated by the ever increasing number of entrants and the logistical problems they created at small and remote Kawākiu, where there are no fresh water outlets and no facilities. The proximity of Hale o Lono Harbor was also attractive to the small flotilla of escort boats that accompany the canoes across the channel.

In 1959 Minvielle was instrumental in starting another long-distance canoe race, the Catalina Channel race from Catalina Island to the California mainland. Again he could not find any local backers for the event, so it was sponsored finally by the owner of the Newport Dunes, a California beach resort. On September 20, 1959, two California crews and one Hawaiian crew participated in the first Catalina Channel race, now an annual event. From that time on, California has also participated in the Moloka'i Channel race.

In the early 1960s Minvielle organized the International Hawaiian Canoe Racing Association, Inc., to promote outrigger canoe racing as an international sport and to seek financial support for other races. He was instrumental in contacting canoe paddling enthusiasts in Tahiti and Japan and getting crews from both places to enter the Moloka'i Channel race.

In 1978 another channel crossing that Minvielle had originally proposed in the 1960s became a reality. On June 14, 1978, nine men from Hawai'i paddled across the English Channel in an outrigger canoe from Calais, France, to Dover, England. The twenty-mile crossing, completed in four hours and fifteen minutes, was part of the festivities commemorating the 250th anniversary of Captain James Cook's birth, on October 28, 1728, as well as his sighting of the Hawaiian Islands in 1778.

For his great contributions to the sport of Hawaiian canoe racing that began with the first Moloka'i Channel race from Kawākiu to Waikīkī in 1952, Minvielle was inducted into the Hawai'i Sports Hall of Fame on August 21, 1978.

Kawākiu was again brought to the public's attention

in July 1975 by Hui Alaloa, a group formed specifically to seek public access to parts of Moloka'i that have been kept off-limits to the general public. Kawākiu is located on land previously belonging to Moloka'i Ranch, Ltd. The ranch was started in 1897 by a group of men who purchased the *ahupua'a* of Kaluako'i I and II and the Kaunakakai ranch lands formerly owned by Kamehameha V. These combined holdings encompassed almost one-third of the island of Moloka'i and the entire west end. Since the formation of the ranch, this entire area including all of its beaches had been accessible only to Moloka'i Ranch employees, stockholders, and guests with passes. Hui Alaloa members and supporters marched from Mo'omomi Beach to Kawākiu on the Fourth of July weekend in 1975 to demonstrate the public's need and desire for access. Kawākiu has since been opened to the public. On October 18, 1975, Hui Alaloa led another march along the Pālā'au Pond to Hale o Lono, to protest restricted access along the portion of the Pālā'au Pond controlled by Moloka'i Ranch, Ltd.

Kawākiu Beach is a wide crescent of white sand at the head of Kawākiunui Bay. The beach has a moderately steep slope, and the offshore bottom drops off quickly to overhead depths. Kawākiu is safe for swimming when the ocean is calm, primarily during the summer months. During times of heavy surf, however, especially during the winter and spring, the bay's waters are very dangerous, with powerful rip currents and a pounding shorebreak. To the rear of the beach is a *kiawe* grove that provides a shady picnic area. The area is totally unimproved except for the dirt access road which begins at Maunaloa Highway. The turnoff is marked by a public right-of-way sign and is located 2.5 miles north from the turnoff to the Sheraton Moloka'i.

Kawākiuiki Bay, located just beyond the north point of Kawākiu Beach, is a smaller version of Kawākiunui Bay, except that the beach is primarily rocky with small pockets of sand. It is not particularly appealing as a swimming area and is very dangerous during the winter months.

(19–21)
Mo'omomi Beach

Mo'omomi is a very large coastal area that extends several miles inland from the ocean and encompasses a por-

tion of one of the most impressive sand dune developments in the Hawaiian Islands. These dunes are still being formed and expanded by sand from the beaches within the Mo'omomi shoreline. This side of the island is exposed to prevailing trade winds which sweep almost continuously across the area. Over centuries these winds have created the massive dunes in this northwestern corner of Moloka'i by carrying the shoreline sand inland, in some places for over four miles. This desolate, sandy region, which includes some older, solidified sand dunes, is sometimes referred to as the Desert Strip. It is also known as Keonelele, "the wind-blown sands."

Mo'omomi was once a popular fishing area. One traditional story says that before the turn of the century the inhabitants of Pelekunu, an isolated valley eighteen miles away, often journeyed by canoe during the summer to Mo'omomi. There they caught and dried fish to take back to Pelekunu. Pelekunu is accessible from the ocean only during certain months of the year. Heavy winter surf prevents boats from landing. Pelekunu also has very high valley walls which permit direct sunlight in the valley's interior only for five hours a day, and during the winter months the valley experiences heavy rains. All these factors, in addition to the better shallow-water fishing grounds and the hotter drying areas at Mo'omomi, made the expedition a travel outing as well as a food-procuring trip. Fishing and drying were also done at Kalawao and Kalaupapa.

Besides being a fishing grounds for the people of Pelekunu as well as others, Mo'omomi was also a quarry site for stones to make adzes. The name of the *ahupua'a* which encompasses the entire west end of the island including most of Mo'omomi is Kaluako'i, "the adze pit." Although stone was quarried at Mo'omomi, the largest quarries in Kaluako'i were located at Maunaloa and covered an area of thirty acres. Prior to their contact with foreign cultures, the Hawaiians had no sources of metal. For weapons and tools they were entirely dependent on shell and bone, and wood and stone, so hard rocks that could be quarried were very valuable.

To longtime residents of Moloka'i, Mo'omomi Beach is the entire three-mile length of the shoreline from the Hawaiian Home Lands recreation center to the high sea cliffs that run past Mokio to 'Ilio Point. This long

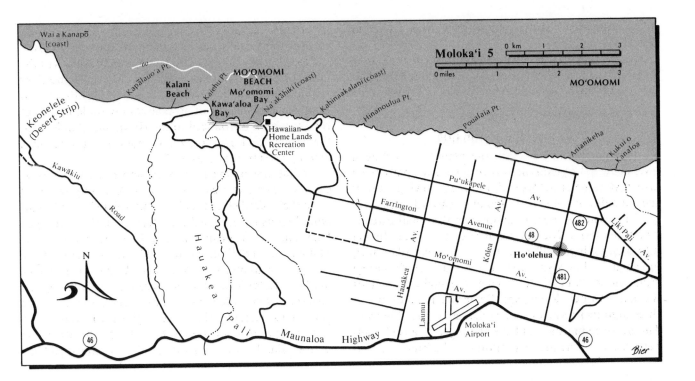

stretch of shoreline, however, includes three distinct beaches, Keonelele, Kawaʻaloa, and Moʻomomi.

Keonelele is a storm beach that fronts the seaward edge of the Desert Strip. Beachrock lines the length of the beach. Inland of the rock is a wide white sand beach created by storm surf carrying sand over the rocks. This shoreline is assaulted by the prevailing trade winds and heavy winter surf. High surf sweeps across the beach and deposits driftwood, bottles, and other debris from the ocean. The nearshore bottom is deep and subject to strong longshore currents. The backshore consists of sand dunes, many of which have solidified into interesting sculptures.

Kawaʻaloa means "the long canoe." Kawaʻaloa Beach is a long, wide crescent of white sand at the head of a large bay. The sand is subject to seasonal erosion and accretion. The west end of the beach is wide and flat, and strewn with driftwood, seaweed, and other items deposited by heavy surf. As the beach progresses to the east, it gets narrower and is very steep at the water's edge. This end of the beach is somewhat pro-

tected by the right point of the bay and the broken reef offshore, offering a cleaner, calmer, and safer swimming area than does the left end. Occasionally the waves offshore are good enough for surfing. Inshore, on a bluff above the beach, is a large beach house that was built by the Del Monte Corporation for its white-collar employees. Both Kawaʻaloa and Keonelele are sometimes called Ranch Moʻomomi because Molokaʻi Ranch, Ltd., owns all of the land *mauka* of these beaches.

The section of the Moʻomomi shoreline that is called Moʻomomi Beach is the bay where the Hawaiian Home Lands Commission has a community recreation center. The large pavilion is located on the low escarpment above the beach. The small pocket beach of white sand in the inner east corner of the bay is shallow and rocky, but a good swimming area for children. The bay is well protected by its fairly long east point. To the west of the sheltered bay is a rocky headland with several small sand pockets fronted by rocks and tidal pools. This area is frequented primarily by fishermen. It is sometimes

87

called Homestead Moʻomomi to differentiate it from Ranch Moʻomomi.

There is no public access to any part of the three-mile length of the Moʻomomi shoreline. The gates leading to the beaches are all controlled by private concerns.

(22)
Kalaupapa Peninsula

Kalaupapa translates as "the flat plain" or as "much level land." The peninsula was formed principally from lava that came from Kauhakō Crater, flowing against the sea cliffs of the main island and seaward of the crater. The crater is more than 450 feet deep and extends below sea level. The inner slopes of the crater funnel into a large, high-walled pit that is partially filled with bluish-green brackish water. The pond is easily visible from the lookout at Puʻu ʻUao, the highest point of Kauhakō Crater. Kalaupapa Peninsula is made up of three *ahupuaʻa*: Kalaupapa, Makanalua, and Kalawao. The entire peninsula is called Kalaupapa because Kalaupapa has been the primary landing and center of popu-

lation since the late 1800s. No one has lived permanently on the peninsula outside of Kalaupapa since the 1930s.

Prior to the mid-1800s Kalaupapa Peninsula was the home of a community of Hawaiian fishermen and their families. In 1866, however, the Board of Health selected Kalawao to be the site of an exile colony for lepers. Leprosy had been introduced to the Hawaiian Islands from the Orient and had grown to epidemic proportions among the Hawaiian people.

At that time no means were available to arrest the disease, so those who contracted it were simply removed from their families and society, and isolated. The Kalaupapa Peninsula provided a perfect natural prison. The Hawaiian government had acquired the *ahupuaʻa* of Makanalua and Kalawao in 1848, which included the valleys of Waikolu, Waiʻaleʻia, and Waihānau. The *ahupuaʻa* of Kalaupapa was purchased in 1873, giving the government complete ownership of the peninsula. The Hawaiians residing there were given the option of remaining or of relocating to Kainalu, on the other side of the island. Almost forty of the original residents

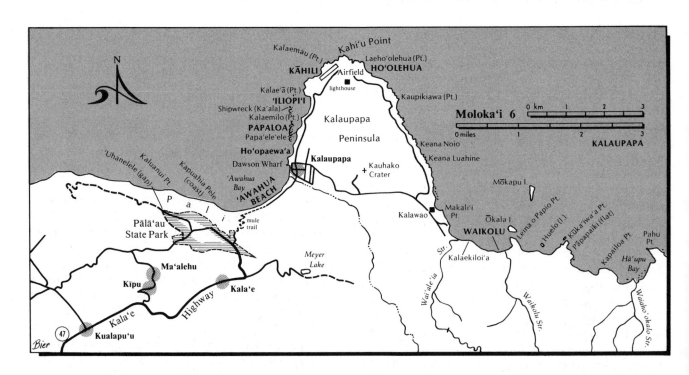

chose to remain and were given access to all areas of the settlement. This intermingling was allowed until 1895, when the Board of Health decided that the situation was unhealthy and evicted all the nonleper residents.

When the settlement at Kalaupapa was created, the Board of Health had felt that the lepers would be able to support themselves by working the land and fishing, as the residents before them had done. The officials thought that after a few years the epidemic would abate and then end once all the lepers had been isolated. The epidemic escalated into the twentieth century, however, and the settlement never became self-sufficient. The first boatload of lepers landed on the peninsula on January 6, 1866. As more and more people were exiled, the conditions at Kalawao, the site of the original settlement, became unbelievably bad. The Hawaiian monarchy had established an organized hospital settlement on paper, but in reality there was very little order, very little help, and every conceivable type of crime. Many lepers were simply left to die when they could no longer care for themselves. Boatloads of new patients were greeted with this phrase of despair: " 'A'ole kanawai ma keia wahi"—"In this place there is no law."

In 1873, seven years after the start of the settlement, a young Catholic priest named Father Damien arrived at Kalaupapa on a small vessel carrying fifty lepers and a few head of cattle. Damien was the first resident priest on the peninsula, and his work among the lepers is legendary. Joseph De Veuster was born at Tremelo, Belgium, on January 3, 1840. He entered the Congregation of the Sacred Hearts in Louvain, taking the name of a physician-saint, Damien; volunteered for duty as a missionary in Hawai'i; and arrived in Honolulu on March 19, 1864. Shortly after, he was ordained a priest in the Cathedral of Our Lady of Peace in Honolulu and was assigned to the island of Hawai'i. Damien spent nine years on the Big Island, first in Puna and then in the Kohala and Hamakua districts.

In 1872 a Sacred Heart brother spent six weeks at Kalawao erecting St. Philomena Church. Damien and three other priests decided to rotate the duties at the new church. Damien drew the first tour of duty, arrived on May 10, 1873, and stayed for the next sixteen years.

Damien contracted leprosy and died at the settlement on April 15, 1889. His remains were returned to Louvain, Belgium, in May of 1936 and buried in the crypt of the church where he first entered religious life. Pope Paul VI declared him the Venerable Father Damien on July 7, 1977. Veneration is the first step toward sainthood in the Catholic church; the second is beatification, and the third and final step, canonization.

On November 11, 1977, the Damien Museum and Archives were blessed and opened to the public. Located on O'ahu, at St. Patrick's Church in Kaimuki, the museum contains personal possessions, papers, letters, and other memorabilia of Father Damien. Although many individuals assisted and followed Damien, it is his name that has become synonymous with the settlement on Kalaupapa Peninsula. The museum and archives are a good place to start for anyone seeking more information about Damien or the settlement.

Today the leprosy treatment center at Kalaupapa Peninsula is administered by the State Department of Health. The thirteen-square-mile district is a county of its own, Kalawao County, although it has no formal county government. There are 125 patient-residents, 37 non-patient employees, and three members of religious orders living on the peninsula (as of October 1979). No new patients are admitted to Kalaupapa. The median term of residence of the present patients is 33.5 years, the median patient age is 58.8 years, and only eight of the 95 patients over 50 years of age are able-bodied. Kalaupapa Peninsula and the entire county of Kalawao are closed to all outsiders. Official visitors and guests of the patient-residents are allowed limited stays by permit only. Trespassers are subject to arrest by the resident sheriff or his deputies. Signs are posted in conspicuous places to advise visitors of the laws and the consequences. Authorized guided tours of the peninsula are available to the public through several commercial firms.

There are five beaches on Kalaupapa Peninsula: 'Awahua, Papaloa, 'Iliopi'i, Kāhili, and Ho'olehua. All of them can be seen from the public lookout next to the start of the *pali* trail 1,664 feet above the peninsula. None of the beaches is good for swimming. The residents use them primarily for fishing.

'Awahua Beach is a long, fairly wide detrital sand beach located at the foot of the *pali* trail. 'Awahua is said to have been the name of a chief, the complete

'AWAHUA BEACH. This long, wide, detrital sand beach graces the bottom of the foot trail that begins at Pala'au State Park and ends on the Kalaupapa Peninsula. Although Kalaupapa has no formal government, it is a county of its own, Kalawao County, and is administered by the State of Hawai'i as a leprosy settlement. The entire peninsula including the trail leading down the cliffs is off limits to all unauthorized visitors.

name of the beach being Ke Ono Ne'e o 'Awahua, "the slowly moving sands of 'Awahua." The sand is subject to seasonal erosion and accretion, eroding during the winter and accreting during the summer. The beach has a moderately steep slope to the water's edge and the offshore bottom drops off quickly to overhead depths. There is no protective reef, so the beach is continually subject to very strong alongshore and rip currents, especially when the surf is big. Dangerous Swimming signs are posted in the area. 'Awahua Beach is more popularly known as Black Sands Beach, for the dominant color of the detrital sand. The beach is also known as Puahi Beach or Pikoone Beach, from shoreline place names in this area of Kalaupapa.

Papaloa means "long flat" and it includes not only the beach and the graveyard to the rear of the beach, but a *mauka* area as well. The inland region of Papaloa is said to have been a garden area for watermelons and other edible plants. Papaloa Beach is a long and fairly wide white sand beach that fronts the settlement proper. The backshore is marked by low sand dunes covered with strand vegetation; it is also the site of an extensive graveyard. Small sections of beach rock and lava line the water's edge of the beach. The offshore bottom is very shallow and rocky with scattered patches of sand. Many boulders are visible above the surface of the ocean. At the south end of the beach is a narrow, sand-bottomed channel that usually has a steady rip current

90

running seaward. The beach area inshore of the channel was called Hoʻopaewaʻa, "to land (a) canoe." On calm days this channel can provide a relatively safe canoe landing. The center of Papaloa Beach is known to many of the residents as Boat House, because of a canoe storage shed that once stood to the rear of the beach. A shallow, sandy, rock-free pocket here provides the best swimming area on the peninsula. At the north end of the beach is Papaʻeleʻele, "black flat," a low flat lava shelf containing many tidal pools. Papaloa Beach ends at Kalaemilo Point, the site of Ocean View Pavilion. Ocean View was formerly the site of the home of the man who ran the Kalaupapa Laundry. The tsunami of 1946 washed his house out to sea, and in 1952 the Kalaupapa Lions built a pavilion for their community on the same site.

ʻIliopiʻi, "climbing dog," is the name found on most maps for the beach and the inland area to the north of Kalaemilo Point. Some sources say this name should be ʻIliopī, the "stingy dog." ʻIliopiʻi is said to have been the site of an old, pre-settlement village. ʻIliopiʻi Beach is a long and fairly wide crescent of white sand bordered by Kalaemilo Point to the south and Kalaeʻā Point to the north. The backshore is low and almost totally devoid of any trees or vegetation. There are five beach houses clustered inshore of Kalaeʻā. The offshore bottom at ʻIliopiʻi is shallow and very rocky, with a few scattered pockets of sand. Large boulders are visible above the surface of the ocean. Beyond the shallows fronting the beach is the wreck of the *S.S. Kaʻala,* a portion of whose structure is still visible from the beach as well as from the Kalaupapa Lookout at the top of the

PAPALOA BEACH. Papaloa Beach is one of two long white sand beaches located on the leeward side of Kalaupapa Peninsula. This view of the beach from Kalaemilo Point also shows how the rest of the island appears from Kalaupapa. From this vantage point it is easy to see why the residents of the settlement invariably refer to the rest of the island as "Topside."

pali. In 1932 the *Ka'ala* had been making her way at night from 'Ilio Point to Kalaupapa. The crew spotted a red light that they thought marked the channel into the wharf, but as the vessel came in to make her landing, she went aground. The light the crew had spotted was from a house at 'Iliopi'i.

The last two beaches, Kāhili and Ho'olehua, are examples of storm beaches created by heavy surf carrying sand over rocks and depositing it inland. Both of these beaches are located some distance from the ocean and are separated from the water by wide, barren expanses of tide pools and rocky shelves. Kāhili, "the feather standard," is a long, wide, and steep strip of coral rubble and white sand *makai* of the airport pavilion. The beach offers a beautiful view inland of Kauhakō Crater and three valleys, Waihānau, Wai'ale'ia, and Waikolu. The beach was named for Kāhili'ōpua, a chiefess from the village at 'Iliopi'i who moved to the present airport area, where she lived with only female retainers. Seating herself on Kanohopōhaku o Kāhili'ōpua, "the rock chair of Kāhili'ōpua," she would act as an intermediary for any man seeking a wife or a *kōko'olua,* a "companion." The rock can still be seen near the airport gate.

Ho'olehua Beach is a wide, sloping white sand beach to the east of Lae o Kahi'u, the outermost point of the peninsula. The shoreline in this area is primarily rocky and composed of low sea cliffs. To the west of Ho'olehua Beach is a wide expanse of shallow tidal pools that is a favorite salt-gathering place for the residents during the summer months.

Other than the storm beaches of Ho'olehua and Kāhili, and the leeward beaches of 'Iliopi'i, Papaloa, and 'Awahua, the coastline of the Kalaupapa Peninsula is composed totally of sea cliffs. Over the years many residents of Kalaupapa have lost their lives after being swept from the rocks by heavy surf, usually while fishing. At least four points are named for men who were caught by the surf and drowned: Monkey's Point (a man's nickname), Sinsato Point, John Davis Point, and Jack Miyoshi Point. A fifth point, Kamahana, was named for David K. Kamahana (1880–1955), who had a beach house there. He is buried to the rear of John Cambra's beach house at Papaloa.

Kalaupapa has a small harbor that was improved by the Corps of Engineers in 1967. A 114-feet-long rubble-mound breakwater was constructed and a half-acre entrance channel and basin were dredged through a reef shelf. The wharf is named P. O. Dawson Ramp and a small plaque explains that it was "dedicated to the memory of a beloved friend of the people of Kalaupapa."

Beyond Kalaupapa Peninsula is Wai'ale'ia, the "gulped water," a very narrow valley with a steep boulder beach at its mouth. Prior to 1946 a seasonal dark detrital sand beach periodically covered the boulders, but it never returned after the devastating tsunami of that year. The present boulder beach begins at Wai'ale'ia, or Waile'ia as the name is invariably pronounced and spelled by the residents, and continues along the shoreline to Waikolu, "three waters." Waikolu Valley is an extremely important and sensitive area for the Kalaupapa settlement. Waikolu Stream is the single source of fresh water on the peninsula. Waikolu Valley is also the major source of fresh water for "Topside," as the rest of Moloka'i is known to the residents. In 1960 a 5.5-mile water tunnel was built into the western side of Waikolu Valley to tap the extensive water resources. The water is stored in a large reservoir at Kualapu'u.

An extremely high sea cliff separates Wai'ale'ia and Waikolu valleys, so the heavy-gauge water main that comes out of Waikolu runs over the surface of the boulder beach at the base of the cliffs, the topography of the area offering no alternate route.

During the history of the settlement the pipe has been smashed and repaired numerous times because of landslides and falling boulders. Broken and discarded sections of old pipe litter the length of the long boulder beach. In an effort to prevent breaks, many of the exposed sections of the pipe are roofed with heavy timber. In many places these 6″ × 12″ planks have been splintered into kindling. This is visible testimony to the very real danger of falling rocks at the base of this high sea cliff, as well as of those from Waikolu to Hālawa.

The ocean offshore from both Wai'ale'ia and Waikolu is deep and often turbulent with strong currents. Both valleys are part of Kalawao County, so the regulations prohibiting landing are applicable and enforced there as well as on the peninsula. Warning signs are posted near the shoreline end of Waikolu Stream. Occasionally, but unpredictably, a dark detrital sand beach forms at Waikolu between Kalaekiloi'a and the mouth of Waikolu Stream.

23

Pelekunu Valley

Pelekunu is a narrow valley with very high walls which allow the sun to shine directly into the interior of the valley for only four to five hours a day. The ridge separating Pelekunu from Wailau Valley is over three thousand feet high. The valley is subject to extended periods of heavy rain, especially during the winter and spring months. Beginning in 1936, a two-year survey was conducted at both Wailau and Pelekunu. The final report, dated June 1938, noted that in the two years of keeping records of rainy days in the two valleys, there was not a single month with fewer than ten days of rain in either valley, and the average was nearly as many rainy days as clear ones. In December 1936 there were twenty-one days of rain, most of it heavy. This tremendous volume of rain has had marked effects on the valley, from giving rise to its name—Pelekunu means a "moldy smell (from dampness and a lack of sunshine)"—to contributing to the depopulation of the valley by 1917.

Archaeological evidence has shown that the upper regions of Pelekunu were once the home of a large population of Hawaiians. They were taro farmers who sup-

plemented their diet by fishing. From roughly October to April, however, the ocean at Pelekunu is often much too rough and dangerous for fishing. Even if the ocean was calm, the continued rains and lack of sunshine in Pelekunu made drying fish almost impossible. For these reasons the inhabitants of the valley traveled during the summer to Kalawao, Kalaupapa, and even to Moʻomomi, to catch and dry fish. They also gathered salt from the rocks of Hoʻolehua at Kalaupapa. In addition, the journeys offered the valley residents an opportunity to travel and visit with friends and relatives.

During the 1800s many people began to leave the valley, beckoned by the trappings of Western culture and the promise of an easier, more comfortable way of life. By 1900 there were fewer than one hundred permanent residents in the valley. In spite of the decline in population, however, the taro industry flourished. In 1863 the farmers had expanded *makai* and cultivated the lower reaches of the valley floor. Chinese taro farmers were involved in these commercial efforts as well as Hawaiians.

Probably the most famous residents of Pelekunu in the twentieth century were Jennie "Kini" and John H. Wilson, who made their home in Pelekunu during the

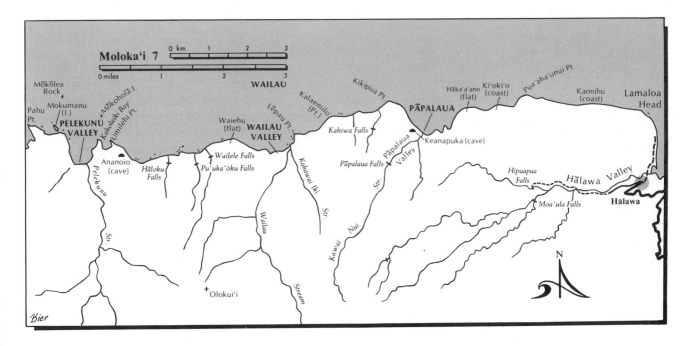

early 1900s. They were involved for a short period of time in a taro raising venture, but abandoned the enterprise in 1911. Wilson was an engineer and his Pelekunu home was his base of operations between contracting jobs elsewhere. He is best known for building the "New Pali Road" from the Pali Lookout on O'ahu to the halfway house where the road forked to Kane'ohe and Waimānalo. Wilson and his partner, Lou Whitehouse, won the contract with a bid of $37,500, began work on May 26, 1897, and finished the project seven and a half months later. Wilson in later years was mayor of Honolulu several times. The Wilson Tunnels on Likelike Highway are named in his honor.

Wilson also utilized his engineering talents in Pelekunu. The valley is often inaccessible from the ocean for long periods throughout the year because of heavy surf. At Wa'a'ula Landing Wilson constructed a derrick with a boom sixty-two feet long that reached out from the cliffs over the breaking waves to the calmer waters beyond. After it was completed, people and supplies could be landed and taro shipped out during the worst surf conditions. In 1914 Kini Wilson, who had served as the postmistress of the village, tired of the isolation and the continuous rains, left the village of Kamalō on the other side of the island. Shortly after her departure the remaining families also began to leave. The interisland steamers had stopped calling regularly because there was no longer a post office. During this period the Pelekunu farmers, underbid by farmers on O'ahu, lost their primary taro market, Kalaupapa. The Pelekunu School closed in 1915 and was relocated to Wailau. By 1917 the valley was virtually uninhabited, although one family remained until 1932.

Even though the farmers of Pelekunu were gone, the water buffalo they had introduced as beasts of burden remained. These animals, multiplying and thriving in the valley, became wild and ferocious. Molokai residents began to hunt them during the 1920s. None of the buffalo remain today.

In 1936 a semipermanent base camp for a water supply study was set up at the site of the old hand-powered derrick by the U.S. Geological Survey. The engineer in charge of the project was Hugh Howell and his field assistant was A. E. Minvielle, Jr., a well-known local surveyor. Minvielle and his crew replaced the rusted and decaying derrick that Wilson had installed with a narrow catwalk of steel beams and wooden planking resting on a concrete foundation and supported by cables. A hanging rope ladder completed the access to the vessels below. They also constructed one shack on the rocky ledge above the landing and one in the rear of the valley. During the long periods that the engineering crew remained in the valley to record rainfall and stream flow information, they hunted for goats and sharks. They shot the goats, and caught the sharks with heavy hooks from the end of the catwalk. Among the many large sharks they hooked was one they caught using a goat carcass which they identified as a great white shark.

The devastating tsunami of 1946 penetrated twenty-eight feet above sea level in Pelekunu and obliterated the old *makai* taro patches and the abandoned village. Only the shack above the old landing remains. Pelekunu Beach is a boulder beach for most of the year while the surf is heavy. During the calmer summer months a small dark detrital sand beach occasionally appears, covering a portion of the boulders. The offshore bottom drops quickly to overhead depths and is subject to strong seaward currents. Five streams from the valley cross the beach. The massive volumes of fresh water flowing into the ocean for untold centuries have scoured the ocean bottom to the west of the bay in the direction of the prevailing currents. There is very little marine life in this area. Access to the beach is possible only on calm days by boat.

(24)
Wailau Valley

Wailau is an immense valley amphitheater, the largest one on Moloka'i. The steep valley walls, rising to a minimum of 3,000 feet and a maximum of 4,970 feet, are laced with numerous waterfalls. The entire valley floor is cut by innumerable watercourses fed by the waterfalls' runoff, by springs, and by the enormous yearly rainfall. These watercourses form Waiakeakua and Pūlena streams, which in turn join to form Wailau Stream, running almost the entire length of the valley. Wailau means "many waters."

The history of Wailau is similar to that of Pelekunu. The valley once supported a large farming and fishing community that began to disperse in the 1800s. The promise of an easier and more comfortable way of life lured many of the inhabitants to more populated areas on Moloka'i and on the other islands. Commercial taro production continued into the twentieth century, however, in spite of the population decline. During the early 1900s low prices for taro and high costs of transportation contributed to the demise of taro operations in the neighboring valley of Pelekunu. Pelekunu residents left their valley and some of them settled in Wailau. The Pelekunu School was relocated to Wailau in 1915. However, the same economic pressures eventually shut down the commercial taro operations in Wailau as well. By 1920 the school was closed, and the valley was abandoned by the forty or so Hawaiian and Chinese families that had been making their home there.

What little remained of the former village was obliterated by the tsunami of 1946. The inundation reached inland heights of twenty-five feet above sea level, depositing large amounts of sand in the mouth of the valley. Wailau Beach today is a wide boulder beach crossed by Wailau Stream. During most of the year heavy surf closes off all access to the valley from the ocean. During the calmer summer months a dark detrital sand beach covers the left corner of the boulder beach. The offshore bottom drops off quickly to overhead depths and is subject to strong alongshore currents. The continuous flow of fresh water into the ocean has scoured the ocean bottom to the west of the stream in the direction of the flow. There is very little marine life in this area. Access to the beach by boat is possible only on calm days, primarily during the summer.

(25)
Pāpalaua

Pāpalaua Valley is another place where taro was grown on the "backside" of Moloka'i. Pāpalaua Falls is one of the highest on the island and provides the water for a stream that flows into the ocean. The shoreline is a boulder beach bordered on both sides by wide, flat peninsulas, Kikipua to the west and Hāka'a'ano to the east. Both of these wide rocky points are covered with trees and shrubbery and fronted by their own boulder beaches. None of these boulder beaches experiences sand accretion during the summer months, unlike Wailau and occasionally Pelekunu and Waikolu. The off-

shore bottom is deep and exposed to the open ocean. Inshore currents are strong, and heavy surf shuts out all possible entry from the ocean.

(26)
Hālawa Beach Park

Hālawa means either "curved," possibly for its naturally curving stream, or "ample taro stems," for the plant that was once the mainstay of the valley. Hālawa is one of four amphitheater valleys in East Moloka'i and is the only one easily accessible by land. The fertile valley

95

HĀLAWA VALLEY. Storm clouds hang over the ocean just outside of the entrance to Hālawa Bay. The inlet on the left was called Kamaʻalaea and is the primary anchorage in the bay area. The inlet on the right was called Kawili. Hālawa was once a major taro-producing valley, but shifts in population and several devastating tsunami ended all commercial cultivation of the plant in the valley.

was once extensively cultivated with taro. Jules Remy, a French naturalist who visited Hālawa in 1854, compared the area to Waipiʻo on Hawaiʻi, probably the most famous taro-producing valley in the Hawaiian Islands. Prior to and during the 1800s, Hālawa supplied most of the taro for the entire island of Molokaʻi as well as for places across the channel on Maui. Taro continued to be raised on a large commercial scale well into the twentieth century, but the population of the valley declined steadily as the people were drawn to more exciting and less vigorous ways of life in other places.

In 1935 a local real estate firm announced that Paul Irving Fagan had purchased the 9,000-acre valley from the Bishop Estate. Fagan, a millionaire sportsman, rancher, and part-owner of the San Francisco Seals baseball team, wanted to see the old life-style preserved and offered his new holdings in Hālawa for this pur-

pose. However, no one ever took up the opportunity to revert to the rigors of the old subsistence life-style. Fagan became disenchanted with the area and concentrated his attention in Hāna, where he developed Hāna Ranch and the Hotel Hāna Ranch (now the Hotel Hāna Maui).

In the ensuing years the few people who continued to grow taro in Hālawa were hit hard by two destructive tsunami, one in 1946 and one in 1957. The 1946 waves devastated the two major irrigated complexes in the lower valley and marked the end of commercial growing. The 1957 waves again inundated the valley and brought about the end of all taro growing. Today a handful of families still live in Hālawa, but the taro complexes are overrun by vegetation.

The lone road that skirts the East Molokaʻi coastline ends at Hālawa. Two of the main attractions in the valley, besides its general beauty and its historic sites, are its waterfalls, Moaʻula and Hīpuapua. Moaʻula is probably the most famous and most easily accessible waterfall on Molokaʻi. Tradition has it that the pool at the base of the falls is the home of *moʻo*. Visitors must drop a *ti* leaf on the surface of the water and only if it floats can they swim safely.

The shoreline of Hālawa Bay is divided into two pocket beaches by a low rise consisting of boulders. The two detrital sand beaches, Kawili and Kamaʻalaea, are backed by low sand dunes covered with strand vegetation. Kamaʻalaea to the west, also called Māʻalaea by the older residents, is situated on a small bay of its own that offers a somewhat protected anchorage for small boats. The inshore waters are shallow and safe for swimming, but the water is usually murky. Hālawa Stream empties into the ocean at the east end of the beach. In the middle of the beach a small patch of reef lies just offshore. During heavy surf a strong rip current runs seaward through the outer channel. Kawili on the east side of the rocky point is much straighter and not as protected from the open ocean. It is subject to strong alongshore currents and rip currents when the surf is big, but is usually safe for swimming on calm days. The offshore bottom is moderately rocky and slopes gently to overhead depths. Hālawa is one of the favorite surfing spots among the island's surfers. Just inland of the shoreline are the facilities of Hālawa Beach Park. Completed in 1968, the park includes a pavilion, restrooms, barbecue grills, and an unmarked parking area. A sign posted in the park warns visitors against drinking the brackish water. Hālawa Beach Park is reached by following Kamehameha V Highway to its end.

(27)
Fagans Beach

Fagans Beach is a small, narrow pocket of white sand located at the head of a small bay. A small stand of ironwood and coconut trees lines the backshore. The shore crescent beach has a shallow, safe swimming area that is protected by a reef offshore. A narrow but fairly deep sand-bottomed channel runs into the shallow water inshore and can be easily negotiated by small boats on a calm day. The secluded beach, probably the best swimming beach on the *manaʻe* (east) side of Molokaʻi, is not visible from the public road and is not accessible to the

public. At the mouths of Moakea and Lupehu, the two gulches on either side of Fagans Beach, are small pockets of sand and coral rubble, but these are not good swimming areas.

Fagans Beach, formerly known as Pōhaku Pili, was named for Paul I. Fagan, a millionaire from California who once owned Puʻu o Hoku Ranch, which includes this beach, and other Molokaʻi real estate. The ranch was purchased by George Murphy from the Ward family in 1955, and its pastures are leased by Molokaʻi Ranch, Ltd.

Offshore to the north of the beach are two rock islands. Kanahā, "the shattered (thing)," is the name of the smaller of the two rock islands. Moku Hoʻoniki, the name of the larger island, means "pinch island" (as a lover pinches). This island, whose name is commonly shortened to Moku Niki, was once famous for two large pits which traditional stories say were a burial pit and an *imu* pit. In more recent years the island acquired many additional pits when it became a bombing target during World War II. The bombing continued long after the end of the war and was not halted permanently until 1958, when the numerous complaints from Molokaʻi residents about the noise and the dangers of possible airplane crashes were finally heeded. Today both islands are bird refuges under state control.

(28)
Sandy Beach

Sandy Beach is a small pocket of white sand located at the mouth of the first gulch past Honouli Maloʻo. This popular roadside beach has a rocky but fairly deep inshore bottom that can accommodate adult swimmers. A shallow reef not far offshore protects most of the beach from strong currents, but a rip current usually runs out along the south point of the beach. It can prove dangerous during periods of heavy surf. Beyond Sandy Beach the Kamehameha V Highway begins its climb toward Puʻu o Hoku Ranch.

(29)
Honouli Maloʻo

Honouli Maloʻo means "dry dark bay." The inner shore of the bay contains a small, narrow detrital sand beach. The offshore bottom is rocky and shallow, deepening in the center of the bay where a channel cuts through the

SANDY BEACH. This tiny pocket of white sand is one of the most popular swimming beaches on Moloka'i. Located alongside the road to Hālawa Valley, it can be found by traveling *mana'e* or "toward the east" on Kamehameha V Highway. In the distance the West Maui Mountains are visible across Pailolo Channel.

reef. The area attracts divers and other fishermen, and provides an anchorage for small boats that is somewhat protected from the prevailing trade winds. Almost exactly the same shoreline features are found at Honouli Wai, a short distance away. Honouli Malo'o is located alongside Kamehameha V Highway.

(30)
Honouli Wai

Honouli Wai means "wet dark bay." The inner shore of the bay contains a small, narrow dark detrital sand beach. The offshore bottom is rocky and shallow, deepening in the center of the bay where a channel cuts through the reef. The bay attracts divers and other fishermen, and like Honouli Malo'o it provides a somewhat protected anchorage for small boats. Honouli Wai is located on Kamehameha V Highway.

Between Honouli Malo'o and Honouli Wai is a high rocky headland that is known as Pōhakuloa, the "long stone." When the shoreline road was constructed around the base of Pōhakuloa, the tip of the point was left standing *makai* of the road. It is commonly called Rocky Point and is a popular surfing area.

(31)
Murphy Beach Park

Murphy Beach Park is located in the land division of Moanui, "big chicken." The park was created as a community service project by the Moloka'i Jaycees, who wanted to provide Moloka'i with a public park on a sandy swimming beach. In 1970 the Jaycees named Ralph Kanemitsu and Greg Helm as co-chairmen of the project to clean up the former rubbish dump and erect the present facilities. The state assisted in the clean-up and the Jaycees spent $3,000 on materials. The park land is owned by Pu'u o Hoku Ranch. Permission to use the site as a park was given to the Jaycees immediately upon their request by George Murphy, the ranch owner. The park is officially named George Murphy Beach Park in recognition of Murphy's contribution to the island of Moloka'i. The park is also known to the local residents as Jaycees Park, for the men who created it. Another name that has occasionally been used for the area is Kūmimi Beach Park, which refers to a neighboring section of shoreline.

Murphy Beach Park is a small wayside park shaded by ironwood trees and fronted by a narrow white sand beach. It has three small pavilions with picnic tables and barbecue grills. The ocean bottom offshore is very rocky and shallow with scattered sand patches. It is a safe swimming area, especially for children, and a popular fishing grounds. Snorkeling and diving are good outside the reef, but only on calm days. The currents outside the reef can be very strong.

The land division of Moanui marks the beginning of the long, wide fringing reef that borders almost the entire length of Moloka'i's southern shore from the park to Kolo Wharf. This extremely shallow reach is said to have given rise to a saying, *"Moloka'i ko'o lā'au"* or "Moloka'i, polling with a stick," which alludes to the formerly common practice of using pole instead of paddles to propel the canoes.

In the early 1870s E. Baldwin established a sugar plantation at Moanui and erected a mill on the beach. The processed sugar was shipped in barrels out of Pauwalu Harbor, where schooners paid periodic visits. The plantation closed in the 1880s after fire destroyed the mill. The ruins of the mill are located along the highway near the beach park.

The shoreline from Moanui to Kaunakakai Wharf

KAMILOLOA. Kaloko'eli, a well-preserved precontact Hawaiian fishpond located in Kamiloloa, is typical of the numerous fishponds found along almost the entire length of Moloka'i's leeward coast. Creeping along the far end of the pond wall is a growth of mangrove, an introduced plant which has proliferated in the shoreline areas. The island of Lana'i is visible across Kalohi Channel.

contains most of the ancient Hawaiian fishponds along the coastline of Moloka'i. Between the fishponds are several narrow white sand beaches very similar to the one at Moanui, but the majority of the beaches in this area are composed of detrital sand. Shingle beaches are found occasionally at the small deltas fronting stream mouths. The bottom along this entire reach is shallow and rocky, often becoming a mudflat in the near shore areas. There are a number of natural channels through the wide reef that form harbors inshore. These inlets are used by many local boat owners. Other than at Murphy Beach Park, only three places along this long stretch of shoreline are accessible to the general public, Puko'o, Kakahai'a Beach Park, and Oneali'i Beach Park.

(32)
Pūko'o Beach

Pūko'o means "support hill," but the origin of the name is unknown. Inland in this district is the oldest and largest *heiau* on Moloka'i, 'Ili'ili'ōpae, located in Mapulehu Valley. The *heiau* site also marks the beginning of the Wailau Trail, the only access to Wailau Valley from the leeward side of the island. Pūko'o was once

the county seat of Moloka'i. In the early 1900s the village was the site of the courthouse and jail, a dairy, an ice and cold-storage plant, a bakery, the Maunakulawai Hotel, and the Hawaiian Sugar Planters Association quarantine station. A wharf at Pūko'o was used to land goods brought inshore by lighters. Larger vessels anchored outside the reef. None of these facilities is in use today.

Pūko'o Beach is a narrow detrital sand beach with a shallow and rocky offshore bottom. It is the only shoreline area with a public right-of-way between Murphy Beach Park and Kakahai'a Beach Park, a distance of nearly fifteen miles. The area is frequented primarily by fishermen. Pūko'o Harbor is a small pocket in the reef with a privately maintained landing. A narrow dirt road from Kamehameha V Highway leads to Pānāhāhā, a state-owned fishpond.

(33)
Kakahai'a Beach Park

Kakahai'a means "fish slicing" and is the name of an inland fishpond. In 1907 the pond's area was recorded as thirty-one acres and it was partially filled. Its area

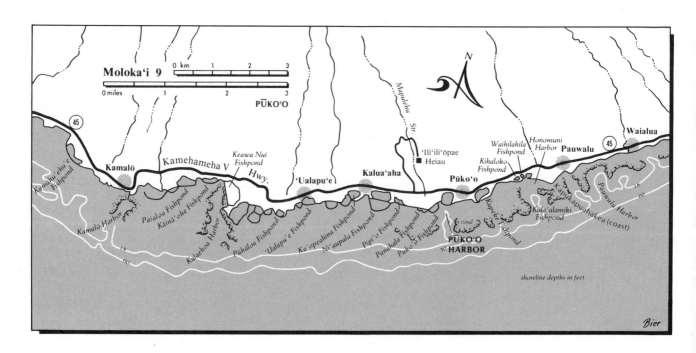

today is considerably less, and the pond is overgrown with bullrushes. This swampy area is commonly called Rice Patch for the food plant that was once grown there. Today Kakahai'a is one of the refuges in the Hawaiian Islands National Wildlife Complex. The forty-two-acre site offers a nesting and feeding area for native as well as migratory birds.

Kakahai'a Beach Park is a narrow, landscaped roadside park with several picnic tables. The beach is a narrow detrital sand beach with a very shallow and rocky offshore bottom. It is visited primarily by fishermen and picnickers. The only real danger in the area is from automobiles passing by on Kamehameha V Highway. Young children should be carefully watched, especially since there is only roadside parking.

(34)
Oneali'i Beach Park

Oneali'i means "royal sands" and is the name of an old Hawaiian fishpond located near the park. Oneali'i is also known as Ali'i fishpond. There are over fifty ancient fishponds in the reef shallows between Honouli Wai and Kolo. These ponds were probably used as hold-

ing and fattening pens for various types of fish, and provided not only a convenient source of food but status symbols for the chiefs who owned them as well. Today all of these old ponds are in various stages of disrepair or ruin. Most of them are filled with mud, a result of soil runoff from the mountains, and many of them are being choked by thick growths of mangrove trees.

In 1965 Oceanic Institute, based on O'ahu, leased Oneali'i (or Ali'i) and 'Ualapu'e fishponds as research centers for aquatic farming. The researchers expected that within five years they would be able to produce more mullet, clam, and shrimp per acre than any similar farm in the world. By 1972 the project had still not realized its goals and was abandoned because of the distressed finances of Oceanic Institute and its parent, Makai Foundation.

Oneali'i Beach Park was the first and only public beach park on Moloka'i for many years. The County of Maui purchased the original six acres from Moloka'i Ranch, Ltd., for $30,000 in 1959 and signed a lease with an option for an additional six acres. In 1963 the County Board of Supervisors exercised the option and acquired the additional park area. In 1964 banyan and

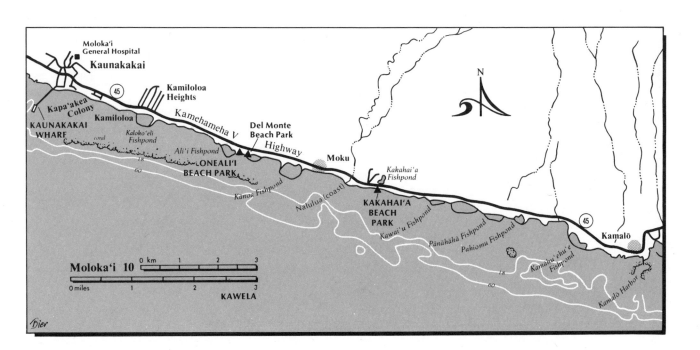

shower trees were removed from other areas and re-planted in the park. Coconut trees were brought in from the University Extension facility at Pūko'o. The fully grown plantings brought some shade and verdancy to the formerly barren park.

The beach fronting the park is a narrow white sand beach. The offshore bottom is very shallow out to the edge of the reef. The inshore areas are a mixture of sand, silt, and rocks, providing a swimming area generally attractive only to children. Facilities in the park include a pavilion, restrooms, and an unimproved parking lot. There are two stone monuments in the park, making the 75th and 100th anniversaries of the Japanese immigration to Hawai'i.

To the east of Oneali'i Beach Park is Del Monte Beach Park, a private park maintained by the Del Monte Corporation for its employees. The park and its facilities are also available to the public for group functions such as wedding receptions and similar events. A small utility fee is charged and reservations must be made in advance. The land is leased from Moloka'i Ranch, Ltd.

KAKAHAI'A BEACH PARK. The long reach of shoreline from the district of Waialua to the ruins of Kolo Wharf is bordered by narrow detrital sand beaches such as this one fronting Kakahai'a Beach Park. The inshore waters are shallow, rocky, and often murky, generally attracting only local fishermen. Good recreational swimming beaches are few and far between on Moloka'i.

Island of Lāna'i

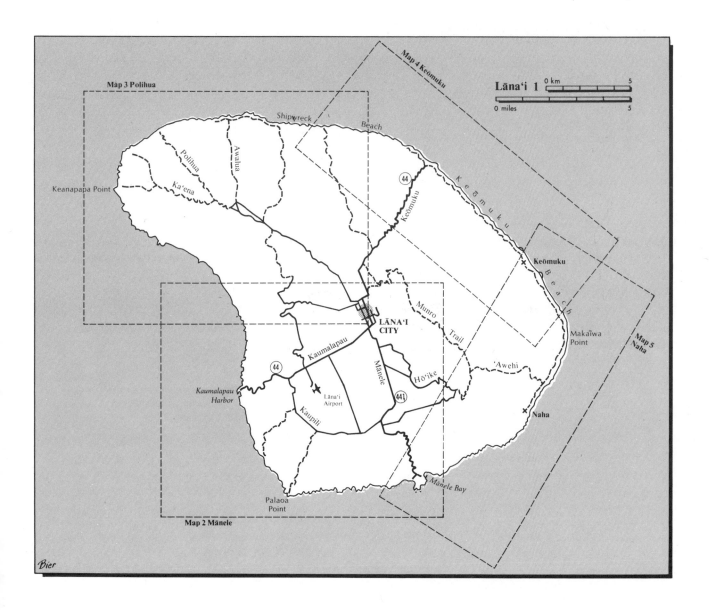

Bier

BEACHES OF LĀNA'I

BEACH & LOCATION	BEACH ACTIVITIES				PUBLIC FACILITIES			BEACH COMPOSITION			ACCESS	
	SWIMMING	SNORKELING	SURFING	BODY-SURFING	COMFORT STATION	PICNIC EQUIPMENT	PAVED PARKING	SAND	DETRITAL SAND	ROCK	PUBLIC	PRIVATE
1) MĀNELE BAY, MĀNELE	✓	✓			✓	✓				✓	✓	
2) PU'U PEHE COVE, MĀNELE	✓	✓						✓				✓
3) HULOPO'E BEACH PARK, HULOPO'E	✓	✓	✓	✓				✓				✓
4) KAUNOLŪ BAY, KAUNOLŪ									✓			✓
5) KAUMALAPAU HARBOR, KAUMALAPAU	✓								✓			✓
6) POLIHUA BEACH, POLIHUA	✓		✓	✓				✓				✓
7) SHIPWRECK BEACH, FROM POLIHUA TO KAHŌKŪNUI	✓	✓						✓				✓
8) KEŌMUKU BEACH, FROM KAHŌKŪNUI TO HALEPALAOA		✓							✓			✓
9) HALEPALAOA BEACH, HALEPALAOA	✓	✓						✓				✓
10) LŌPĀ BEACH, LŌPĀ	✓	✓	✓	✓				✓				✓
11) KAHEMANŌ BEACH, KAHEMANŌ		✓							✓			✓
12) NAHA BEACH, NAHA		✓							✓			✓

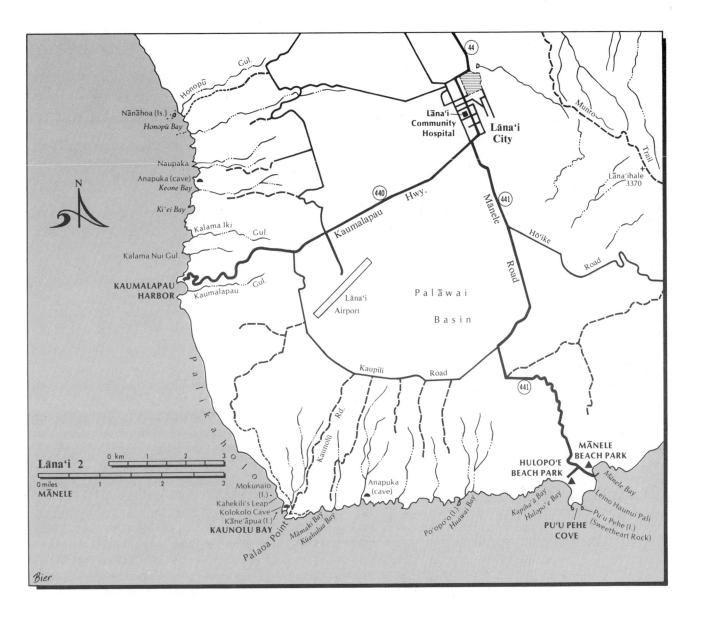

(1)
Mānele Bay

Eight miles below Lāna'i City is the ancient fishing village of Mānele. The village ruins begin in the *kiawe* forest directly inland of Mānele Small Boat Harbor and extend into adjoining Hulopo'e Beach Park, where they are most apparent in the designated camping area. The word *mānele* means "sedan chair," but how it came to be the name of the village is not known. The village was deserted by 1853, when Elder Francis A. Hammond organized a branch of the Mormon church there upon first landing on the island. A year later the small Mormon community reestablished themselves upland of the

105

MĀNELE BAY. Mānele Bay offers the only public boat harbor on the island of Lānaʻi. The harbor and its facilities are situated just *mauka* of this old cattle-loading ramp. When the ramp was in operation, a retractable wooden extension completed the connection from the structure on the rocks to the steamer anchored below.

shoreline in Pālāwai Basin. A permanent settlement was constructed and named Iosepa, for Joseph Smith, the founder of the faith. The settlers erected homes and a school to teach the Hawaiians the English language. Plagued with problems from the beginning, primarily lack of water and insects attacking the crops, the colony floundered and was abandoned by 1857. In 1861 Walter Murray Gibson arrived and repopulated the deserted Mormon colony at Pālāwai with another group of Mormon missionaries. Like their predecessors, however, Gibson and his colonists were beset by innumerable troubles. In addition, Gibson himself became a colorful and controversial figure. He was often involved in bitter conflicts with members of the Hawaiian government and members of the Hawaiian business community. Gibson also ran afoul of the Mormon church when he

refused to deed to them the Lānaʻi lands under his control. This refusal ultimately resulted in his excommunication in 1864. When he died in 1888, his property went to his daughter, Mrs. Talula Lucy Hayseldon.

In 1899, with the financial support of W. G. Irwin, Lucy and her husband, Frederick Hayseldon, attempted to grow sugar cane commercially as the Maunalei Sugar Company. The venture began in August 1899 and ended in March 1901. With the close of the plantation, the Hayseldons divested themselves of most of their interests on Lānaʻi. In 1902 Charles Gay began acquiring acreage on the island, and in 1904 he landed his family at Mānele Bay and began the task of upgrading the ranching operations started by Gibson. By 1909 Gay was forced, primarily by a long period of drought, to sell his lands. A group of local businessmen formed the

Lāna'i Company, Ltd., and purchased most of Gay's holdings. They decided to change the focus of the ranch from sheep to cattle. George Campbell Munro was brought in as ranch manager in 1911 and under his direction the ranch prospered. Cattle bound from the Honolulu markets were herded down to Vancouver Bay, as Hulopo'e was then commonly known, and forced to swim out to the ships anchored offshore. There they were hoisted aboard in a sling, completing a cattle-loading operation that was also performed at many other undeveloped island harbors. In 1917 Harry and Frank Baldwin purchased the island and formed the Lāna'i Ranch Company to concentrate on raising Hereford cattle.

In 1921 the Kahului Railroad Company was contracted under their direction to build a cattle-loading chute at Mānele Bay to facilitate the operation. The old wooden chute is still standing just beyond the present breakwater where it is anchored with concrete into the low sea cliffs. A secondary chute that rested inside the main one was extended and attached to the side of the ship to complete the shore-to-ship connection. From a holding pen on top of the hill, the cattle were herded down through the chutes and aboard ship. Just inland of the old cattle-loading chute are two large, shallow, adjoining concrete pans that upon casual inspection resemble the foundation of a building. These pans, also constructed under the direction of Lāna'i Ranch, were used to make sea salt. Water was pumped up from the ocean below and allowed to evaporate. The salt was scraped and bagged and used primarily for salt licks for the cattle.

In 1922 James Dole bought the island for the express purpose of growing pineapple. The ranching operations became secondary to pine, and Mānele Bay was superseded as a major landing with the completion of Kaumalapau Harbor in 1926. Mānele Bay then assumed the role of the primary anchorage on Lāna'i for pleasure craft, both fishing and sailing, a role it still maintains today.

In 1965 a small boat harbor was completed in the west corner of Mānele Bay, the first jointly constructed federal-state small boat harbor in Hawai'i. Artificial structures that make up the 4.6-acre harbor include navigational aids, berthing facilities for 60 small craft, a 570-foot rubblemound breakwater, and a launching ramp. Almost all trailered launches are made from this ramp, the only one on the island. *Mauka* of the harbor is an artificial silting basin that was built to inhibit sedimentation within the harbor caused by heavy rains. The 10-acre area of the harbor and the surrounding shoreline is administered by the State Division of Harbors. Harbor facilities include picnic tables and barbecue grills, restrooms and showers, and several large unmarked parking areas for automobiles and trailers.

Prior to construction of the harbor, a dark detrital sand beach existed at the head of Mānele Bay that was known as Black Sand Mānele Beach. The beach was eliminated almost entirely by the harbor construction. Within Mānele Bay there is one remaining sand beach, a tiny pocket of white sand in the east corner of the bay. The offshore bottom fronting it is shallow and rocky. The remaining shoreline is primarily shingle. Mānele Bay as a whole is not highly regarded as a recreational swimming area, but it is an excellent snorkeling, diving, and fishing grounds. All water enthusiasts, however, should be aware that in 1976 the Board of Land and Natural Resources established the Mānele-Hulopo'e Marine Life Conservation District to preserve, protect, and conserve the marine resources and geological features within the district. The only taking of fin fish and crustaceans now allowed in Mānele Bay (subzone B) is by legal methods except for spears, traps, and nets other than throw nets. Large signs with maps are posted throughout the conservation district, listing the restrictions and showing the boundaries.

Mānele Bay is generally calm and safe for various water activities, but swimmers and divers should always be alert to the boat traffic. Dangerous currents usually occur only during heavy *kona* weather when the swells are coming directly into the bay. The bay can be reached by following Mānele Road from Lāna'i City.

(2)
Pu'u Pehe Cove

Mānele Cone, a volcanic cinder and spatter cone, separates Mānele Bay from Hulopo'e Bay. The seaward edge of the cone has been extensively eroded by the ocean, creating a large cove that is lined with a white sand beach. Just offshore from the east point of the cove is a

MĀNELE-HULOPOʻE MARINE LIFE CONSERVATION DISTRICT. Tucked into the *makai* end of this rocky headland is a small pocket of white sand called Puʻu Pehe Cove. The waters offshore from the cove are excellent for snorkeling and are part of the Mānele-Hulopoʻe Marine Life Conservation District. The conservation district also includes Hulopoʻe Beach, the long stretch of white sand beyond the cove, and Mānele Bay, located on the opposite side of the headland.

sea stack that was also sculptured by the ocean. This little rock island was once part of the mainland but has been separated from it by the erosive action of the waves. The cove takes its name from that of the sea stack, Puʻu Pehe. One translation of Puʻu Pehe is "owl trap hill," the explanation being that a platform of stones located on top of the rock was once a shrine for bird hunters. In 1921 Dr. Kenneth Emory, of the Bishop Museum in Honolulu, Hector Munro, and another Lānaʻi resident scaled Puʻu Pehe to examine the rock platform in question. Their examination revealed nothing to refute or confirm the theory of the shrine's usage as reflected in the name "owl trap hill." Another interpretation is simply that Puʻu Pehe is a proper name. The sea stack is more popularly known as Sweetheart Rock or Sweetheart Island, names that have their origin in a Hawaiian legend. Puʻu Pehe, a beautiful girl from Maui, was captured by a young warrior from Lānaʻi. He brought her home and made her his wife, but he feared he would lose her, so he kept her hidden in a sea cave. One day when he had gone to a *mauka* spring to get fresh water, a tremendous *kona* storm arose and the huge waves that ensued devastated the cave, killing Puʻu Pehe. The young warrior retrieved her body and carried it to the top of the rock island for burial. Then he took his own life by jumping into the sea below. This story, which accounts for the English and Hawaiian names, has a number of variations.

Puʻu Pehe Cove is also known as Sharks Bay or Sharks Cove. Some shoreline fishermen say this name originated in times past when sharks were frequently spotted cruising through the cove's waters, although they are not commonly seen there today. Pu'u Pehe Cove is an excellent area for swimming and snorkeling. The water is usually very clear and contains an abundance of marine life. Adverse water conditions occur only during *kona* storms or strong southerly swells, both of which will bring surf and create hazardous currents inshore. Pu'u Pehe Cove is part of the Mānele-Hulopo'e Marine Life Conservation District, so all divers and fishermen should be aware of the restrictions and restricted areas. Informational signs are posted in conspicuous places throughout the district.

One danger in the area that may not be apparent to the average beachgoer is not in the ocean, but on the lava terrace that goes out the left point of the cove. The sea cliffs above the terrace are composed of very loosely packed volcanic material. This cinder stone often breaks away and falls, as evidenced by the numerous heaps of rock slides and large boulders on the terrace below. Anyone who walks in this area should be aware of this everpresent danger. Pu'u Pehe Cove is most easily reached by following the shoreline from the east side of Hulopo'e Beach.

(3)
Hulopo'e Beach Park

The origin and meaning of the name Hulopo'e remain obscure to this day. One possibility is that Hulopo'e was the name of a man who lived in this area of the shoreline, where he performed fishing rites. Another suggestion is that Hulopo'e, which has no meaning, is a variation of *huelopō'ai,* "swirling tail." The name Huelopō'ai is said to be descriptive of the currents in the bay when the ocean is rough. Some residents even refer to the west side of the bay as the "Toilet Bowl" because of this meeting-and-circling action.

In 1921 Dr. Kenneth Emory of the Bishop Museum made an archaeological survey of Lāna'i which recorded not only ancient Hawaiian sites but Hawaiian place names as well. It was during his residency on the island that the name Hulopo'e was reintroduced. Prior to Emory's work, the bay was commonly known as Vancouver Bay. Captain George Vancouver explored the Hawaiian Islands extensively and sailed around Lāna'i in March 1792. However, as he did not land anywhere on the island, the origin of that name is still somewhat of a mystery.

The most common contemporary name for Hulopo'e is White Sand Mānele Beach. Before the Mānele Small Boat Harbor was constructed, there was a dark detrital sand beach in Mānele Bay that was known as Black Sand Mānele Beach. Hulopo'e, or Vancouver Bay, received its corresponding name simply by virtue of proximity and color comparison.

In 1961 the Kō'ele Company of Lāna'i, the managers of the land surrounding the beach, installed some facilities and created a private beach park. They named it Hulopo'e Beach Park, once again reintroducing the Hawaiian name of the area. All of the beach facilities, which include picnic tables, barbecue pits, showers, and restrooms, are located on property owned by Castle and Cooke, Inc. Use of these facilities by the public, as well as by commercial charter boat cruise companies, is strictly regulated by permits which are frequently checked by a privately employed warden. With the exception of the harbor facilities at Mānele Bay, Hulopo'e Beach Park is the only beach on Lāna'i with restrooms and showers. For a variety of reasons it is also the most popular picnic site on the island, and it has the best swimming beach. Commerical cruises are allowed use of the facilities only on weekdays during specified daylight hours.

Hulopo'e Beach is a long, wide crescent of white sand bordered on either end by boulders lying against lava points. The foreshore is usually moderately steep, a result of the swells that come into the bay. The surf is occasionally good enough for bodysurfing and board surfing. The offshore bottom slopes quickly to overhead depths—a danger to little children and nonswimmers, especially if there are sizable waves in the shorebreak that could knock them off their feet. Small rip currents sometimes form, but they generally terminate a short distance offshore and are of minor concern to a strong swimmer. Dangerous water conditions, however, may be created by severe *kona* storms or by heavy south swells.

On calm days the bay is excellent for snorkeling. Divers and fishermen should be aware that Hulopo'e Bay is part of the Mānele-Hulopo'e Marine Life Conservation

HULOPO‘E BEACH PARK. A father and son share a peaceful moment at otherwise deserted Hulopo‘e Beach Park. This large tidal pool was blasted out of the rocky shoreline in 1951 by Lāna‘i residents to create a safe swimming pool for little children. The boats anchored offshore from the beach date the picture before September of 1979, when a law was enacted prohibiting any vessel from anchoring in the Mānele-Hulopo‘e Marine Life Conservation District.

District (subzone A). Fishing for fin fishes and crustaceans is permitted by hook and line from the shoreline only. Large signs with maps giving the restrictions and showing the boundaries are conspicuously posted throughout the district. Other signs, also posted in the park, note that "the beach park land above the upper reaches of the waves evidenced by the vegetation line is private property owned by Castle and Cooke, Inc. for the benefit of the owner, and Lāna‘i residents and their guests. No commercial tours, operations, or activities are allowed on this private property without the consent of the owner."

The east point of Hulope‘e Bay is actually a wide lava terrace that harbors several small inlets and large tidal pools, all of which contain an abundance of marine life. Also on the terrace is a small wading pool for children, with concrete steps leading down to it from the dirt road above. The pool was excavated in 1951 during a six-month strike by plantation workers. It was constructed in a joint effort by both the members of the union and the plantation management.

Hulopo‘e is the most popular picnicking and swimming beach on Lāna‘i. It was also a well-used anchorage until September 1979, when an amendment governing boating in the Mānele-Hulopo'e Marine Life Conservation District came into effect. The amendment prohibits operating, anchoring, or mooring any vessel within the boundaries of subzone A (Hulopo'e Bay), except for persons with a permit or those engaged in law enforcement, rescue, or other emergency operations. During the winter months these waters are occasionally visited by whales and schools of porpoises. Inshore in the *kiawe* forests to the rear of the beach park is also an abundance of animal life, primarily birds. Commonly seen are turkeys, quail, Francolins, chukkar, and pheasants. These ground-nesting birds thrive on Lāna'i only because there are no mongooses on the island.

(4)
Kaunolū Bay

Kaunolū is the site of an ancient fishing village whose ruins are among the best preserved of any in Hawai'i. There are numerous house sites, stone shelters, animal pens, graves, fishing shrines, and *heiau*. The village obtained its fresh water from a well located in a gulch about 250 feet inland from the ocean. This well was reportedly destroyed in 1895 by someone who was trying to improve it.

Kaunolū was one of the favorite fishing spots of King Kamehameha I. The offshore waters provided good trolling grounds for *aku* and still do to this day. In 1868 King Kamehameha V also visited his grandfather's famous fishing resort. During his stay he is reported to have ordered hidden a stone image of Kū'ula, the god of Hawaiian fishermen. In the years following, the area continued to be visited by fishermen, but the village itself was abandoned. Today the Kaunolū Village Site, still a popular fishing area, is a registered National Historic Landmark. A plaque set in a stone in the village notes this information and is dated 1963. The only other contemporary addition to the village besides the plaque is Palaoa Point light, a navigational aid located on the edge of a cliff about ninety feet above sea level.

The shoreline at Kaunolū is made up primarily of sea cliffs interspersed with occasional boulder beaches. It is typical of the reach of shoreline from Hulopo'e Beach Park to Polihua Beach. There are no sand beaches along this coast, although there are offshore deposits of white sand in several areas.

To the north of Kaunolū is Pali Kaholo, the highest sea cliff on Lāna'i's shoreline, rising over one thousand feet above sea level. Pali Kaholo is of interest not only because of its height but because it is located on the southwest side of the island. Usually sea cliffs in Hawai'i are much higher on the northern side of the islands, where the prevailing wind and waves maintain a constant erosive assault. Lāna'i is an exception because Moloka'i and West Maui shield her northern side, leaving only her southerly shores exposed to severe storms.

The road to Kaunolū from the edge of the pineapple fields is strictly for vehicles with four-wheel drive. A sign marks the *makai* turnoff.

(5)
Kaumalapau Harbor

In 1922 James Dole, the founder of the Hawaiian Pineapple Company, paid Harry and Frank Baldwin $1,100,000 for most of the island of Lāna'i. Dole's express reason for the purchase was to turn the island into the world's largest pineapple plantation. Once the land was secured and the pine operations were underway, Dole turned his attention to constructing a harbor, a necessity for shipping pineapples by barge to the cannery in Honolulu. Kaumalapau, located directly below the newly laid out Lāna'i City, was the selected site. The old name Kaumālapa'u means "soot (from burning) placed (in) gardens."

Hawaiian Dredging began blasting the first of the 116,000 tons of rock that eventually came out of the sea cliffs adjoining Kaumalapau Gulch. The wharf area, formerly a series of small shelves of reef, was formed by using boulders as fill. A small section of railroad tracks was layed out from the gulch to the wharf to transport the fill material. Piles were driven at random as they were needed. In 1926 Kaumalapau Harbor was completed and included a 400-foot-long concrete wharf, a 250-foot-long breakwater on the right side of the harbor entrance, and a large harbor basin with a minimum depth of 30 feet. The harbor is Lāna'i's only interisland shipping terminal and is still in use today as a shipping point for the island's pineapple. The fruit is crated in upland fields and then trucked to the harbor, where it is loaded aboard the barges and towed to Honolulu.

When commercial shipping operations are not in

progress at Kaumalapau, the wharf becomes a popular shoreline fishing spot. The water in the harbor, which is almost invariably crystal clear, also occasionally attracts a few swimmers. Various privately owned fishing craft are moored inshore of the working area within the harbor. Adverse water conditions occur infrequently, usually during westerly or *kona* weather. Even the devastating tsunami that struck the Hawaiian Islands on April 1, 1946, was of no consequence. The rise and fall of the ocean was so gentle that the pineapple loading operations continued uninterrupted. The harbor is located at the bottom of Kaumalapau Highway.

Two and a half miles away from Kaumalapau Harbor is a well-known coastal feature of Lāna'i, Nānāhoa, a cluster of five sea stacks. These rocks are remnants either of the collapse of a sea arch or simply of erosion of the main island by the ocean. One of the stacks is tucked well into the shoreline and is not immediately obvious. Two of the offshore stacks stand side-by-side on the same rock island, so from a distance there appear to be only three sea stacks, grouped together, giving rise to their popular local name, Three Stone. Also known as the Needles, the pinnacles are among the best examples of sea stack rocks in Hawai'i. Their Hawaiian name, Nānāhoa, is the name of a legendary man who was a symbol of sexuality. The outer rock is said to be female while the inner three are male.

The access road begins at the edge of the pineapple fields where the turnoff is marked with a sign. The *makai* road, strictly for vehicles with four-wheel drive, stops half-way down the slope. A foot trails decends the rest of the distance to the boulder beach and sea cliffs inshore of Nānāhoa. The area is visited almost exclusively by shoreline or boat fishermen.

(6)
Polihua Beach

Polihua literally means "eggs (in the) bosom" and is perhaps a poetic way of expressing "egg nest." Polihua was once one of the most famous green sea turtle nesting beaches in Hawai'i, and its name reflects this distinction. Green sea turtles, *honu,* are the most abundant of the two species of marine turtles native to Hawai'i. Their common name comes from the color of the fat found inside their bodies. The *honu* nest on sandy beaches, the females coming ashore at night to bury their eggs several times during the breeding season from mid-May to August. The other turtle native to Hawai'i is the hawksbill, *'ea,* which is easily recognized by its hawklike beak. The fame of the turtles of Polihua is noted in the following lines of an old chant:

Ua ono 'o Pele i kana i'a	Pele enjoys eating her meat
O ka honu o Polihua	From the turtles of Polihua

Another reference to Polihua appeared in the Hawaiian newspaper *Ka Nūpepa Kū'oko'a* in 1902. The fishing-lore writer Kahaulelio noted that the Hawaiians formerly visited the beach to catch turtles if they needed meat. During the summer when the turtles came ashore at night in large numbers, they layed their eggs in the sand above the high water mark. At these times they could be easily caught, because of their sluggishness on land. One of the last known nestings of green sea turtles at Polihua was in 1954. Today the turtles are considered an endangered species and are protected by law. A ban on the taking of all sea turtles has been in effect since July 1978, when the green sea turtle was placed on the list of threatened species under provisions of the Endangered Species Act. The only exceptions are in the Trust Territory of the Pacific, where limited taking of turtles is permitted for subsistence and under special permit for scientific, zoological, and educational purposes. All turtle products that are available commercially come primarily from out-of-state commercial turtle farms. Besides being noted for its turtles, Polihua is also known as a good place to watch whales. They often pass by very close to shore.

Polihua Beach, over a mile and a half long, is the longest and widest white sand beach on Lāna'i. It looks directly across Kalohi Channel at Moloka'i, providing an excellent view of the entire length of the island. On a clear day O'ahu can also be seen past Lā'au Point on West Moloka'i. For all of its beauty, Polihua is not frequently visited. During most of the year the trade winds blow across the beach with such intensity that they create stinging sand storms. Anyone standing out in the open is literally sand-blasted. The beach is tolerable only during mild *kona* weather or on a windless day. Another detracting factor at Polihua is its dangerous currents. The foreshore is usually steep and the sandy

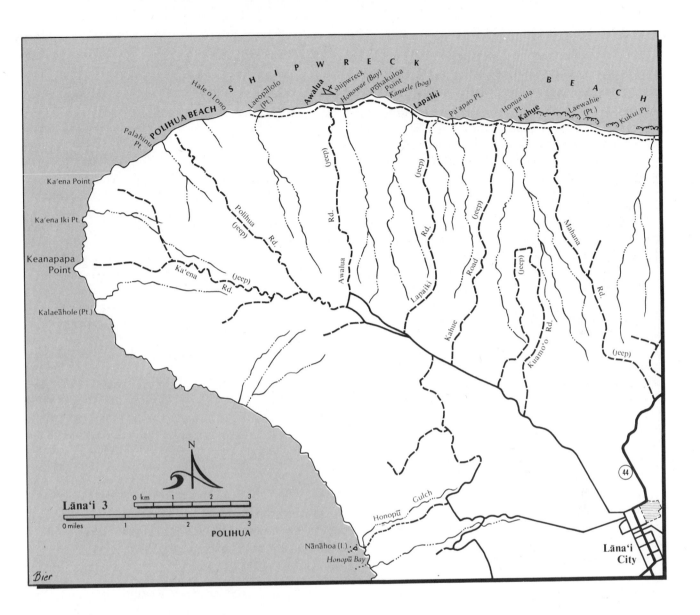

Lāna'i 3

POLIHUA

Bier

bottom drops sharply to overhead depths. The entire beach is completely exposed to the open ocean, with no protective reef or rocky points. The prevailing current which runs from east to west is always strong and will pick up any swimmer in its path. Even during relatively calm *kona* weather there is a powerful alongshore current usually running in the opposite direction. Polihua Beach is not safe for swimming at any time of the year.

The beach is subject to seasonal changes. During the late fall the sand shifts to the east end of the beach and by winter it often reaches widths of over 350 feet. The reverse occurs during the summer, when the sand shifts to the west end. The steep foreshore is a result of the strong currents and heavy surf that often hit the beach. The debris line often reaches to the middle of the beach or even higher as the waves wash up and inland. The

113

POLIHUA BEACH. A young early morning explorer wanders along the water's edge on the largest white sand beach on the island of Lāna'i. This remote beach can be reached on land only by using a vehicle equipped with four-wheel drive. The mountains of East Moloka'i are visible across Kalohi Channel.

access road down to Polihua from the edge of the pineapple fields is marked by a sign. The road is passable only for a vehicle with four-wheel drive.

One mile along the low sea cliffs to the west of Polihua is Ka'ena Point, once an exit colony for women who had committed adultery or theft. The first women were sent to this remote prison camp probably about 1830. After being convicted and sentenced in Lahaina, they were taken by schooner to Ka'ena. There they were left to eke out whatever existence they could in this barren, desolate region. One well at least provided fresh water. By 1850 the exiling practice had been discontinued and the colony was abandoned. The Ka'ena area is also important because of its many archaeological sites, including the largest *heiau* on Lāna'i, at Ka'enaiki. The area can be reached in a four-wheel drive vehicle by following an access road that begins near the top of Polihua Road. The turnoff is marked with a sign.

(7)
Shipwreck Beach

Shipwreck Beach is a name that encompasses the eight miles of shoreline stretching from Polihua Beach to Kahokunui. This long stretch of beach is littered with a vast array of flotsam and jetsam, although driftwood comprises the bulk of the material left onshore. The two most treasured finds for beachcombers are the hand-blown glass balls used by Japanese fishermen as floats and the rare pelagic paper nautilus shells.

The shipwrecks that gave this northern Lāna'i coast-

114

line its popular name have been numerous. Two of the earliest recorded groundings were of the British ship *Alderman Wood* and the American ship *London* in the 1820s. Many more followed, including the *Helene,* a four-masted schooner, the *Charlotte C,* a 45-foot yawl, and the *Tradewind,* a 34-foot auxiliary. During World War II three 60-foot navy Landing Craft Mediums (LCMs) ran aground on the reef and were abandoned. Unintentional shipwrecks such as these, however, have constituted only a portion of the total number of wrecks. Many of them have been deliberate. In former years old vessels that were no longer useful were either run aground or towed offshore and allowed to drift onto the shallow reef. Such deliberate wreckings included wooden steamers from the former Inter-island Steam Navigation Company, old pineapple barges, and assorted pleasure craft.

The beach served as an isolated disposal site for the unwanted relics and allowed their destruction by the ocean without posing any hazard to navigation. The name Shipwreck Beach was a natural outcome of all this activity. Most of the local residents who frequent the beach, however, particularly the shoreline fishermen, do not use the name Shipwreck Beach. They call the various sections of the eight-mile shoreline by more specific local names, primarily the major Hawaiian shoreline names. The best-known areas are Awalua, Lapaiki, Kahue, Yamada, Pō'aīwa, and Federation Camp.

Shipwreck Beach, the shoreline from Polihua Beach to Kahokunui, consists of numerous stretches of narrow white sand beach alternating with points of beach rock backed by low sand dunes. The rocky offshore bottom is shallow in most places, sloping gently to the outer reef. There are occasional channels through the reef, affording shallow-draft boats access to the beaches. The currents inside the reef are usually insignificant, but during most of the year the inshore waters are murky, choppy, and cold as a result of prevailing winds, precluding snorkeling or diving. Mud and gravel are frequently washed into the ocean by heavy rains, but the water is clear on windless days or during *kona* weather. The primary activities at Shipwreck Beach are beachcombing and shoreline fishing. Walking the beach is easy, but one feature may present a problem to some people. Scattered along the entire length of Shipwreck

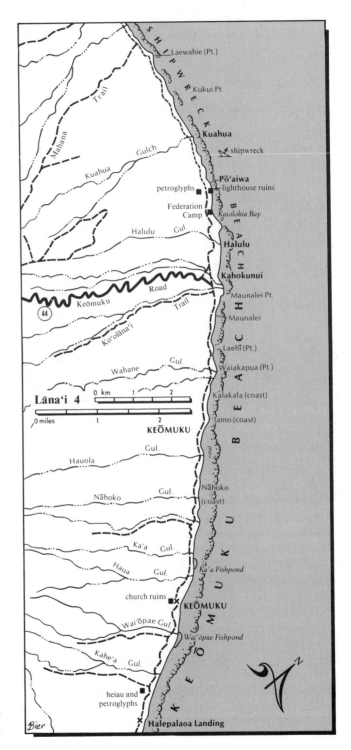

115

SHIPWRECK BEACH. One of the two shipwrecks still visible at Shipwreck Beach sits on the shallow reef bordering Awahua Harbor. Awahua Harbor, the large, deep section of calm water between the log and the beached ship, was formerly an important landing site on the island.

Beach are many freshwater seeps, especially in the rocky areas. These places are often marked by *limu 'ele'ele,* a seaweed that grows only where fresh and salt water mix, by occasional bird and animal tracks in the surrounding sand, and also by hundreds of bees and wasps foraging for a drink of water. Anyone allergic to insect stings should be alert to these seeps, especially on calm, windless days when access to them is easier for the insects.

Awalua, one large section of Shipwreck Beach, means "double channel." It was one of the major boat landings on Lāna'i, along with Halepalaoa and Mānele. Today it is probably best known as the site of one of the two wrecks still visible on Shipwreck Beach. Early in the 1950s a shipyard oil tanker was presumably under tow from the mainland to Japan when it broke loose and

went aground at Awalua. The exact circumstances surrounding its sudden appearance are still somewhat of a mystery. The wreck is located directly offshore from the *makai* end of Awalua Road.

Another major section of Shipwreck Beach is Lapaiki, "small ridge." A small, crudely built fisherman's shack and storage shed at the end of Lapaiki Road are easily recognizable features of the area. Midway between Awalua and Lapaiki is Pōhakuloa Point, which is marked by a navigational light. The point is so low and rounded that it is difficult to recognize it as the northern extremity of Lāna'i.

Kahue, "the gourd," is another large shoreline area. Located at the *makai* end of Kahue Road, its most outstanding feature is Lae Wahie, "firewood point." Lae

116

Wahie, the widest and most prominent rock point on the shoreline of Shipwreck Beach, is better known to Lāna'i residents as Yamada. Yasukichi Yamada, for whom the point is named, ran a fish market in Kahuku on O'ahu during the 1920s, but moved to Lāna'i about 1929 to work in the plantation's butcher shop. He started selling fish there about the same time. Yamada used to travel on muleback to Lae Wahie, where he had a fishing shack, and transported his catches back to Lāna'i City the same way. In 1945 he left Lāna'i for Maui and ran the restaurant in the Kahului Hotel. In 1947 Yamada opened his own restaurant, the No Ka 'Oi Inn, which is still in operation.

Shipwreck Beach is most easily accessible from the road leading to Pō'aiwa. When the Keōmuku Road comes down from Lāna'i City and reaches the shoreline, the pavement ends and the unpaved road branches left and right. The right branch, the main road, continues on to Keōmuku and finally ends at Naha. The left branch passes through Federation Camp and ends at Pō'aiwa. Pō'aiwa, the "ninth night," is the site of a former lighthouse as well as of some Hawaiian petroglyphs. A short walk along the beach beyond the end of the road leads to the second of the two wrecks aground on Shipwreck Beach, a concrete mud barge. The story of the appearance of this wreck in 1960 is also obscured by cloudy circumstances.

Federation Camp is located on Kaiolohia, "tranquil sea," a beautiful little bay with a crescent of white sand. The camp takes its name from the Filipino Federation of America, a religious, cultural, and social organization founded by Hilario Camino Moncado on December 25, 1925. After Moncado's death in 1956, the Lāna'i Federation, like the Federation branches on the mainland and in Honolulu, split into two groups. The main group built their camp at Kaiolohia during this period. The Lāna'i Company had made the land available on a leased basis several years earlier. The camp is still used today by Federation members.

The white sand of Shipwreck Beach ends at Kahokunui. From Kahokunui to Halepalaoa the shoreline is made up of dark detrital sand beaches. Pō'aiwa, Federation Camp, and Kahokunui are all accessible in an ordinary vehicle, but the Awalua, Lapaiki, and Kahue roads are only for vehicles with four-wheel drive.

Keōmuku Beach

Keōmuku Beach is a name that encompasses the six miles of shoreline stretching from Kahokunui, a small cluster of beach homes near the bottom of the Keōmuku Road, to Halepalaoa, the site of an old landing just beyond the village of Keōmuku. The geographical features of this entire reach are almost unchanging. The shoreline consists of a long series of narrow black detrital sand beaches between low points of shingle and cobblestone. Offshore is a portion of one of the longest stretches of fringing reef in Hawai'i, which is more than a half mile wide in several places. The ocean bottom between the beaches and the outer edges of the reef is primarily shallow and rocky with a few scattered pockets of white sand. The water is usually murky, choppy, and cold, because of the strong prevailing trade winds. All these factors tend to discourage most swimmers and snorkelers. The area is frequented primarily by fishermen, beachcombers, and a variety of shoreline seabirds such as the *'akekeke,* the *hunakai,* the *kōlea,* and occasionally the *kioea.* The beach to the north of Lae Hī at Kahokunui is used as a mooring site for small shallow-draft boats. Keōmuku Beach is separated along its entire length from Keōmuku Road by shoreline vegetation, primarily *kiawe.* There are numerous access roads from the main road to the beach.

There are three well-known landmarks along the beach. The first is Lae Hī, commonly called White Rock, a wide limestone ridge that extends *mauka* from the beach and forms a large hill over which the Keōmuku Road passes. Lae Hī means either "casting (for fish) point" or "flowing point." It is an important location in the most famous legend of Lāna'i, the story of Ka'ulalā'au. Ka'ulalā'au was the mischievous son of Kaka'alaneo, a former chief of Maui. As the boy grew older his penchant for playing pranks grew progressively worse until finally his weary parents, partly pressured by the people of Lahaina, took him to Lāna'i, where he was abandoned. Lāna'i at that time was inhabited only by ghosts who killed all human intruders. Guided by his guardian sprit, however, Ka'ulalā'au found a cave in which he secretly slept at night while the ghosts hunted for him. Eventually he managed to rid the entire island of all its evil spirits, making Lāna'i for the first time safe for human habitation. The cave in which Ka'ululā'au found shelter and safety was located at Lae Hī.

The other well-known landmarks on Keōmuku Beach are the ruins of the two ancient fishponds of Ka'a and Wai'ōpae, located at the water's edge on either side of Keōmuku village. Apart from their location, little is known about these two fishponds. They cannot be seen from the main road and are visible only at low tide from the beach.

Near Lae Hī, the Keōmuku Road passes through Maunalei, a small cluster of beach homes situated near the shoreline of Maunalei Gulch. In his book *Stories of Lanai* Lawrence Gay relates that Maunalei was the only place on the island where wetland taro was grown. The stream then had plenty of water to irrigate the taro patches and flowed into the ocean continuously throughout the year, except during times of severe drought. By 1900, however, the taro operations in Maunalei had been completely abandoned. The vegetation along the face of the cliffs above the patches had by that time been totally destroyed by the thousands of wild goats and sheep running rampant on Lāna'i. Landslides and falling boulders loosened by the ensuing erosion ruined the patches below and made cultivation in the gulch much too dangerous. The Maunalei water supply was eventually tapped and pumped upland to Kō'ele and later to Lāna'i City when it was constructed in the 1920s. Today Maunalei continues to serve as the primary source of fresh water for Lāna'i. Lawrence Gay also supplies an interesting explanation of the meaning of Maunalei, "*lei* mountain." He writes that at certain

KEŌMUKU BEACH. On the shoreline on either side of Keōmuku Village are the remains of two of Lāna'i's four precontact Hawaiian fishponds. Visible in this aerial photograph is Wai'ō-pae, the larger of the two. The pond walls are discernible only at low tide.

118

times of the year clouds drifting in from the ocean seem to form a white *lei* that stretches across the summit of the island. This phenomenon is best observed from a vantage point some distance from the island.

Midway between Maunalei and Keōmuku is the deepest gulch on the island, Hauola Gulch, more than two thousand feet deep. Although the origin of the name Hauola, "dew (of) life," is now unknown, it is interesting to note that dew was formerly an important source of water. In *The Island of Lanai* Kenneth Emory notes that before the destruction of vegetation on the plateau lands by the introduction of grazing animals, dew was collected from thick shrubbery by whipping the moisture into large bowls or squeezing the dripping brush tops into the vessels. Oiled *tapa* was also spread on the ground to collect the dew.

The village of Keōmuku is the focal point of one of the most easily accessible historical areas on Lāna'i. Keōmuku has been variously translated as "the shortened sand" (the *o* being an abbreviated form of "one" or "sand"), "the digging stick," "the stretch of white," and finally as "the spars (of a) ship" from the alternate pronunciation and spelling, Keomoku. Keomoku was a small, unpretentious fishing village until the summer of 1899, when a major change occurred. Talula and Frederick Hayseldon decided to try to grow sugar cane on Lāna'i and selected Keōmuku as their plantation site. By August 1899 sugar-cane-growing operations were well underway. Over five hundred laborers, primarily Japanese, were brought in to work in the fields. In addition to the living quarters and other buildings that were erected, a pier was constructed at Halepalaoa, the only major landing in the area. A railroad was laid out from Keōmuku to the landing to transport the harvested sugar cane overland. The cane was then shipped to Olowalu on Maui, where it was milled. The venture was proceeding smoothly until the plague of 1900, which began in Honolulu, reached the outer islands. The Lāna'i plantation's work force was hit hard. Disaster followed disaster when the fresh water sources for irrigating the fields turned brackish. The Maunalei Sugar Company folded by March 1901.

Today Keōmuku is deserted. With only a few scattered wooden houses still standing, the main building to be seen is Ka Lanakila o Ka Mālamalama Church, completed in 1903 and located in the midst of the extensive

KEŌMUKU VILLAGE. Ka Lanakila o Ka Mālamalama Church was built in 1903 in the now deserted village of Keōmuku. The village flourished only from 1899 to 1901, when an attempt was made to establish a sugar plantation in the area. Today the church is the last structure still standing intact and is surrounded by a large coconut grove bordering both sides of Keōmuku Road.

coconut grove. Directly *makai* of the church are the decaying remains of three large whaleboats that formerly operated out of Keōmuku. Their location marks the shoreline of the ocean in 1935, when they were abandoned. Since then an almost unbelievable five hundred feet of new shore has been created by soil runoff from the mountains.

(9)
Halepalaoa Beach

Halepalaoa, also commonly called Kahalepalaoa, means either "whale house" or "whale ivory house," but how the name came to be applied to this area is now unknown. Halepalaoa is best known as the site of a former landing that was built to service the Maunalei Sugar Plantation. On the shoreline a few of the old rock-and-concrete pilings are still visible. Just inshore of them in the *kiawe* are the ruins of a wooden warehouse built with the pier. Also in the underbrush are the remains of an old boiler and the metal frames of several railroad handcarts. The carts were used to transport sugar cane and supplies to and from the end of the pier. *Mauka* of the landing, across the road, a short trail leads to an old abandoned locomotive with its tender that was used to haul cane from the Keōmuku fields to Halepalaoa. The locomotive first belonged to the Hawaiian Commercial and Sugar Company on Maui and arrived on that island in 1883. It was shipped to Lāna'i in 1899 and then abandoned in 1901. Its name may have been the Waiāhole.

A short distance farther down the road toward Naha is another reminder of the former sugar venture, a large stone monument with an inscription in Japanese. It is a memorial to the many Japanese plantation workers who died at Keōmuku during the plague of 1900. The Buddhist community of Lāna'i holds commemorative services there once a year.

The site of the Halepalaoa Landing is the dividing point on the shoreline between the dark detrital sand beach of Keōmuku and the white sand beach of Halepalaoa. About a mile long, Halepalaoa Beach winds around and beyond Makaīwa Point. It is one of the nicest beaches on the northeastern side of the island. To the rear of the south half of the beach are sand dunes covered with *kiawe* and lantana. The beach ends at Kikoa Point where the ocean has eroded these dunes, undermining the *kiawe* trees and exposing beach rock. The fallen trees block easy passage along the shoreline.

Halepalaoa Beach provides fair swimming, mostly at high tide. There are scattered pockets of sand in the primarily shallow and rocky bottom. Swimming is safe inside the reef, but the water is often murky. The area is frequented by fishermen. The most convenient access to

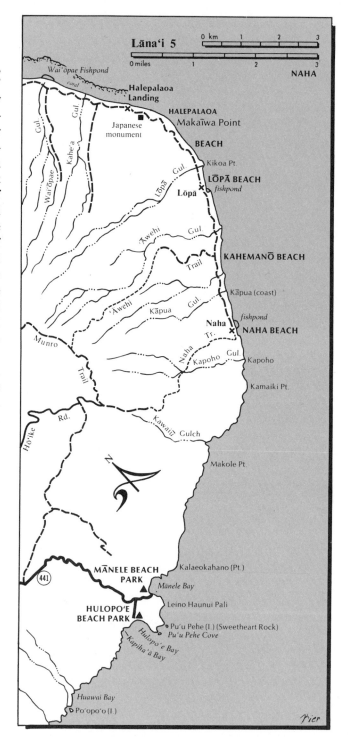

the beach is the short trail to the old Halepalaoa Landing. Except for the private estate to the south of the landing, the entire backshore of Halepalaoa Beach toward Naha is a dense entanglement of *kiawe* and lantana with only a few narrow animal trails leading from Keōmuku Road to the shoreline. A jeep trail goes out to Kikoa Point at the end of the beach.

(10)
Lōpā Beach

Lōpā means "tenant farmer," but the origin of the name as applied to this former village site is now unknown. The name is also pronounced and spelled Lopaʻa, as on Brown and Monsarrat's 1878 government survey map of Lānaʻi. The most outstanding feature at Lōpā is its fishpond, sometimes called Loko Lōpā. In *The Island of Lanai*, the results of an archaeological survey carried out in 1920–1921, Kenneth Emory offers this information:

> Fish ponds or traps are found only on the east coast where the fringing reef is far from shore. I have seen only one true fishpond. The west point of Lōpā beach has been bridged to the shore by a sea wall 217 feet long forming a fishpond above sea level but fed by the wash of waves at high tide and by the seepage of brackish water.

LŌPĀ BEACH. Small surf breaks on the shallow reef fronting the rocky point at Lōpā. The two low concrete rock walls in the foreground are the crumbling remains of the *mākāhā* or sluice gate that once connected Lōpā fishpond with the ocean. The pond has been designated as a bird sanctuary to accommodate some of the many shoreline birds that frequent the beaches from Polihua to Naha.

Today the pond is part of a private estate but can easily be seen from the beach. The area is marked by a small cluster of coconut trees. The long wall described by Emory has been buried by drifting sand that has formed additional beach around the point. However, portions of the *mākāhā,* the sluice gate, are visible near the ocean. The pond itself is completely overrun by mangrove.

Lōpā Beach is a fairly long white sand beach that begins on the south side of Kikoa Point and ends just past the old fishpond. The offshore bottom is rocky and very shallow even at high tide. Swimming is safe for everyone, but probably more suitable for children than for adults. The long, wide fringing reef offshore from Keōmuku Beach begins to narrow at Lōpā, so that the distance from the beach to the outer edges of the reef is considerably reduced. Occasionally the waves are good enough for surfing. The prevailing winds, which blow forcefully into Shipwreck and Keōmuku beaches, begin to lose their power here as the island curves southward. The beach is frequented primarily by fishermen and is accessible from several jeep trails branching off the Keōmuku Road. The shore beyond Lōpā is a narrow brown detrital sand beach completely overhung with *kiawe.*

(11)
Kahemanō Beach

Kahemanō means "school (of) sharks." The name refers to the occasional appearance at the beach of small numbers of sharks. The specific attraction that draws them to the area and inside the reef is not known, but the phenomenon still continues. The sharks that come inshore through shallow channels in the narrow reef are usually *lālākea,* the common Hawaiian reef shark.

Kahemanō Beach is located at the *makai* end of the 'Āwehi Trail, a well-known landmark in this region. The long winding beach is made up of brown detrital sand combined with coral rubble and shingle. *Kiawe*

trees overhang the right end of the beach. The reef is very narrow, often extending no more than fifty feet offshore. The inshore bottom is very shallow and rocky. The area is frequented primarily by fishermen and can be reached by several jeep trails leading from the Keōmuku Road.

(12)
Naha Beach

The word *naha* means "bent, curved, or bow-legged," but its origin as a name for this area is now unknown. Naha is mentioned in one version of the legend of Ka'ululā'au, one of the most famous stories of Lāna'i. The young man Ka'ululā'au was banished to Lāna'i from Lahaina. After defeating all the evil spirits living on the island, he built a huge fire on the beach at Naha, a signal of his success to the people of Maui. Lāna'i was then inhabited by humans for the first time in its history.

Naha, a former fishing village, is presently the site of a crumbling shack, a concrete water trough, a small cattle pen, and one of the four fishponds on Lāna'i. The walls of the old pond, easily discernible at high as well as at low tide, are the most outstanding feature of the Naha shoreline. Adjoining the north side of the pond is a narrow brown detrital sand beach overhung with *kiawe* trees. The offshore bottom is shallow and rocky with a few scattered pockets of sand. Naha marks the end of the Keōmuku Road, the end of the narrow sand beaches that begin on Lāna'i's northern coast, and the end of the fringing reef. The area is frequented primarily by fishermen.

Beyond Naha the rocky shoreline passes through several small pockets of shingle, cobblestone, and white sand before it reaches Kapoho, a small gulch with a fishermen's shelter constructed of cobblestone and driftwood. Midway between Naha and Kapoho is the *makai* end of an old paved Hawaiian trail that runs *mauka* into Pālāwai Basin. Beyond Kapoho are high sea cliffs that continue on to Mānele Bay.

Island of Kaho'olawe

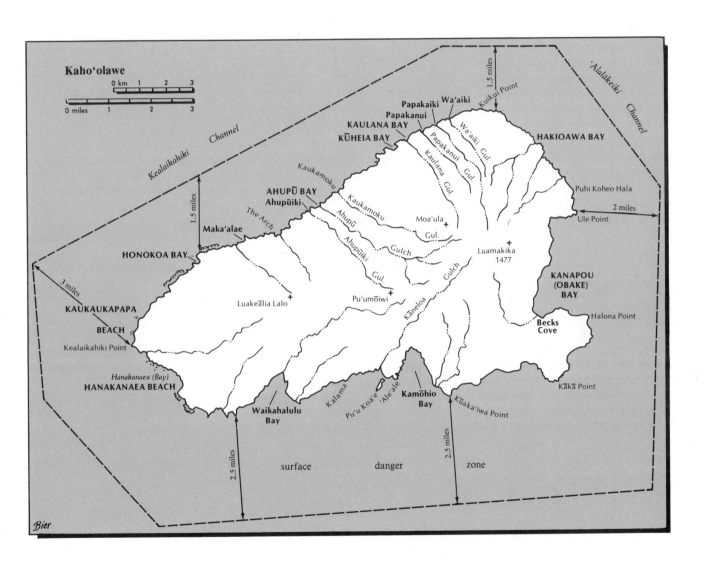

BEACHES OF KAHO'OLAWE

BEACH & LOCATION	BEACH ACTIVITIES				PUBLIC FACILITIES			BEACH COMPOSITION			ACCESS	
	SWIMMING	SNORKELING	SURFING	BODY-SURFING	COMFORT STATION	PICNIC EQUIPMENT	PAVED PARKING	SAND	DETRITAL SAND	ROCK	PUBLIC	PRIVATE
1) HANAKANAE'A BEACH, HANAKANAE'A	✔	✔		✔				✔				✔
2) KAUKAUKAPAPA BEACH, KEALAIKAHIKI	✔	✔	✔	✔				✔				✔
3) HONOKOA BAY, HONOKOA	✔	✔							✔			✔
4) AHUPŪ BAY, AHUPŪ	✔	✔							✔			✔
5) KŪHEIA BAY, KŪHEIA	✔	✔							✔			✔
6) KAULANA BAY, KAULANA	✔	✔							✔			✔
7) HAKIOAWA BAY, HAKIOAWA	✔	✔		✔					✔			✔
8) KANAPOU BAY, KANAPOU	✔	✔	✔	✔				✔				✔

(1)
Hanakanae'a Beach

Hanakanae'a, once the site of a small fishing village, is located at the southern extremity of Kaho'olawe. The name is probably a shortened form of Hanakanaenae, "the resting bay." Hanakanae'a is more popularly known as Smugglers Cove, a name with verifiable origins. Beginning in the days of the Hawaiian monarchy, ships from the Orient slipped into Hawai'i carrying contraband cargoes of opium. Often these illegal goods were cached on the remote beaches of Lāna'i and Kaho'olawe. A fishing boat from Maui would pick up the opium there and return to Maui with it. From any of the ports on Maui it could be transported to Honolulu on the interisland steamers without the danger of discovery by customs officials. Isolated Hanakanae'a was a natural choice because it offers one of the best anchorages on Kaho'olawe, except during periods of severe *kona* weather. In addition, at the head of the small bay is a white sand beach that affords easy landings and departures for small craft. In her book *Born In Paradise* Armine Von Tempski writes: "As we suspected, opium was still being landed on Kaho'olawe for distribution. Mac and Yamaichi ran into a cache sufficient enough to take care of most of his debts—if he didn't turn it over to the authorities. He did." "Mac" was Angus Mac-Phee, who ran cattle on Kaho'olawe from 1919 to 1941, and "his debts" allude to the financial problems Mac-Phee had encountered establishing a ranch on the island. Opium smuggling continued to be a major problem for health and legal authorities well into the twentieth century.

Smugglers Cove may also have been a burial site for stolen treasure. One account reports that in about 1880 Captain Alfred Deveroux stopped at the beach and buried a fortune in silver and gold coins. Deveroux caught one of his crew watching him bury the loot and killed the man on the spot. The crewman's ghost is said to haunt the area. Deveroux himself is reported to have died a violent death before he was able to return to retrieve the treasure.

Today the entire island of Kaho'olawe is used as a military training complex, and Hanakanae'a, or Smugglers Cove, serves as the base camp for the personnel who maintain a communication and medivac station during military exercises. Structures at the camp include Montague Hall, a combination mess hall and barracks building, and a small shack providing separate quarters for the explosive ordnance disposal specialists. The use of Kaho'olawe as a training area began in 1941 when the U.S. Army subleased the island from the Kaho'olawe Ranch Company for unrestricted military operations. The sublease allowed the prime lessee to maintain ranching opreations, which was continued until the United States entered World War II. The bombing of Pearl Harbor on December 7, 1941, resulted in the termination of all civilian use of Kaho'olawe. Formal notice of intention to use the entire island was given by Presidential Executive Order 10436 on February 20, 1953. This order reserved the island for the use of the United States government and placed it under the jurisdiction of the Secretary of the Navy for use by the armed services. The order also stipulated that when the island is no longer needed for military purposes, Kaho'olawe would be rendered "reasonably safe for human habitation" and returned to the territory (now the state) without cost to the local government.

From 1941 to 1969, the entire island was used as an impact area for training, and significant quantities of unexploded ordnance contaminate nearly all of the island, both below and on the surface. In addition to the land areas, the waters surrounding the island contain many unexploded shells, bombs, and torpedoes dating from World War II. As unexploded ordnance ages, it becomes more unstable, posing an even greater hazard. Military personnel and visitors to the island must have explosive ordnance disposal specialists as escorts. There have been no accidents involving ordnance to date because military personnel are alert to the dangers and visits by the general public have been kept to a minimum.

In 1969, in an effort to avoid any excessive noise disturbance on the neighbor island of Maui, the central one-third of Kaho'olawe was established as the ordnance impact area. Within this area, only designated targets specifically designed and built to meet the needs of realistic training and readiness requirements are used. Off the northern shore, Navy ships fire in such a direction that Maui is never placed in any danger. Military

125

HANAKANAE'A BEACH. A bodysurfer, almost hidden in the shadows of the wave, streaks through the Hanakanae'a shorebreak. This beautiful white sand beach is popularly known as Smugglers Cove. In former times opium was illegally shipped into the Hawaiian Islands from the Orient and deposited on this remote beach for local pickup and distribution. The building visible among the *kiawe* trees is Montague Hall, the military's combined mess hall–barracks. Kealaikahiki Point in the background points the way to Tahiti for navigators.

planes approach from the south toward mock airfields and missile sites. Aircraft do not carry live ordnance over any populated areas. The western one-third of Kaho'olawe is used as a troop movement area where Marines maneuver in coordinated exercises involving infantry, artillery, and air strikes. The eastern one-third of Kaho'olawe is dominated by Luamakika, elevation 1,477 feet. This high ground helps act as a buffer against noise for residents of Maui.

Today the island of Kaho'olawe is the principal training area in the mid-Pacific. It is used by Hawaii-based units of the U.S. Navy, Marine Corps, Air Force, and Army. In addition, ships and aircraft carriers en route to the western Pacific use Kaho'olawe for final qualifications before joining America's first line of defense in the Far East.

Military training activities, while extensive, are able to coexist with other important events taking place on Kaho'olawe, activities designed to preserve and protect the island. In 1978 the U.S. Navy and the State of Hawai'i negotiated a Memorandum of Understanding concerning Kaho'olawe. This document provides the basis for a series of management actions by which the Navy and state will cooperate in archaeological and conservation programs. The Memorandum calls for programs that include, but are not limited to, the following:

1. A program already begun by the State of Hawai'i and the Navy to rid Kaho'olawe of all cloven-hooved animals as a necessary step toward rehabilitation of Kaho'olawe.
2. A soil conservation program evolving from the cooperative experimental planting programs jointly conducted by the state and the Navy since 1970.

126

3. A program wherein the Navy and the state will continue to cooperate in inventorying archaeological sites on Kaho'olawe. The Navy will continue to plan operations so as to protect such sites.

Stretching from Kealaikahiki Point to Hanakanae'a is a long, wide white sand beach broken in several places by rock. Almost this entire reach of shoreline is rocky at the water's edge, but provides good snorkeling and diving opportunities. The waters inshore are usually safe for water activities, with adverse conditions occuring primarily during periods of heavy surf or *kona* storms. The best section of beach is Hanakanae'a, or Smugglers Cove, where a wide white sand beach slopes gently into the ocean. The bottom immediately offshore is also very sandy. The cove is safe and offers protection from the strong prevailing winds offshore.

To the east of Hanakanae'a is a large crater in the rocky shoreline, the result of Operation Sailor Hat. During April 1965 the Navy simulated an atomic explosion by detonating five hundred pounds of TNT to test the effect of nuclear-sized blasts on warships anchored nearby. The test not only created the crater but destroyed the mothballed and unoccupied cruiser *Atlanta* as well.

(2)
Kaukaukapapa Beach

Kaukaukapapa Beach is a long, wide white sand beach that begins near Kealaikahiki Point and runs along the coast toward Maka'alae. In the middle of the beach a point of rock splits the beach into two halves. This division is responsible for the beach's popular name, Twin Sands Beach. Kaukaukapapa has a moderately steep slope to the ocean, a result of the surf and the powerful currents that wash the length of its shoreline, generally from the north end of the beach to the south. The inshore bottom drops quickly to overhead depths, and this feature combined with the fast currents makes the waters dangerous. Directly offshore from the beach are many shallow, isolated rock piles that pose a hazard for any boats maneuvering in the inshore waters.

Kaukaukapapa Beach is one of the few white sand beaches on Kaho'olawe. From the north end of the beach to Honokoa Bay are several tiny pockets of white sand, but with the exception of the white sand beach in Becks Cove in Kanapou, all the rest of the island's beaches are composed of grey or brown detrital sand, the result of widespread soil runoff into the shoreline after heavy rains.

To the south of Kaukaukapapa Beach is a rocky point called Kealaikahiki, "the route to foreign lands (Tahiti)." Legend says that when Kila, the son of the great navigator Moikeha, led an expedition to Tahiti, the point of departure from the Hawaiian Islands was this western point of Kaho'olawe. Modern navigators, including those of the Polynesian voyaging canoe *Hokule'a,* have also acknowledged the point's importance as a landmark indicating the direction of the islands to the south of Hawai'i.

Just offshore from Kealaikahiki Point is a small rock island commonly called Black Rock. It is an important landmark for fishermen passing the area, as it marks the point and also the outer edge of the shallow Ku'ia Shoal.

(3)
Honokoa Bay

Honokoa, "brave bay" or "harbor (of) soldiers," is a large bay that is a popular boat anchorage. The long, wide north point of the bay provides excellent protection for the inner waters. A wide, deep channel runs almost all the way into shore. A large rock juts above the water along the north side of the channel about midway to the beach. The calm, protected waters are good for snorkeling and diving. The beach inshore is a pocket of detrital sand and shingle. *Kiawe* lines the backshore.

Honokoa Bay marks the beginning of the detrital sand beaches that are typical on Kaho'olawe from this area to Hakaioawa. Honokoa is popularly known among local fishermen as Tickman Bay, for a man by that name whose boat was wrecked there in the 1920s.

(4)
Ahupū Bay

The long reach of shoreline from Honokoa to Kūheia is composed of numerous pockets of rubble and detrital sand. There are at least eight large beaches located primarily at mouths of the larger gulches. Examples can easily be located at Maka'alae, Ahupūiki, Ahupū, and Kaukamoku. These beaches are all typically flat with gentle slopes to the deeper waters offshore. They are generally good snorkeling and diving areas when the ocean is calm. Adverse water conditions occur after heavy rains, when soil runoff floods the inshore areas. All of these secluded beaches are backed by stands of *kiawe*.

Ahupū Bay, located in the center of this long reach of shoreline, is typical of the area and has one of the largest beaches. It is a well-known landmark to fishermen. Ahupū means "heaped together." Another prominent landmark along this shoreline is The Arch, a naturally eroded hole in a rocky point. It is located in the Maka'alae area.

(5)
Kūheia Bay

Kūheia means "to stand entangled." The bay is also known as Conradt's Cove, for former Judge Christian Conradt of Maui, who purchased the Kaho'olawe lease in December 1903. Kūheia has played an important role in the various attempts to wrest financial profit from the island. Beginning in 1858 Kaho'olawe was leased a number of times to various individuals for use as a grazing land for cattle, sheep, and goats. Several of these leases were successive assumptions of a single lease that was originally for fifty years, but none of the lessees retained

KŪHEIA BAY. Just inland of this section of detrital sand beach on Kūheia Bay are the ruins of Kaho'olawe Ranch. The ranch was started by Angus MacPhee, a cattleman from Wyoming who had made his home on Maui, and was operational from 1919 to 1941. Kūheia Bay is more commonly called Pedro Bay, after Manuel Pedro, MacPhee's foreman who lived alone on the island for most of each year of the ranch's existence.

use of the island for that long a period. The lessees were able to support livestock by building catch basins for retention of rainwater and occasionally, during periods of extreme drought, by bringing in additional water and feed by boat. The lessees, including one who never received approval, are as follows:

August 18, 1854. Z. Ka'auwai applied to lease the island for fifty years at two hundred dollars a year. This application appears never to have been approved.

1858. R. C. Wyllie leased the island as a sheep ranch. The sheep were brought to the island but the venture failed because all the sheep were diseased.

March 11, 1864. Elisha H. Allen leased the island for a period of fifty years at an annual rent of two hundred fifty dollars. He reportedly had twenty thousand sheep and ten horses on the island in 1876. All subsequent leases, until 1909, were assumptions of this lease.

1880. Albert D. Courtney and William H. Cummins assumed the lease. They planned to replace the two thousand goats and one thousand sheep they found on the island with cattle. This was the first time cattle were introduced to Kaho'olawe.

April 27, 1887. The Kynnersley brothers and Randall Von Tempsky assumed the lease. They had nine hundred cattle and twelve hundred sheep on the island.

1898. In that year, the U.S. government acquired fee title to the entire island of Kaho'olawe by the annexation of the Hawaiian Islands. The title to all public lands of the Republic of Hawai'i (lands in the Hawaiian Islands classified as government or crown lands previous to August 15, 1895, and lands subsequently acquired by the government) was given to the United States. Kaho'olawe, overlooked in the Great Mahele, was designated as government land on June 7, 1848, by a law which confirmed the division of government and crown lands. The Organic Act of 1900, which created the Territory of Hawai'i, confirmed the United States' title to all public and crown lands, although use and possession were assigned to the territory pending use by the United States.

1901. B. F. Dillingham Company, Ltd., assumed the lease for the purpose of raising sugar cane.

December 28, 1903. Christian C. Conradt assumed the lease to raise sheep.

December 28, 1906. Eben P. Low assumed the lease to continue the ranching operation. By 1909 the vegetation had deteriorated very badly and soil erosion by wind and water was so severe that the legislature voted not to renew the fifty-year lease.

August 25, 1910. The island was proclaimed a Territorial Forest Reserve. The Board of Forestry did not have sufficient resources to eliminate all the sheep and goats, however, and by 1918 the reclamation project was abandoned.

1919. Angus MacPhee, a cowboy from Wyoming and the ex-manager of Ulupalakua Ranch, secured the Kaho'olawe lease. Within two years MacPhee was able to slaughter or capture and sell over twelve thousand goats and sheep. Although he was never able to exterminate all the goats and sheep, he succeeded in greatly reducing their numbers. He then built a fence across the island to confine the remaining animals to the rocky hills on the east side of the island. Governor Wallace R. Farrington was pleased with MacPhee's accomplishments, so MacPhee went ahead with his ranch plans. He erected ten redwood water tanks, each with a ten-thousand-gallon capacity, and several smaller ones. He built a house at Kūheia Bay, refurbished the bunkhouse, and constructed corrals and fences. Thousands of trees were planted, mainly *kiawe,* along with several varieties of grasses.

In 1922 MacPhee enlisted the financial support of Harry A. Baldwin of Maui, and together they formed the Kaho'olawe Ranch Company. By 1938 six hundred cattle were being fattened on the island and a small annual profit was being made. The ranch looked as if it would eventually be successful.

In 1939 MacPhee was asked to sublease half of the island to provide a military bombing range. He agreed, believing it would provide a good opportunity to rest his pastures. All the cattle were shipped back to Maui. With the involvement of the United States in World War II through the bombing of Pearl Harbor on December 7, 1941, MacPhee's sampan, used for transporting his horses, cattle, and supplies, was commandeered, and he, along with the rest of the civilian population, was forbidden to set foot on the island. As a target complex during the years 1941 to 1945, Kaho'olawe became the most shot-at island in the Pacific.

Although MacPhee's lease was good until 1953, the island was not returned to him after the war ended in 1945. The Navy convinced local administrators that the needs of military preparedness should be met before those of private interest. In 1946 MacPhee filed suit against the Navy when he realized that the federal government would not allow him to reclaim his property or compensate him for his financial losses. He died in July 1948 without compensation. When MacPhee's lease expired, President Dwight Eisenhower officially transferred jurisdiction from the Territory of Hawai'i to the Navy by executive order. The Navy has retained absolute control since then. When Hawai'i was admitted to the Union as the fiftieth state in 1959, all public lands except those set aside for the use of the federal government were transferred to the State of Hawai'i. Since Kaho'olawe had been thus designated by the 1953 executive order, it remained the property of the federal government and was therefore not transferred when Hawai'i became a state.

Kūheia Bay is known to local fishermen as Pedro Bay. Manuel Pedro was MacPhee's foreman on Kaho'olawe for almost the entire period from 1919 to 1941. He was born in 1875 in the Azores, a group of islands off the coast of Portugal. His family came to Hawai'i in 1878 with the first group of Portuguese who migrated to the Hawaiian Islands. He was raised in Kapa'au, Kohala, on the island of Hawai'i and was very loyal to the kingdom. Pedro never got over the bitterness he felt when the Hawaiian Islands were annexed by the United States. Pedro lived alone on Kaho'olawe except during the summer when his four children came over from Maui to visit. Hattie Pedro, his wife, died in childbirth in Wailuku in 1933. Her infant son died a month and a half after she did and was buried with her in the graveyard of St. Anthony's Church. Pedro's job on the island was to check the water troughs, repair the fences, and hunt the goats. Kūheia's alternate name, still in use today, is a recognition of the last permanent resident of Kaho'olawe.

On August 8, 1975, a small party of goat hunters, local residents of Maui, was camped at Pedro Bay, as they prefer to call Kūheia. They were on the island illegally and began discussing the possibility of getting Kaho'olawe returned to civilian use. They envisioned the island's remaining undeveloped, for the protection and preservation of its numerous historic sites, and then using it as a natural museum for Hawai'i's people.

Many discussions on Maui followed the hunting trip. The men decided the best way to call attention to their plans would be to land a group of people on Kaho'olawe and then report the landing to the Navy. When the landing party was subsequently arrested, their program would be brought into the open in the courts. Previous efforts to get the island returned, in 1964 by the Hawai'i State Legislature, and from 1969 to 1974 by a handful of local political figures including Patsy Mink, Elmer Cravalho, Hiram Fong, Daniel Inouye, Mamoru Yamasaki, and Goro Hakama, had not succeeded.

On January 4, 1976, about thirty-five people on boats started out for Kaho'olawe from Maui. The military got wind of the invasion and warned them from a helicopter to return. Everyone went back to Mā'alaea, but later the same day nine of their members succeeded in landing on the island. All nine were arrested and taken off the island. This was the beginning of the Protect Kaho'olawe 'Ohana, a group dedicated to stop the bombing on Kaho'olawe and to preserve the historical, cultural, and environmental intergrity of the island. Members and supporters of the Protect Kaho'olawe 'Ohana made a series of landings on the island a year later, in January, February, July, and August of 1977. During this period two of their members, George Helm and Kimo Mitchell, were lost at sea trying to reach the island on a surfboard from Mākena. In August 1977 Walter Ritte and Richard Sawyer were fined five hundred dollars each and sentenced to six months in jail, the severest sentences given to any of the individuals arrested and convicted of trespassing. Since then, the Protect Kaho'olawe 'Ohana has continued to work for the transfer of Kaho'olawe to the State of Hawai'i. The 'Ohana would like to protect the entire island from any desecration or development and to see it maintained as a spiritual sanctuary for the people of Hawai'i.

Kūheia is a horseshoe-shaped bay with two pocket beaches of detrital sand separated by a rocky bluff. *Kiawe* lines the entire backshore. The inshore waters of the bay are shallow and safe for snorkeling and diving. The south pocket beach is fronted by a very shallow *papa* that extends ten to fifteen yards offshore. The north pocket beach has a small entrance channel with a gentle, sandy slope. The ocean is often muddy after heavy rains. *Mauka* of the north pocket beach, ruins of the Kahoʻolawe Ranch buildings and corrals can still be found in several places.

The common denominator among all the civilian lessees of the island was their use of Kūheia as the site for their headquarters on the island. Kūheia Bay provided a suitable anchorage, a white sand beach for easy landings, and convenient access from the Maui landings at Mākena, Kīhei, and Māʻalaea. In addition, Kūheia was centrally situated among the five former natural reservoirs on the island, located in the uplands of Ahupū, Kūheia, and Papaka Nui. Several of these craterlike depressions, or tanks, retained water for many months after heavy rains.

One of the most distinguished visitors to Kahoʻolawe was King David Kalākaua, who visited the island in 1875. The Hawaiian newspaper *Ka Lahui Hawaii* reported that the entourage left Māʻalaea in the steamer *Kinau* and landed at Kūheia. There they found two men, two women, two children, two dogs, four houses, and ten horses. The article noted that a Mr. Lewis, a Frenchman, was king of the island, which was also the home of hundreds of goats and twenty thousand sheep. Kalākaua and his company spent the morning visiting and then returned to Maui.

(6)
Kaulana Bay

Kaulana means "(boat) landing." It is probably best known as the primary settlement on Kahoʻolawe when the island was a penal colony, roughly from 1830 to the early 1850s. Any man sentenced to imprisonment there was placed aboard a schooner in Lahaina and transported to the island. Women were segregated and taken to Kaʻena Point on the island of Lānaʻi. One of the most famous convicts was a Maui chief named Kinimaka, who was sentenced to five years for forgery. He was put in charge of the other convicts and all newcomers. Kinimaka and his charges made their home at Kaulana, along with some fishermen already living there. The fishermen eventually left, however, and returned to their permanent homes in Honuaʻula, Maui, as more convicts were sent to the island.

The colony's major problem was the lack of adequate food supplies. By February 1841 the problem was so severe that it precipitated a secret excursion to Maui. A group of the strongest swimmers made their way to Maui with a favorable current. They raided several places for food and canoes and returned to Kahoʻolawe. Other raids followed, including one to Kaʻena Point to pick up the exiled women. Most of this information was related to historian George Thrum by a man born in 1823 whose mother had been sent to Kaʻena Point.

Shortly after these raids on Maui, a party of American explorers and Hawaiians were stranded on the island after their small boat sank in heavy seas. U.S. Navy Lieutenant Charles Wilkes, commander of the United States Exploring Expedition, was not able to pick up his men until six days had passed. During that time Lieutenant Budd, the officer in charge of the landing party, and his crewmen eventually made their way to Kaulana. They later reported that Kinimaka had treated them with kindness and shared dry clothing and food with them.

Probably the last prisoner on Kahoʻolawe was one George Morgan. Convicted of theft, he was deposited on the island in 1847. Five years later he was removed after he became too sick to take care of himself.

The beach in Kaulana Bay is one of five large detrital sand pocket beaches in this area of Kahoʻolawe. The other beaches are Kūheia, Papaka Nui, Papaka Iki, and Waʻaiki. All these beaches have very similar features. Their coastlines are covered with *kiawe,* while their backshores are flat detrital sand beaches. The inshore waters are shallow and sandy with scattered rocks, providing good snorkeling and diving conditions. Adverse water conditions occur after heavy rains, when soil runoff washes into the ocean. The beach sand shifts periodically with variations in the wind and surf. None of these bays has protective reefs, so divers offshore should be alert to strong alongshore currents during certain times of the year.

Papaka Nui, "large drops," is known to fishermen as Water Tank Bay. There were formerly three water tanks in the bay area that were constructed while Kahoʻolawe Ranch was still in operation. The crumbling remains of two of the wooden tanks can easily be seen from a boat offshore. One is located on the north point of the bay and another is visible on the beach just inshore of the first one. Papaka Iki, "little drops," is known to fishermen as Santos Bay. In 1965 two cousins, Rodney and

KAULANA BAY. Two Marines, including an Explosive Ordnance Demolition (EOD) specialist, accompany a member of a
shoreline photography expedition across the beach. Landing
on Kahoʻolawe is prohibited without permission from the
United States Navy, and all personnel allowed on the island
must be escorted by an EOD specialist. The tents under the
kiawe trees were part of a temporary campsite set up by ar-
chaeologists employed by the Navy. The intermittent stream
crossing Kaulana Beach was running because of heavy rains
the previous night.

Herbert Santos, were anchored off Papaka Iki. During the night their boat broke her moorings and was
wrecked on the beach inshore. After the men had been
stranded for some hours, another fishing boat picked
them up. Besides resulting in a new name for this little
bay, the incident was of importance to Maui County for
another reason.

After experiencing the helplessness of being wrecked
on Kahoʻolawe, Herbert Santos decided to help others
in similar predicaments and began using his own boat to
assist other boats in distress. During the mid-1970s Santos was instrumental in helping to organize the Maui
Volunteer Search and Rescue Service, of which he is still

the lead rescueman. Maui County has no police or fire
department rescue service, and the lone Coast Guard
cutter stationed at Maʻalaea cannot cover all of the
numerous and often shallow-water, inshore emergencies. The Maui Volunteer Search and Rescue Service
performs an invaluable function in ensuring the water
safety of Maui County's residents and visitors. Today
there are about seventy members who donate their time,
the use of their boats and equipment, and their expertise
whenever they are called. The members use their personal citizens band (C.B.) radios to coordinate their
operations.

The shoreline from Waʻaiki to Hakioawa round Kui-

kui Point, the northernmost point on Kahoʻolawe. This area of the island is exposed to heavy surf and the powerful currents flowing through Alalākeiki Channel. The waters are safe for diving only on very calm days, and even then the water is often murky from the soil runoff after heavy rains. Large deposits of driftwood and other debris, washed up on the rocks and on the many small detrital sand pockets, can be found all along this shoreline.

(7)
Hakioawa Bay

Hakioawa means the "breaking of (the) harbor." In 1931 archaeologist J. Gilbert McAllister noted that the various historical sites at Hakioawa probably once constituted the most permanent settlement on Kahoʻolawe. He further observed that two *heiau* on the island are located in this area. In more recent times as well, Hakioawa has been visited for the purpose of holding religious ceremonies. In February 1976 more than fifty people, including members and supporters of the Protect Kahoʻolawe ʻOhana and observers such as Maui County Mayor Elmer Cravalho, were permitted by the Navy to journey to Hakioawa to participate in certain Hawaiian religious rites. Three years later, on June 17, 1979, Hakioawa also became the site of the first court-protected landing of Hawaiians on Kahoʻolawe. The landing was a result of the Protect Kahoʻolawe ʻOhana's court request for a deadline on the archaeological survey being conducted on the island by the Navy. The federal judge who ruled on the request ordered the Navy to let members of the Protect Kahoʻolawe ʻOhana land on the island while the survey was being conducted.

During the summer of 1910 a young man named

HAKIOAWA BAY. Hakioawa is considered by many contemporary Hawaiians to be one of the sacred places on Kahoʻolawe. The unusual patterns on the sand were formed by the small shorebreak acting on an unusually large amount of soil left on the beach by heavy rains. The West Maui Mountains are clearly visible across Alalākeiki Channel and East Molokaʻi is also visible, although less distinctly, between Kahoʻolawe and Maui.

Kalua Kaaihue spent three months alone on Kahoʻo-lawe, primarily at Hakioawa. The eighteen-year-old youth from Kaupō, Maui, was on the island as a ranch hand helping with the annual roundup and shearing of sheep. Maikai, the foreman, went to Lahaina to get their wages. Kalua, a Japanese hand named Togo, and a dog were left to tend the sheep and hunt goats. After ten days Togo caught a passing fishing boat to Lahaina to look for Maikai. When Togo also failed to return, Kalua realized that he had been abandoned. He lost the only company he had, the dog, when it was butted over a cliff by a goat.

Kalua left the ranch at Kūheia and moved to Hakio-awa, which faces the small village of Mākena on Maui. There he built a shelter and lit fires to attract attention. His signal fires went unanswered and his two attempts to build a raft were unsuccessful. Finally, late in August, Kalua spotted the *Maui Maru,* a fishing boat, heading for Kūheia. He left Hakioawa on the run and met the boat and his surprised rescuers.

The beach at Hakioawa is a small pocket of detrital sand bordered by two low sea cliffs. The inshore bottom is shallow and sandy with scattered rocks. The water is often murky from soil runoff after heavy rains. Hakio-awa is subject to heavy surf and the strong currents in Alalākeiki Channel. Water activities of any type must be done with caution even when the ocean is calm. This end of the island often experiences sudden changes in water and wind conditions. Hakioawa is commonly known to fishermen and hunters as Big Gulch, for the large gulch that runs down to the shoreline. The beach is located at the foot of the gulch and is backed by a large stand of *kiawe.* The area is usually windy because of the prevailing trade winds.

Around the east point of Hakioawa is another small detrital sand pocket beach fronted by large rocks. Driftwood is plentiful and lines the entire backshore.

(8)
Kanapou Bay

Kanapou is the widest bay on Kahoʻolawe, with a width of two miles between Ule and Hālona point. During rough *kona* weather the bay offers protection to boaters, and small boats can anchor offshore from Becks Cove in the east corner of the bay. Kanapou is com-

monly called Obake Bay by charter and commercial fishermen. *Obake* is the Japanese word for ghost, and the bay was so named by local Japanese commercial fishermen who fished here for *akule* and *ʻōpelu.* Kanapou is subject to extremely abrupt changes in ocean and wind conditions. Calm waters in the bay often will suddenly be devastated by large waves, powerful currents, and strong winds that seem to come out of nowhere, creating unexpected hazards for any boat caught in the area. The bay was called Obake for this reason. Fishermen familiar with the area usually keep an eye on the ocean toward Hāna. If they see white caps coming down the channel, they know they are in for some rough weather. Kanapou, however, provides an excellent anchorage during *kona* storms when the adverse water conditions approach from the opposite direction.

One of the most famous stories of Kanapou is the legend of Kalaepuni and Kalaehina collected by historian Abraham Fornander, although in the story Kanapou is called Keanapou.

> Kalaepuni was a famous strong man in the time of Keaweaumi, a former king of the big island of Hawaiʻi. Keaweaumi was afriad of Kalaepuni and allowed him to take over the island. Later the deposed king asked his priest Mokupane to help him to get rid of Kalaepuni.
>
> Mokupane sent a large work force of men to Kahoʻolawe. They landed at Keanapou where they dug a deep well, lined it with stones, and then returned to Hawaiʻi leaving an elderly couple in charge of the well. The couple were given a description of Kalaepuni and told if they ever saw him, they must only give him dried fish to eat and then direct him to the well for water.
>
> Sometime later Kalaepuni, a great shark fighter, went to Kohala to fight some great school of sharks and a strong current carried him away from Hawaiʻi to Kahoʻolawe. He landed at Keanapou and asked for food and water. Following Mokupane's instructions the old couple gave him the salted dried fish to eat and then pointed out the well to him. While Kalaepuni was inside the well getting a drink, the old couple disposed of him by rolling rocks into the well.

In 1902 A. D. Kahaulelio offered these stories of Kanapou in his fishing lore column in the Hawaiian newspaper *Ka Nūpepa Kūʻokoʻa:*

> The dark makaiauli opihi were gathered by the children at the cliffs of Kaholo, Lanai, a place famed for its

KANAPOU BAY. Members of a shoreline photographic expedition, accompanied by a Navy EOD specialist, rummage through the piles of driftwood on the beach at Kanapou. Both Haleakalā on Maui and the small island of Molokini are visible across Alalākeiki Channel. This large bay was formerly a popular fishing grounds for *akule,* big-eyed scad, and *'ōpelu,* mackerel scad, two schooling fish found in Hawaiian waters and sought by commercial net fishermen.

big opihi. True, but for the size they were not equal to those of Kanapou, Kahoolawe. Your writer is well acquainted with these places. The opihi (of Kanapou) are as large as bowls found in shops, not large ones, but the smaller ones. Goat meat would be boiled in opihi shells.

My grandparents told me why the opihi are so large. A man from Hawaii left Kohala on his small canoe and swamped in the Alenuihaha Channel. He swam for Kahoolawe and an opihi makaiauli appeared beside him. He grabbed it, wondering why it did not sink and why it had appeared. It had been sent by the prophet Moaula, who lived on the only mountain of Kahoolawe. He was sorry for Puuiaiki and sent the opihi to help him. Shortly after the appearance of the opihi a shark swallowed Puuiaiki, who then used the opihi shell to scrape its insides. Three days later the shark died at Kanapou and

washed up on the sand. When Puuiaiki crept out some fishermen saw him and thought he was a supernatural being because the shark had not killed him. They tried to kill him with stones at a spring on the hill above, but Moaula saved him. That is why the opihi of this place are so large.

We got there as castaways in the year 1848 and drank the water of that spring of Puuiaiki's. If it were not for that spring, we eight would have been corpses, six adults and two of us young boys, one thirteen and your writer who was eleven.

Kahaulelio again mentioned Kanapou in another of his columns in 1902: "Many a time your writer fished in lauapoapo fishing from Kaanapali to Kealia (on Maui), all around the island of Lanai, and on the leeward side

135

of Kahoolawe from the canoe landing to Kanapou that is facing Makena and on to the point of Kealaikahiki where it dips into the sea."

The beach at Kanapou, commonly called Becks Cove, is a fairly long and wide white sand beach. After heavy rains the beach often looks like the rest of the detrital sand beaches on the island. However, Kanapou's exposure to the surf from Alalākeiki Channel provides the necessary cleansing to quickly restore the beach to its original white color. Kanapou is a favorite beach of the *ohiki,* the common Hawaiian sand crab, and their holes often line the backshore near the water's edge. The inshore bottom is shallow and sandy out into the shorebreak. From the edge of the shorebreak the bottom drops quickly to overhead depths. Sandy dunes created by the strong winds blowing into the bay are located to the rear of the beach. The dunes are covered with *kiawe.* On calm days the cove provides a good boating area, but adverse water conditions are common and heavy surf comes directly into the beach. Becks Cove is surrounded on three sides by steep, high sea cliffs. The offshore waters frequently are subject to strong currents and strong winds.

The high cliffs that are typical of Kanapou Bay continue around the island all the way to Hanakanae'a. There are two big bays along this reach of rugged shoreline, Kamōhio, "the gust of wind," and Waikahalulu, the "roaring sea." Both of these deep bays are exposed to the powerful prevailing winds and currents. Waikahalulu has one small boulder beach and one small pocket of boulders and detrital sand. Between the two bays is a rock island called Pu'u Koa'e "hill (of the) tropic bird," a common caller in this area. Pu'u Koa'e is also known as Kaho'olawe Li'ili'i, or Little Kaho'olawe, because the small offshore island is said to resemble its larger neighbor.

Molokini

Molokini, "many ties," is a small island located midway across the Alalākeiki Channel between Maui and Kaho'olawe. There are a number of legends explaining the creation of Molokini, but the majority of them agree that the island was once a beautiful woman or a part of a woman that was turned into stone by Pele. The half-moon-shaped rock is part of an eroded volcanic tuff-cone and rises about 150 feet above sea level. The inner side of the west point of the island provides a good landing for small boats in almost all kinds of weather. A navigational light was erected in 1911 and its replacement today is the only man-made structure on the tiny island.

Molokini has no beaches, but the protected inner crescent of the island harbors one of the greatest diversified concentrations of fish in the Hawaiian Islands. It also has some of the most abundant growths of reef corals. This area was once a very popular diving grounds for those seeking reef fish, and a netting grounds for *akule* and *'ōpelu*. The deeper waters around the island formerly harbored extensive forests of black coral, but they were harvested early in the history of the industry.

In June 1977 such activities were ended with the establishment of the Molokini Shoal Marine Life Conservation District. The purpose of the district is to preserve, protect, and conserve the marine resources and geological features within it. The district includes that portion of the submerged lands and overlying waters surrounding Molokini Island from the high water mark at the seashore to a depth of 30 fathoms (180 feet).

The only exception of the fishing prohibition permits trolling for fin fishes, but only with artificial lures. There is also one exception to the prohibition against possessing in the water any device for the taking of marine life or geological features. Divers, snorkelers, and swimmers are permitted to carry for personal safety a knife, a shark billy, a bang stick, a powerhead, or a carbon dioxide injector. This was allowed because of the many sharks that frequent the waters around Molokini, especially around the underwater caves on the Maui side of the inner crescent.

Molokini is accessible only by boat. The distance and the currents across Alalākeiki Channel between the island and the Maui mainland prohibit any attempt at crossing by swimming or by using any paddling device or rowing craft. Anyone interested in visiting the protected waters of the conservation district should contact the commercial charters that visit the island frequently.

Water Safety

Dangerous Water Conditions

Many of the beaches in Maui County are protected by coral reefs, so strong currents are not a serious problem to inshore water activities. However, there are just as many beaches that are not sheltered from the open ocean that are subject to heavy surf and hazardous water conditions. Examples of these dangerous beaches are Kaukaukapapa on Kahoʻolawe, Polihua on Lānaʻi, Pāpōhaku on Molokaʻi, and Mokuleʻia on Maui. Some of the water hazards to be encountered in such areas are:

Shorebreaks

Places where waves break close to shore or directly on it are known as shorebreaks. The ocean swells that hit these beaches generally pass abruptly from a deep bottom to a very shallow one, causing the waves to rise quickly in height and to break with considerable downward force. Shorebreaks usually are very dangerous swimming areas, a fact substantiated by the numerous rescues and injuries that happen each year at places like Paʻiloa Beach and D. T. Fleming Beach Park. Even so, these places are popular recreational beaches because most people enjoy being tossed and rolled around by the big waves, and because, for more experienced swimmers, some shorebreaks provide excellent waves for bodysurfing.

One of the most important points for a swimmer to know, when playing in a shorebreak, is how to go out safely through the surf, to the quieter waters beyond. The trick is, simply, to take a big breath of air and to dive *under* each incoming wave. Many people, especially among our out-of-state visitors, will turn their backs to the cresting waves or will attempt to jump through or over them. This approach may work for waist-high waves or smaller ones, but all too often in the high waves of our Hawaiian surf it invites disaster. The swimmer, receiving the entire force of the wave upon his back, shoulders, and head, is pounded against the bottom and then tumbled and tossed about, often with complete loss of wind, control, and sense of direction. If he's lucky, he comes up with nothing worse than a nose full of salt water and a scoured skin.

Shorebreaks should be approached with a great deal of caution, even by swimmers who think they are experts.

Backwash

After a wave has washed up on the shore, the water it has brought must flow down the beach again as it returns to the sea. Backwash is simply the returning water from the spent wave. Trouble for a swimmer can develop if the backwash gains speed because the beach is steep. When this happens, the rush of the returning water can be almost as forceful as that of an incoming wave. A strong backwash is especially dangerous to small children and elderly people playing near the shore's edge. It can easily sweep them off their feet and carry them out into the surf. All beaches that have a steep slope should be considered dangerous, especially at or near high tide, when some of the bigger waves can rush up to and over the top of the slope. The higher a wave goes up the beach, the greater will be the force of its backwash. Smart people on a beach will keep themselves and their children beyond the reach of *all* waves.

Rip Currents

Rip currents are flowing, riverlike movements of water that run from shallow areas near shore out to sea. They are a major cause of the near and actual drownings that occur every year throughout Maui County. The formation of a rip current is a very simple process. Waves generally come in sets, one after another, with a short lull between sets. After the first wave of a set rolls up on shore, its mass of water washes down the beach into the ocean, but the approach of the second incoming wave prevents the backwash from dispersing completely. After three or four waves of a set have come in, a substantial volume of water is contained inshore. This buildup begins to flow along the shore until it finds a point of release, usually a channel in the reef, a trough gouged in the sand, or other similar bottom conditions. The flowing movement of such a buildup of water is a rip current.

Rip currents can be recognized from the beach by observing their effect on incoming waves and their direction of travel. Strong rips will tend to flatten waves and generally will be heading out to sea, often along a rocky point or through a channel in a reef. On sandy beaches, especially where seaweed is present, rip currents are easily seen. They resemble small rivers of seaweed or sand flowing away from shore.

If you ever get caught in a rip current, don't fight it. Just ride along with the current until it loses its power, which usually happens not far offshore, or try to ease out of it by swimming to one side at an angle to the beach. The disastrous mistake that almost every inexperienced swimmer makes is trying to swim back to shore against the rip to his original point of departure from the beach. This is as effective as swimming upstream in a rushing river and will tire a swimmer to the point of exhaustion. It is also the major reason rip currents are a leading cause of near drownings and actual drownings. If you are swept away from a beach, ride the rip out, and then head for the safest shoreline nearest you.

Rip currents occasionally form undertows where heavy surf occurs in shorebreaks areas, such as Pa'iloa Beach on Maui or 'Awahua Beach on Moloka'i. An undertow occurs when a rip current can find no path seaward other than directly through the incoming surf. When surf breaks on the outgoing rip, a swimmer caught in the current will feel he is being pulled underwater. This is an undertow, a very dangerous water condition for a struggling swimmer trying to keep his head above water. A few seconds underwater may seem like an eternity and may well draw him into it if he yields to panic.

Tsunami or "Tidal Waves"

Tsunami, or seismic sea waves, frequently are called "tidal waves" because as they move up a river or over the land they resemble the bore tidal floods that occur daily in the mouth of the Amazon River, the Bay of Fundy, and other such funnel-like areas. Tsunami, though, have nothing to do with tides. They are set in motion by great disturbances, such as earthquakes, volcanic eruptions, landslides, and other such occurrences. Most tsunami occurring naturally are generated in the oceanic trenches around the borders of the Pacific Ocean, the most active areas being along the Pacific coast of Japan, the Kurile-Kamchatka chain, the Aleutian Island arc, and along the coast of Central and South America.

One of the worst tsunami in modern history occurred early in the morning of April 1, 1946, when a violent earthquake disturbed the northern slope of the Aleutian Trench. Minutes after the earthquake occurred, waves more than 100 feet high smashed the lighthouse at Scotch Cap, Unimak Island, in the Aleutians, killing five people. The first wave struck Hawai'i less than five hours later, having traveled across the north Pacific Ocean at the rate of 435 miles per hour. This wave, and the several that followed it, battered exposed island shores, and penetrated to heights of fifty-five feet in some places. When the destructive waves subsided, 159 persons were dead and 163 injured; 488 homes had been demolished and 936 damaged; and property damage was estimated in the millions of dollars. This tsunami, the most destructive natural disaster in Hawai'i's recorded history, was the last one ever to take the islands by surprise. Since then a seismic sea wave warning system has been established. Fortunately, the Pacific Ocean is so large that waves moving even at high speeds take several hours to cross it, thereby giving the system enough time to warn coastal inhabitants of approaching tsunami.

When the possibility exists of a tsunami reaching Hawai'i's islands, the public will be informed by the sounding of the Attention Alert Signal sirens. This particular signal is a steady one-minute tone on the sirens, followed by one minute of silence, and then a repetition of blast and silence for as long a time as may be necessary. As soon as you hear this signal, you should turn on a radio or television set immediately, and tune it to any station for essential Civ-Alert emergency information and instructions. The initial signals will be sounded not only on the coastal sirens, but on all other sirens as well. This is meant to alert boat owners who do not live near the ocean, and also to alert people with relatives or friends living in threatened areas who are not capable of removing themselves from places in jeopardy. The warning will be broadcast by Civ-Alert, as well as by police and fire department mobile units, and by Civil Air Patrol aerial units. The warning will state the expected time of arrival of the first wave.

Do not take chances! When a tsunami warning is given, move *immediately* out of coastal areas that are subject to possible inundation. Maps defining inundation areas within Maui County are found in the front pages of the Maui County telephone directory. Be aware, however, that the limits of inundation indicated on the maps may be exceeded if a tsunami is generated by a local earthquake. In such an event, moreover, the siren warning may not have time to function. Therefore, any violent earthquake, one that forces you to hold onto something to keep from falling down, should be considered a natural tsunami warning. Immediately evacuate all low-lying areas. If you are in a house, take emergency supplies with you, lock the house, and leave quickly. If you live in an area not mapped in the telephone directory, just remember that an elevation of fifty feet above sea level has been set arbitrarily as ground safe from any likely wave.

Remember also these additional points:

1. A tsunami is not a single wave. It is a series of waves. Stay out of the danger areas until an "All Clear" signal is issued by a competent authority. An "All Clear" signal will *not* be given by the sirens.

2. Never go down to the beach to watch for a tsunami. If you can see the approaching wave, you will be too close to escape from it when it sweeps ashore.

3. Approaching tsunami sometimes are heralded by a sudden noticeable rise or fall of coastal water. This is nature's tsunami warning and should be heeded, instantly.

4. The Pacific Tsunami Warning Center does not issue false alarms. When a warning is issued, a tsunami exists. The tsunami of May 1960 killed sixty-one people in Hilo who thought it was "just another false alarm," and did not run when they should have.

The warning sirens are tested throughout the state on the first working Monday of every month, at 11:00 A.M., to make certain that each siren is operating properly. While the signals are sounding, Civ-Alert announces over all broadcasting stations that a test is underway and explains what is taking place. The entire test lasts only a few minutes. You should listen to them every once in a while just to keep yourself informed.

Warning sirens are located on Maui, Moloka'i and Lāna'i, and each island activates its own sirens. Some are radio-activated and some are activated by direct line. Eventually the sirens on all the islands will be radio-controlled from one central location.

Dangerous Marine Animals

Jellyfish

There are many kinds of jellyfish in Hawaiian waters, but probably the one most familiar to islanders is the Portuguese man-of-war, *Physalia*. The man-of-war is easily recognized by its translucent, crested, blue "bubble," usually less than six inches long, that floats on the surface of the water. Seafarers of old found a resemblance between this crested bubble and sailing ships of their time, so the creature was called the Portuguese man-of-war. The crest on the gas-filled bubble is used as a sail of sorts, and it can be raised, lowered, or curved to help determine direction. The man-of-war, drifting with the winds and currents, has retractable tentacles that are trailed underwater to snare its food. Each tentacle contains thousands of poison-filled nematocysts that sting and paralyse the entrapped prey.

The man-of-war usually is not a problem on most beaches unless there is a strong onshore wind. When such a wind arises, the creatures are blown inshore, where they become a menace to swimmers. The tentacles are capable of delivering a severe sting, causing a burning pain and, quite often, reddened welts. Places so affected should be rubbed immediately, and gently, with clean, wet sand. This treatment will remove any pieces of tentacle still clinging to the victim without exposing the helping hand to stinging. Then the afflicted areas, after being rinsed free of sand, can be washed with freshwater or with a solution of household ammonia or baking soda. Man-of-war stings, like those of certain insects, can cause acute reactions in some people who are allergic to the poisons, so if any extreme symptoms are observed—such as shock, severe swelling, cramps, trouble in breathing, convulsions, vomiting, or anything else unusual—professional help should be sought AT ONCE. Take the suffering person to the nearest physician or hospital.

In addition to the Portuguese man-of-war, the umbrella- or bell-shaped jellyfishes also are found in our waters. In calm or protected places, these jellyfish move under their own power by contractions of the bell, but they, too, depend mainly upon winds and currents. Some of these jellyfish also have stinging tentacles, so contact with all of them should be avoided as much as possible. Even in their smallest stages, when they are almost invisible, they can be bothersome. Swimmers who develop unbearable itching, allergic reactions, and other harmful responses should be taken to a physician as soon as possible.

Coral

Coral is found in abundance throughout Hawaiian waters and accounts for a good portion of the abrasions and lacerations incurred by swimmers, surfers, and divers. Coral cuts, no matter how small, should always be treated and watched carefully, because they are very susceptible to infection and are extraordinarily slow to heal. For cases of severe cuts, where you are required to give first aid, immediately apply direct pressure to involved arteries in order to stop the bleeding. If you are in deep water, take the injured swimmer to shore or to a protected place as quickly as possible. Profuse bleeding in the water may attract sharks.

Eels

Eels are found in almost every reef in Hawai'i. They live in holes, crevices, and under coral heads, where they feed mainly on fish and crabs. Generally, they leave their hiding places only because the prospects of food are better elsewhere or because they have been disturbed. Eels usually are not aggressive unless they are confronted and threatened, so it is best to leave them alone. They have powerful jaws and many sharp teeth, and they can be vicious when they do attack.

Sharks

Sharks are not a problem at Hawai'i's beaches and do not pose any threat to the ordinary swimmer. Generally they are found in the open ocean, and come near shore only where the water is deep and lacks a protecting reef. Sharks in Hawaiian waters are well fed by the natural abundance of reef and pelagic fish, so they do not need to hunt for other kinds of food, as is the case in other parts of the world. In Hawai'i, usually a shark will approach a swimmer only out of simple curiosity and, after it has looked, it will move on. The chief exception to this rule of passing interest is well known to many local divers: sharks are attracted to fish blood, as well as to animal blood, and many a string of fish has been seized by a cruising shark. For this reason, most divers keep a long line between themselves and the catch they've speared.

If you should meet a shark face-to-face, the most important point to remember is not to panic. Avoid creating any commotion, and restrain yourself from making a wild, frenzied sprint toward shore. Although sharks are attracted by the scent of blood or food, as well as by bright or contrasting colors, they are drawn from far greater distances by low-frequency vibrations such as those produced by a wounded fish or by a swimmer thrashing about erratically. Keep the shark in view at all times, and swim smoothly and steadily to safety. Although sharks have been driven off by yelling, and blowing bubbles underwater, and even by charging them aggressively, probably your safest course is an immediate and quiet retreat.

Sea Urchins

Sea urchins, common in all Hawaiian waters, are covered with sharp, brittle, needlelike spines that protect the animals within from predators. They are found in almost all types of underwater terrain, but usually are living in, upon, or close to rocks and coral. If they are stepped on or even brushed against, the tips of the spines easily break off and are embedded in the skin, causing more discomfort than anything else. The fragile slivers are not easily removed, even with a needle, but they will dissolve after a week or so if left alone. The punctured places should be checked occasionally, in any event, to make sure that no infection develops. A common folk remedy in Hawai'i is to urinate on the afflicted area. As strange or distasteful as this may sound, it is effective sometimes. The uric acid is said to hasten the dissolution of the bothersome spines.

Beach Thefts

A major problem at many island beaches is thefts from cars. Many people, especially tourists, lose thousands of dollars every year in cash, cameras, jewelry, and other personal items of value. The thieves operating in the beach areas are often very professional and can break into a locked car or car trunk, loot it, and be gone within a few minutes. Beach-goers, especially tourists, should bring with them only what is necessary and should never leave anything of value in the car even if it is locked. Automobiles from car rental agencies are prime targets.

Emergency Services

Most of the beaches in Maui County are not protected by lifeguards. Rental concession attendants at some beaches offer limited lifeguard service to the areas near their stands, but throughout Maui County beachgoers should be prepared to be their own lifeguards. If you do encounter a life-threatening situation in the ocean, find the nearest telephone and call the fire department for help. They will send rescue units to assist you and dispatch any additional help that is needed such as the Coast Guard, the police, or an ambulance.

Each island in Maui County (except uninhabited Kaho'olawe) has at least one hospital that provides twenty-four-hour emergency medical service. Only Maui, however, has emergency ambulance service.

Pronunciation of Hawaiian

Increasingly, in Hawai'i, concern is felt over the mispronunciation of Hawaiian words, the place names in particular. In an effort to correct this situation many Hawaiian words are now printed with diacritics, modifying marks that indicate a phonetic pronunciation different from that given the same unmarked word. The two common diacritical marks used in the pronunciation of Hawaiian are the macron (¯) and the glottal stop ('), and their use is explained below. In this text diacritics are used on all words where they are applicable. *Place Names of Hawai'i* and the *Hawaiian Dictionary* are the two primary sources for correct pronunciations.

Consonants

p, k	about as in English but with less aspiration.
h, l, m, n	about as in English.
w	after *i* and *e* usually like *v;* after *u* and *o* usually like *w;* initially and after *a* like *v* or *w*.
'	a glottal stop, similar to the sound between the *oh*'s in English *oh-oh*.

Vowels

Unstressed

a	like *a* in above
e	like *e* in bet
i	like *y* in city
o	like *o* in sole
u	like *oo* in moon

Stressed

(Vowels marked with macrons are somewhat longer than other vowels.)

a, ā	like *a* in far
e	like *e* in bet
ē	like *ay* in play
i, ī	like *ee* in see
o, ō	like *o* in sole
u, ū	like *oo* in moon

Diphthongs

(These are always stressed on the first member, but the two members are not as closely joined as in English.)

ei, eu, oi, ou, ai, ae, ao, au

Common Hawaiian Words Used in the Text

'a'ā Lava with a rough, irregular, spiny surface, as opposed to *pāhoehoe,* lava with a smooth, unbroken, ropy-appearing surface.

ahupua'a Land division usually extending from the uplands to the sea, so called because the boundary was marked by a heap *(ahu)* of stones surmounted by an image of a pig *(pua'a),* or because a pig or other tribute was laid on the altar as tax to the chief.

'ape Large taro-like, but nonedible plant.

hala The pandanus or screw pine, a tree native to the region from southern Asia east to Hawai'i. Often incorrectly called *lauhala,* which means "leaf (of the) *hala.*" *Pūhala* is the tree.

heiau Pre-Christian place of worship; some *heiau* were elaborately constructed stone platforms, others simple earthern terraces.

kāhili A feather standard, symbolic of royalty.

kahuna A priest, minister, sorcerer, or expert in any profession.

kalana Land division smaller than a *moku.*

kama'āina Native-born; literally, "land child."

kapu Taboo, prohibition.

kauna'oa A mollusk that becomes solidly fixed to rocks in its adult stage, and is common on boulder beaches. Its sharp edges can cause severe cuts.

kiawe The algaroba tree, a legume from tropical America first planted in Hawai'i in 1828, where it has become very common and useful. The branches are covered with thorns.

koa haole A common roadside shrub or small tree from tropical America, closely related to the *koa;* literally, "foreign *koa.*"

kona Leeward side of a Hawaiian island; also used to denote weather conditions such as wind originating from the leeward side.

kupua A demigod, especially a supernatural being possessing several forms.

lae Cape, point, promontory.

lamalama To spear fish at night by wading through shallow water and using a torch for light.

limu A general name for all kinds of plants living underwater, both fresh and salt. Also a common term for seaweed.

makai Toward the sea, in the direction of the sea.

mauka Inland, upland, toward the mountain.

mo'o	Lizard, reptile of any kind, dragon, serpent, water spirit.	*pānini*	The prickly pear, a Mexican branching cactus; considered a weed in Hawai'i.
muliwai	Pool of brackish water formed by the separation of a stream mouth from the ocean by a sand bar.	*papa*	A flat section of exposed reef at the water's edge or a flat area of submerged reef.
naupaka	Native species of shrubs found in coastal and mountainous areas.	*Pele*	The goddess of the volcano.
'opihi	Any of several species of edible limpets.	*pu'u*	Any type of protuberance such as a hill, a mound, or a heap.

Further Reading

Abbott, Isabella A., and Williamson, Eleanor H. *Limu.* Lawai, Kauai: Pacific Tropical Botanical Garden, 1974.

Adler, Jacob. *Claus Spreckels, the Sugar King in Hawaii.* Honolulu: University of Hawaii Press, 1966.

Adler, Jacob, and Barrett, Gwynn. *The Diaries of Walter Murray Gibson 1886, 1887.* Honolulu: University Press of Hawaii, 1973.

AECOS, Inc. "Maui Island Coral Reef Inventory." Prepared for the U.S. Army Engineering Division, Pacific Ocean. AECOS, Inc., 1980.

Allen, Gwenfread. *Hawaii's War Years.* Honolulu: University of Hawaii Press, 1950.

Apple, Russ and Peg. *Seaflite.* Norfolk Island, Australia: Island Heritage, 1977.

Ashdown, Inez. *Kaho'olawe.* Topgallant Publishing Co., 1979.

———. *Ke Alaloa o Maui.* Wailuku: Ace Printing Company, 1971.

Balaz, George H. *Hawaii's Seabirds, Turtles, and Seals.* Honolulu: World Wide Distributors, 1976.

Baldwin, Arthur D. *Henry Perrine Baldwin (1842–1911).* Cleveland: private printing, 1915.

Beevers, John. *A Man for Now.* Garden City, N.Y.: Doubleday, 1973.

Bescoby, Isabel. *Aloha and Kla-How-Ya (The Story of Maui Lu).* Seattle: Metropolitan Press, 1969.

Blackman, Marilyn. *Hokule'a.* Honolulu: Fisher Printing Company, 1976.

Bone, Robert. *The Maverick Guide to Hawaii.* Gretna, La.: Pelican Publishing Company, 1977.

Boom, Robert, and Christensen, Chris. *The Island of Maui.* Honolulu: Robert Boom Publishing Co., 1974.

Buck, Peter. *Arts and Crafts of Hawaii, Section VI—Canoes.* Special Publication 45. Honolulu: Bishop Museum Press, 1964.

Bunson, Maggie. *Faith in Paradise.* Boston: Daughters of St. Paul, 1977.

Bushnell, O. A., ed. *The Atlas of Hawaii.* Norfolk Island, Australia: Island Heritage, 1970.

Clark, John R. K. *The Beaches of O'ahu.* Honolulu: University Press of Hawaii, 1977.

Cooke, George P. *Moolelo o Molokai.* Honolulu: Honolulu Star Bulletin, 1949.

Corps of Engineers, U.S. Army Engineer Division, Pacific Ocean. "Hawaii Regional Inventory of the National Shoreline Study." Honolulu: Corps of Engineers, 1971.

Damon, Ethel M. *Early Hawaiian Churches.* Honolulu:[ ], 1924.

———. *Siloama, the Church of the Healing Spring.* Honolulu: Hawaiian Board of Missions, 1948.

Daws, Gavan. *Holy Man: Father Damien of Molokai.* New York: Harper and Row, 1973.

———. *Shoal of Time.* Honolulu: University Press of Hawaii. 1974.

Department of the Navy. "A Report on the Island of Kahoolawe." Honolulu: Commander of the Third Fleet, Department of the Navy, 1976.

Dondo, Mathurin. *La Perouse in Maui.* Wailuku: Maui Publishing Company, 1959.

Emerson, Nathaniel. *Pele and Hiiaka.* Honolulu: Honolulu Star Bulletin, 1915.

Emory, Kenneth P. *The Island of Lanai.* Bulletin 12. Honolulu: Bishop Museum Press, 1924.

Emory, Kenneth P., and Hommond, Robert. *Endangered Hawaiian Archaeological Sites within Maui County.* Report 72-2. Honolulu: Bishop Museum Press, 1972.

Farrow, John. *Damien the Leper.* New York: Sheed and Ward, 1937.

Field, W. H. *Maui, the Valley Isle.* Honolulu: Paradise of the Pacific, 1909.

Fleming, Martha. *Old Trails of Maui.* [ ]: sponsored by William and Mary Alexander Chapter, Daughters of the American Revolution, 1933.

Fleming, Mary E. *David Thomas Fleming:* [ ]: private printing, 1956.

Fornander, Abraham. *An Account of the Polynesian Race.* Rutland, Vt.: Charles E. Tuttle Co., 1969.

Foster, Jeanette. *Locked Gates: The Kapu Beaches of Maui.* Wailuku: Maui Sun, 1977.

Gay, Lawrence K. *True Stories of Lanai.* Honolulu: Mission Press, 1965.

Gibbs, Jim. *Shipwrecks in Paradise.* Seattle: Superior Publishing Company, 1977.

Handy, E. S. Craighill. *The Hawaiian Planter.* Bulletin 161. Honolulu: Bishop Museum Press, 1940.

Hawaii Audubon Society. *Hawaii's Birds.* Honolulu: Hawaii Audubon Society, 1967.

Hawaii State, Department of Planning and Economic Development. "Artificial Reefs." Honolulu: Department of Planning and Economic Development.

Hawaii State, Department of Transportation. "Statewide Boat Launching Facilities Master Plan." Honolulu: Department of Transportation—Harbors Division, 1972.

Hawaii State, Legislature. "Kahoolawe: Aloha No." Honolulu: Hawaii State Legislature, 1978.

Honolulu Advertiser. "Pacific Commercial Advertiser Anniversary Edition, July 2, 1856–July 2, 1956." Honolulu: Honolulu Advertiser, 1956.

Honolulu Star Bulletin. "Centenary Number 1820–1920." Honolulu: Honolulu Star Bulletin, 1920.

Howell, Hugh. "Water Supply Studies—Molokai." F.P. no. 45. United States Department of the Interior. Bureau of Reclamation, 1938.

Ii, John Papa. *Fragments of Hawaiian History.* Edited by D. Barrere. Honolulu: Bishop Museum Press, 1959.

Judd, Gerrit P., IV. *Puleo'o—The Story of Molokai.* Honolulu: Porter Printing Company, 1936.

Kane, Herb K. *Voyage.* Honolulu: Island Heritage, 1976.

Kay, E. Alison, and Magruder, William. "The Biology of Opihi." Honolulu: State Department of Planning and Economic Development, 1977.

Kirch, Patrick V., and Kelly, Marion. *Prehistory and Ecology in a Windward Hawaiian Valley: Halawa Valley, Molokai.* Pacific Anthropological Records no. 24, Honolulu: Bishop Museum Press, 1975.

Korn, Alfons. *News from Molokai.* Honolulu: University Press of Hawaii, 1976.

Krauss, Bob. *Travel Guide to the Hawaiian Islands.* New York: Coward-McCann, 1963.

Lahaina Restoration Foundation. *Story of Lahaina.* Lahaina: Lahaina Restoration Foundation, 1972.

McAllister, J. Gilbert. *The Archaeology of Kahoolawe.* Bulletin 115. Honolulu: Bishop Museum Press, 1933.

Macdonald, Gordon, and Abbott, Agatin. *Volcanoes in the Sea.* Honolulu: University of Hawaii Press, 1970.

Malo, David. *Hawaiian Antiquities.* Honolulu: Bishop Museum Press, 1951.

Medina, Teddi; Stephens, Jack; and Johnson, Robert. *Maui Now!* Makawao, Maui: Aquarius Enterprise, 1969.

Merlin, Mark D. *Hawaiian Coastal Plants and Scenic Shorelines.* Honolulu: Oriental Publishing Company, 1977.

Mitchell, Charles, and Shifflette, Colleen. *Hawaii for You and the Family.* Seattle: Hancock House Publishers, 1979.

Moberly, Ralph M. *Hawaiian Beach Systems.* Honolulu: Hawaii Institute of Geophysics, University of Hawaii, 1964.

Munro, George C. *Birds of Hawaii.* Rutland, Vt.: Bridgeway Press, 1960.

National Oceanic and Atmospheric Administration. "United States Coast Pilot 7 Pacific Coast: California, Oregon, Washington and Hawaii." Washington: National Oceanic and Atmospheric Administration, 1977.

Neal, Marie C. *In Gardens of Hawaii.* Honolulu: Bishop Museum Press, 1965.

Nordyke, Eleanor C. *The Peopling of Hawaii.* Honolulu: University Press of Hawaii, 1977.

Palmer, Harold S. "Geology of Molokini." Occasional Papers VIX no. 1. Honolulu: Bishop Museum Press, 1930.

Propellor Club of the United States, Port of Honolulu. "Ports of Hawaii." Honolulu: Red Dot Publishing Company, 1967.

Scott, Sylvia. *Facilities Manual on the Islands of Maui, Molokai, and Lanai: A Reference Guide.* Honolulu: Hawaii Visitors Bureau, 1975.

Shepard, F. P.; Macdonald, G. A.; and Cox, D. C. *The Tsunami of 1946.* Bulletin of the Scripps Institution of Oceanography of the University of California. Berkeley: University of California Press, 1950.

Smith, Robert. *Hiking Maui.* Pasadena: Ward Ritchie Press, 1975.

Speakman, Cummins E., Jr. *Mowee: An Informal History of the Hawaiian Islands.* Salem, Mass.: Peabody Museum of Salem, 1978.

Sterling, Elspeth. "The Sites of Maui County." 14 unpublished volumes. Bishop Museum, Department of Archaeology, and Hale Hō'ike'ike, Wailuku.

Stearns, Harold T. *Geology of the Hawaiian Islands.* Honolulu: Advertiser Publishing Company, 1946.

Summers, Catherine C. *Molokai—A Site Survey.* Pacific Anthropological Records 14. Honolulu: Bishop Museum Press, 1971.

Sutherland, Audrey. *Paddling My Own Canoe.* Honolulu: University Press of Hawaii, 1978.

Tabrah, Ruth. *Lanai.* Norfolk Island, Australia: Island Heritage Press, 1976.

Tinker, Spencer W. *Pacific Sea Shells.* Rutland, Vt.: Charles E. Tuttle Co., 1952.

———. *Sharks and Rays.* Rutland, Vt.: Charles E. Tuttle Co., 1973.

Titcomb, Margaret. *Native Use of Fish in Hawaii.* 2nd ed. Honolulu: University Press of Hawaii, 1972.

Von Tempski, Armine. *Born in Paradise.* New York: Duel, Sloan and Pierce, 1940.

Wenkam, Robert. *Maui, the Last Hawaiian Place.* San Francisco: Friends of the Earth, 1970.

Wilcox, Charles. *Kalepolepo.* Honolulu: Paradise of the Pacific, 1921.

Wood, Amos L. *Beachcombing for Japanese Fish Floats.* Portland, Oregon: Binford and Mort Publishers, 1967.

Wright, Bank. *Surfing Hawaii.* Los Angeles: Tivoli Printing Company, 1972.

Index

About the Author

John R. Kukeakalani Clark is the author of a series of books on Hawaiian beaches. His other works include *The Beaches of O'ahu, Beaches of the Big Island,* and *Beaches of Kaua'i.* He was employed by the City and County of Honolulu in 1970 as a lifeguard and then in 1972 as a fire fighter. Now a captain in the Honolulu Fire Department, he is also self-employed as an ocean recreation and water safety consultant. He holds an A.S. in Fire Science and a B.A. in Hawaiian Studies.